WMU Studies in Maritime Affairs

Volume 9

WMU Studies in Maritime Affairs was launched in 2013 to inspire scholars from all walks of maritime life to contribute to the creation and advancement of knowledge in the numerous maritime disciplines through publications of the highest order of excellence. With this book series, the World Maritime University aims to lead an expansion of scholarly pursuits, particularly in the areas of maritime law and policy, maritime safety and environmental administration, maritime education and training, marine environmental and ocean management, port management, and shipping management.

More information about this series at http://www.springer.com/series/11556

Victor Oyaro Gekara • Helen Sampson
Editors

The World of the Seafarer

Qualitative Accounts of Working in the Global Shipping Industry

Springer

Editors
Victor Oyaro Gekara
School of Accounting, Information Systems and Supply Chains
RMIT University
Melbourne, VIC, Australia

Helen Sampson
Seafarers International Research Centre
School of Social Sciences
Cardiff University
Cardiff, Wales, UK

ISSN 2196-8772 ISSN 2196-8780 (electronic)
WMU Studies in Maritime Affairs
ISBN 978-3-030-49824-5 ISBN 978-3-030-49825-2 (eBook)
https://doi.org/10.1007/978-3-030-49825-2

This Springer imprint is published by the registered company Springer Nature Switzerland AG.
The registered company address is: Gewerbestrasse 11, 6330 Cham, Switzerland

Acknowledgements

We are extremely grateful to The Nippon Foundation for generously supporting both the publication of this book and the work which underpins it. We would like to extend our thanks to all those who contributed to the data which was collected by contributors in the course of their projects. Particular thanks are due to Anne Kennedy for providing specialist copy editing of the manuscript.

Contents

Chapter 1
Introduction

Helen Sampson

The shipping industry transported a total volume of 10.3 billion tons of cargo in 2017 (UNCTAD 2017) and is estimated to employ 1.5 million workers (http://www.ilo.org/global/standards/subjects-covered-by-international-labour-standards/seafarers/lang%2D%2Den/index.htm accessed 1/2/18) who are classed as seafarers. Such workers are employed on different vessel types in the cruise and cargo sectors. Sailors working for the military are not classed as seafarers. However, seafarers may be employed on board in a variety of roles which are not directly associated with marine navigation (as croupiers or entertainers on a cruise ship for example) but their ship should be engaged in a voyage which would differentiate them from taking a 'fishing trip' for example. Doumbia-Henry describes some of the provisions of ILO Convention No. 185 stating that:

> Article 1 defines the seafarer as "any person who is employed or engaged or works in any capacity on board a vessel, other than a ship of war, ordinarily engaged in maritime navigation". This is a very broad definition of seafarers, extending the term seafarer to persons working on board a ship who may not be ship's crew. It covers all those who work on a ship and need an identity document for the purposes of shore leave, joining ship or transit to join a ship or repatriation. (Doumbia-Henry 2003, p. 135)

This edited collection, focuses on those seafarers who work in the cargo sector of the industry on board a variety of ships such as oil and chemical tankers, gas carriers, bulk carriers (carrying minerals or wood products for example), refrigerated cargo vessels, container ships, and what are termed 'general cargo ships'. Most of these workers are men (Belcher et al. 2003; http://www.ilo.org/global/publications/world-of-work-magazine/articles/WCMS_081322/lang%2D%2Den/index.htm) who have acquired a range of internationally recognized certificates to qualify for work on board. Such seafarers are employed in various roles relating to navigation, engine

H. Sampson (✉)
Seafarers International Research Centre, School of Social Sciences, Cardiff University, Cardiff, Wales, UK
e-mail: sampsonh@cf.ac.uk

V. O. Gekara, H. Sampson (eds.), *The World of the Seafarer*, WMU Studies in Maritime Affairs 9, https://doi.org/10.1007/978-3-030-49825-2_1

performance, and vessel/crew maintenance. They are drawn from a range of traditional (e.g. European, OECD) and 'new' (e.g. China, Philippines, Myanmar, Indonesia) labour supply countries and frequently work as part of a mixed nationality crew. The vast majority of seafarers are employed by third party crew agencies who are contracted to supply workers to shipowners and shipmanagers on temporary contracts. Typical voyages last for between three and 12 months and many seafarers are technically 'unemployed' during their leave periods ashore and uncertain of when, or indeed if, they will be re-called by their agency to join a vessel. As such, although they are relatively well-paid whilst they are on board, seafarers are generally temporary workers employed on precarious contracts.

The global nature of the industry is a challenge to nations which seek to protect their shorelines from pollution/'security' threats, and to implement both labour and environmental laws within their territories (including territorial waters). Major pollution incidents and those involving loss of life (particularly amongst passengers) can be seen to have been instrumental in driving change in international regulations covering safety and environmental protection. Such regulations (as well as those relating to security) are produced and amended at the International Maritime Organization which is a United Nations (UN) agency with responsibility for regulating ships as technical entities. The International Labour Organization (another UN special agency) also plays a significant role in the regulation of the sector but this is restricted to matters pertaining to labour standards and seafarers' rights.

Not only does the industry present challenges to states wishing to safeguard their national economic and security interests, it also presents difficulties for worker representation and protection. Employers tend to operate different wage scales for different nationalities on board and on multinational vessels it also common for the duration of a contracted voyage and arrangements for overtime payments to vary with nationality. Thus one third officer from the Philippines (at the end of his contract) may be replaced by another from Ireland who is paid more per month and expected to remain on board for a shorter period of time. Such inequities are accepted by seafarers, who are also acutely aware of their vulnerability in the labour market and for whom the competition for jobs between labour supply countries could easily translate into a classic 'race to the bottom'. In this context the role of the International Transport Workers' Federation (ITF) has been critical in protecting wages. The ITF is one of a small number of Global Union Federations and is unique in negotiating wages for seafarers employed on open register vessels which are not covered by a recognized collective bargaining agreement. In practice the wage scales negotiated with employers by the ITF play a key role in setting an international benchmark for wages, and the role of national collective bargaining agreements in determining wages has diminished. This leaves many trade unions occupying rather curious positions as job brokers and service providers (Yang 2010) and weakens their capacity, or willingness, to defend the interests of seafarers in dispute with vessel operators.

The shipping industry can be seen to be at the forefront of globalization, and it provides us with a good example of the associated challenges for labour, regulation and standards. As a crucial part of the transport infrastructure that facilitates trade between nations it has indeed 'driven' globalization. At the same time, it has, been transformed by globalisation as ships have ‘flagged out’ and labour recruitment has been outsourced and off-shored. These processes have been written about and analysed by a number of authors (e.g. Sampson 2013). However the kind of broad perspective contained in such accounts is necessarily produced at the expense of an in depth and detailed consideration of many of the individual elements which comprise the industry. This book addresses the gap in the literature and provides a detailed account of the industry which can be metaphorically likened to a mosaic—or to filling in some of the pieces of a complex jigsaw. The collection is largely based upon chapters produced by the authors of a variety of PhD theses all of which related to the shipping industry but which were otherwise unrelated to one and other constituting free-standing research projects and pieces of work. Students were from a variety of backgrounds and nation states and came together in Cardiff as part of a large postgraduate programme led by Helen Sampson who also makes a contribution to this work as co-editor with Gekara (a member of the first cohort of PhD students starting in 2004) and as the author of Chap. 8. This PhD programme, the scholarships that emerged as a part of it and this book, have only been possible because of generous funding from The Nippon Foundation. The Nippon Foundation funded the PhD programme in full from 2004–2017. Ten cohorts of PhD students were recruited numbering 37 individuals in total. The theses were varied and rich and in this text we attempt to weave a selection of them together to provide a unique insight into a very complex global industry.

The book is organised into three parts which reflect the trajectory of seafarers as they enter the industry.

‘Part I’ considers where seafarers hail from, why they join the industry, and some of the barriers that particular seafarers face in finding and keeping jobs. As such the component chapters discuss: the history of the Philippines as the leading global labour supply nation; the recruitment practices of agencies operating in China; the policy challenges associated with maintaining adequate training and supply of junior officers in traditional maritime nations in the current labour market jobs; seafaring as a portfolio career and the opportunities and threats to the industry that are presented by current recruitment practices; and the barriers presented to would-be women seafarers who seek a career in this highly male-dominated industry.

Overall, ‘Part I’ provides a better understanding of why it is that the industry may find it challenging to recruit good quality deck officers, and engineers, in the future. Officer shortages have been predicted by analysts for several decades (BIMCO ISF 2015) but the reasons behind such predicted shortages have been less-well described. Whilst relatively poor members of developing (labour export) societies such as the Philippines may continue to seek a career at sea they may be deterred by the costs of training and education in the largely private maritime education and training sector. Meanwhile, Chinese seafarers are less likely than originally predicted to make up any shortfall in the global supply of officers as a result of the operational constraints on Chinese crewing agencies which result in the payment of inflated wages to ratings and inadequate salaries to officers in comparison to international wage rates. These practices deter Chinese officers from continuing to work at sea and may explain why it is that China has not come to dominate the global labour market for seafarers as had previously been predicted by academics and industry insiders. Meanwhile we have seen a reluctance amongst employers to invest in the higher salaries demanded by junior European officers despite the fact that European senior officers remain in demand. This has undermined labour supply in Europe. When these factors are set in a broader context in which seafarers find the life at sea less attractive than it once was, and half of the potential labour force are excluded from seafaring careers as a consequence of their gender, then the long-term prospects for the global supply of high quality officers to the international fleet may indeed seem bleak.

The first three chapters in 'Part II' of the book provide an insight into the day-to-day life of seafarers on board. Chapter 7 describes the transitions and adjustments required of seafarers as they leave home to join a vessel, progress through a 'tour of duty' and prepare for the end of their voyage. Chapter 8 discusses issues of nationality and hierarchy in the context of a strong occupational culture and the overwhelming dominance of work on board merchant cargo vessels. Chapter 9 reports on research that focussed upon Filipino seafarers in lower ranking positions and discusses what it is like to live and work on board alongside powerful supervisors and managers.

Seafarers constantly live and work under threat of severe sanctions whether these relate to instant dismissal (a potential consequence of the displeasure of a captain or chief engineer) or to the imposition of personal fines and imprisonment by port authorities charged with enforcing international regulations. These chapters convey a great deal about life on board a commercial cargo vessel and the ways in which seafarers' activities are constrained and monitored. Such institutionalized and regulated lives can produce high levels of occupational stress. In a context where seafarers' opportunities for 'resistance' and indeed for psychological 'restoration' are highly circumscribed such stress is likely to produce a variety of health problems and the potential for high levels of seafarer attrition.

The final three chapters in 'Part II' direct our attention to some of the specific challenges of working at sea. Seafaring is known to be a relatively dangerous occupation characterized by high rates of occupational illness and work-related fatalities. In 2014 Roberts et al. estimated that the mortality rate for British seafarers over the period 2003–2012 was 21 times higher than that found in the general UK working population (Roberts et al. 2014). However, shipping is also an industry that has been associated with headline-grabbing oil spills which produce a great deal of pollution and more recently it has been characterized by some states as constituting a potential threat to national security as well as playing a role in the facilitation of covert (undocumented) migration. As a result of these combined 'threats' the industry has been increasingly regulated and Chaps. 10, 11 and 12 deal with some of the intended and unintended consequences of such regulation. Chapter 10 describes the ways in which regulatory requirements (in this case relating to environmental protection) structure the experience of work and the ways in which work is conducted on board. In Chap. 11 Xue sheds light on the management of safety on board vessels crewed and managed within China, and in Chap. 12 Senu describes the rarely considered impact, on seafarers, of attempts to prevent the carriage of shipboard stowaways and to deter the rescue of undocumented migrants imperilled at sea.

In 'Part III' we look beyond the ship to consider the shore-based and computer-facilitated mechanisms which are currently available to support contemporary seafarers and their families as they grapple with challenges associated with participation in the industry. As such Gekara considers the challenges that are posed to national trade unions attempting to support and represent seafarers participating in a global sector; Buiser reflects on the limits to trade union support in the Philippines; and Tang discusses the on line support that has developed in China to support seafarers' partners and assist them in enduring the consequences of the long absences of serving seafarers.

In combination these chapters provide a wealth of detail about a range of key actors and stakeholders engaged in the cargo shipping sector. The book is organized with a logic that allows it to either be read from start to finish or in a more piecemeal fashion. However it is used, it serves to provide a remarkable insight into a poorly understood, global, fragmented, industry of considerable scale.

References

Belcher, P., H. Sampson, M. Thomas, J. Veiga, and M. Zhao. 2003. *Women Seafarers – Global Employment Policies and Practices*. Geneva: International Labour Office. 92-2-113491-1.

BIMCO ISF. 2015. *MANPOWER REPORT The global supply and demand for seafarers in 2015 (Executive Summary).* www.bimco.org. Accessed 9 Feb 18.

Doumbia-Henry, C. 2003. Current Maritime Labour Law Issues – An Internationally Uniform Identity Document for Seafarers. *WMU Journal of Maritime Affairs* 2 (2): 129–148.

Roberts, S., D. Nielsen, A. Kotłowski, and B. Jaremin. 2014. Fatal Accidents and Injuries Among Merchant Seafarers Worldwide. *Occupational Medicine (London)* 64 (4): 259–266. https://cronfa.swan.ac.uk/Record/cronfa18992. https://doi.org/10.1093/occmed/kqu017.

Sampson, H. 2013. *International Seafarers and Transnationalism in the Twenty-First Century.* Manchester: Manchester University Press.

UNCTAD. 2017. *Review of Maritime Transport 2017.* Geneva: UNCTAD. http://unctad.org/en/PublicationsLibrary/rmt2017_en.pdf

Yang, P. 2010. *Romance of the Three Unions: A Comparative Study of the Identity Discourses of Three Indian Maritime Trade Unions.* PhD Thesis, Cardiff University. http://www.sirc.cf.ac.uk/Uploads/Thesis/Yang.pdf. Accessed 1 Feb 18.

Part I
Going to Sea

Chapter 2
A Taste of the Sea: Artisanal Fishing Communities in the Philippines

Nelson Turgo

Introduction

The Philippines remains one of the top suppliers of seafarers to the global merchant fleet. In the 2015 BIMCO Manpower Report on seafarer supply countries, the Philippines ranked first for ratings and second for officers with 363,832 Filipino seafarers deployed to ocean-going merchant vessels in 2014 and accounting for 28% of the global supply of seafarers (MARINA 2015). Seafarers are crucial in keeping the Philippine economy afloat and in 2018, Filipino seafarers sent home USD 6.14 billion (Hellenic Shipping News 2019), accounting for about a fifth of the USD 32.2 billion overseas workers sent home that year (Inquirer 2019). The Philippines has developed as a major player in the crewing sector of the global maritime industry primarily because of its maritime history (Giraldez 2015; Mercene 2007; Schurz 1939), its maritime geography and the continued centrality of the sea to many people's lives (as attested to by the presence of the myriad fishing communities dotted around the many islands of the country) (Warren 2003, 2007), the economic liberalisation of the 1970s and the concomitant institutionalisation of the labour export policies as enacted by Philippine governments since the presidency of Ferdinand Marcos whose latter policy saw many Filipinos seeking employment overseas (Asis 2017; Kaur 2016; Wozniak 2015).

This concatenation of circumstances can be seen to have produced the dominant contemporary role of Filipino seafarers. Some of these have been drawn from traditional fishing communities where precarious lives are endured, by many who are subject to exploitation and at times violence on board commercial fishing vessels. This provides a backdrop to the economic and geographical context of how the

N. Turgo (✉)
Cardiff University, Seafarers International Research Centre, School of Social Sciences, Cardiff Wales, UK
e-mail: turgon@cf.ac.uk

V. O. Gekara, H. Sampson (eds.), *The World of the Seafarer*, WMU Studies in Maritime Affairs 9, https://doi.org/10.1007/978-3-030-49825-2_2

Philippines became a leading provider of seafarers to the world. This chapter reviews the existing literature on the topic including international and Philippine government reports and statistics on seafarers and the maritime industry. Previous interviews with fishermen and data from fieldwork in the fishing community which contributed to a PhD thesis by the author are also used.

The Importance of the Sea

As an archipelago of 7107 islands, the Philippines has an extensive coastline of 17,460 km in length and about 26.6 million ha of coastal waters and 193.4 million ha of oceanic waters. The country exercises authority over 2.2 million square kilometers (or 220 million ha) of territorial ocean waters including its Exclusive Economic Zone (EEZ) (BFAR 2014). Prior to colonization, the sea and bodies of inland waters provided a means of transportation and trade for indigenous people.[1] All over the country, archaeological finds attest to the extensive connection of the archipelago to ancient kingdoms like Siam (now Thailand) and the Middle Kingdom (now China) and the far-reaching travels of the native people to other ancient realms like Srivijaya (largely in what is now Indonesia) (Corpuz 2005). In Butuan in Agusan del Norte (a province in Mindanao, one of the Philippines' three major island groups) massive wooden boats called 'balangay' pre-dating the arrival of the Spaniards by hundreds of years, were unearthed in the 1970s, clear testimonies to the mobile ways and sea prowess of the ancient Filipinos (Clark et al. 1993). By riding the crest of waves in their wooden boats, they established connections to their Southeast Asian neighbours, learnt of their cultures and imbibed their ways of life (Warren 2003, 2007). Later under the rule of Spain, from 1815 onwards Philippine products were sent to the Spanish empire via Mexico in what historians call the galleon trade. In this intercontinental exchange, many Filipinos served as crew and had a taste of foreign cultures and the joys and perils of life on board (Aguilar 2012; Guevarra 2011; Mercene 2007). When the Philippines became a US territory at the beginning of the twentieth century, Filipinos were recruited to serve in the US Navy. In 1903 just nine Filipinos were recruited to join the US Navy; but by the First World War their number had risen to 6000 (Aguilar 2012, p. 384). Given this continuing engagement by Filipinos with the sea across time, it is not surprising that Filipinos have come to dominate employment at sea, bringing with them hundreds of years of sea-going tradition and culture.

In addition to travel, the sea has presented a myriad of opportunities to Filipinos providing the means to barter with people in other locations as well as furnishing them with a much-needed regular diet of protein for everyday sustenance. Thus,

[1]The Philippines was never called by its present name until 1543 when the islands Samar and Leyte, two big islands south of Manila, were named after Prince Philip, Prince of Asturias, by the explorer Ruy Lopez de Villalobos and the name stuck until it referred to the entire archipelago.

fishing communities are a regular feature of many islands in the Philippines. Currently, it is estimated that there are over 1.5 million fishermen in the country whether large-scale (meaning commercial and on the high seas) or small-scale (within the municipal waters) (BFAR 2018).

The Philippines is one of the major producers of fish in the world and in 2016, it ranked 10th amongst the top fish producing countries, with a total production of 1.87 million metric tonnes of fish, crustaceans, molluscs and aquatic plants including seaweed (FAO 2018). Some nine million more Filipinos indirectly depend on the fishing industry through fish trading, fish food production and the manufacturing of boats, fishing gear, and related products (PSA 2017). In the fourth quarter of 2018, the fisheries sector contributed 8.9% to the country's GDP (DTI 2019).

Fishermen in the Philippines can be divided into two types. The first type comprises those employed by big fishing companies whose fishing vessels are engaged in commercial[2] fishing outside the country's municipal waters. The second type is made up of small-scale fishermen whose fishing is limited to the country's municipal waters[3] and could be characterised as 'subsistence', does not require fishing boats or whose fishing boats weigh not more than three gross tons (see also Kurien 1998, 2003; Stobutzki et al. 2006). In many cases, the former earn a monthly wage of PHP12-15,000 (USD250-315) a month with add-ons and bonuses depending on the volume of catch per fishing season[4] while the latter's remuneration is governed by a system unique to the fishing industry called clear or broken lay (see also St Martin 2005, 2007). The cited monthly income of fishermen aboard commercial fishing vessels is based on an assumed wage arrangement prescribed by the national government for fishermen working on commercial fishing vessels. However, reports state that in many cases, "fish workers" all over the country receive an average daily pay of between PHP150-180 ($3.30-4)—way below the minimum wage set by regional wage boards for agricultural and non-agricultural workers in rural Philippines (Corpuz 2014).

Poverty remains a constant defining feature of many, if not all, fishing communities in the Philippines (Eder 2005; Guieb 2009; Mangahas 1993, 2000; Turgo 2010; Ushijima and Zayas 1994). According to Pamalakaya (an NGO working for the welfare of fishermen in the Philippines) surveys conducted by the National

[2]Commercial fishing involves catching of fishery species by passive or active gear for trade, business or profit beyond subsistence or sports fishing to be further classified as: 1. small scale—with passive or active gear utilizing fishing vessels of 3.1 GT up to 20 GT; 2. medium scale—utilizing active gears and vessels of 20.1 GT up to 150 GT; 3. large scale—utilizing active gears and vessels of more than 150 GT. Commercial fishers cannot conduct fishing activities within the 15 km municipal waters unless the local government concerned allows them from 10.1 km to 15 km. They can also operate in foreign or international waters. (Primer RA8550, p. 2).

[3]Municipal waters as defined in Republic Act 8550 are marine waters 15 km from the coastline including streams, rivers, public forest, timber land, forest reserve or fishery reserve within the municipality except those under the NIPAS Law (BFAR 2015).

[4]Targets are usually set by fishing companies and if these are met and at times surpassed, bonuses are paid to fishermen. On the other hand, skippers are paid differently depending on the arrangement they have with company officials.

Statistical Coordination Board (NCSB) in 2006, 2009 and 2010 revealed that the *fisherfolk* sector has the highest poverty incidence in the country. Furthermore, the NSCB revealed that the *fisherfolk*, farmers and children comprised the poorest segments of the population across the country with poverty incidence of 49.9%, 44% and 40.8% respectively (Corpuz 2014). This is not new and a visit to many fishing communities in the country reveals the appalling quality of life for most fishermen and their families. They live in houses where basic sanitation is almost non-existent; there is no running water and no electricity. Hygiene is, to say the least, dismal.[5]

These communities are also the most vulnerable to the consequences of climate change. Since they live close to the shore, their houses and properties are prone to destruction brought about by strong wind and tidal surges. Fatalities are therefore an inevitable consequence. This vulnerability was clearly displayed in catastrophic events in the Philippines and other countries like Thailand, Indonesia, and Sri Lanka, during the 2004 tsunami, caused by an Indian Ocean earthquake. Recently, typhoon Haiyan's (locally known as Yolanda) land-fall in the Philippines in November 2013 further illustrates the extreme vulnerability of people living in fishing communities. A report produced by OXFAM, stated that 30,000 boats were lost to the typhoon. Furthermore, in the aftermath of the typhoon, the Philippine Department of Agriculture estimated that 202,410 fishing households, a total of 865,305 individuals, had been affected (OXFAM 2014).

Fishing is considered to be the most dangerous occupation in the world (FAO 2018). In this regard, commercial fishing is more prone to accidents and deaths at sea. Furthermore, exploitation, violence and slavery characterise employment in the commercial fishing sector (Couper et al. 2015; Pocock et al. 2018). The length of time out at sea and the intensity of fishing activities taking place on commercial fishing vessels make it more open to fatal accidents. In addition, while small-scale fishing recruits people of the same kinship network, which limits if not constrains the likelihood of exploitation, abuse and violence, commercial fishing does not.[6] Commercial fishing operators recruit personnel from the provinces and require them to fish for weeks and months on end which limits, if not totally cuts off, their communication with people ashore (Couper et al. 2015).[7] This increases the

[5]In the fishing community that I studied, I once interviewed a couple in their living room that was so dirty and the smell of dried feces and rotten animals (maybe rats, I thought) was so nauseous that I had to terminate the interview at some point before I got overwhelmed by the smell. This is of course not generic as some other houses tried to be as clean and orderly as possible.

[6]In most fishing communities, fishing is usually conceived to be a family enterprise, and crews are drawn from within the family or immediate relations. In such an arrangement, as fishermen come from the same family or kin (both real and fictive), exploitation is almost nil as taking advantage of others could create rifts amongst family members and endanger close relationships in the community.

[7]Unlike modern day merchant vessels, commercial fishing vessels rarely have internet provision or any other means of communication to the shore aside from satellite phones which are kept most of the time by the skipper or captain and can only be used in emergency situations.

possibility of exploitation since fishermen are at the mercy of owners. Cases of exploitation of Filipino fishermen aboard commercial fishing vessels registered in Taiwan, South Korea, Singapore, New Zealand, the UK and many others are well documented (Couper et al. 2015; Howard 2012; Yea 2014).

As attested to by many studies, working conditions in many commercial fishing boats are appalling (see, for example, Couper et al. 2015; Simmons and Stringer 2014; Brown 2009). Sleep is a scarce commodity on board; fishermen may be required to work 24 hours a day regardless of the weather and their levels of fatigue. Sleeping quarters may be equipped with simple hammocks and rooms are not insulated from the cold weather. A fisherman I interviewed told me how he had to endure sleeping in a very cold room (or very hot depending on the season of the year) together with some five other men for one entire year. In 2019, I visited a fishing vessel anchored in a port in Taiwan and saw for myself the very basic and uncomfortable living quarters of fishermen. A Filipino crew member told me that on some fishing vessels that he had been on, they had to schedule their sleeping time since the room was very small and could only accommodate five people at a time. Medical treatment was also non-existent for many of fishermen falling ill on the vessel. The same fisherman also told me that when a young fisherman from Vietnam (14 years old) fell grievously ill (he had a recurring stomach ache), the owners of the fishing vessel did not allow them to moor the boat to unload the sick fisherman to seek treatment. They were told to make use of the available medicine on board instead. The young fisherman soon died and again the owners did not allow them to berth in the nearest port. They kept his body in the cold storage together with their catch. Before going back to the Philippines (they fished mostly in the area between the Philippines and Indonesia), they were ordered to dispose of the body since it was considered by the vessel owners to be too costly to repatriate it to Vietnam. The company then reported to his family that he absconded in a fishing port and was not seen again.[8]

In many places in the Philippines, fishing communities have become a fertile ground for recruitment to these fishing vessels. With their experience at sea, many small-scale fishermen are lured to working on fishing vessels overseas with a promise of a better salary than they would get working on small scale fishing boats or local commercial fishing vessels. In recent years, for example, Scotland has seen the rise of Filipinos employed in many of its commercial fishing vessels (Howard 2012; Ross 2015). However, many of them have been victims of exploitation both by their employers and their recruiters in the Philippines (Couper et al. 2015). For example, their monthly salary is lower than their European counterparts

[8]However unfortunate, I was told that this is the usual practice on most commercial fishing vessels operating in the Philippines, Singapore and Taiwan and employing fishermen from the Philippines, Cambodia, Thailand and Vietnam. In his first day on the fishing vessel (the vessel was moored in Singapore and he flew there from Manila), he was told pointblank by the Taiwanese captain not to fall sick or otherwise they would have to throw him overboard if he dies. He thought it was a joke until it happened to one of their crew. He stayed on the ship for a year and when he signed off, he did not renew his contract.

though they perform the same job on board and may work longer hours. In addition, instead of receiving their monthly salary in full, it is often remitted to their recruiters in the Philippines who then send the money to their families' bank account, with large, unaccounted deductions. To illustrate, another Filipino fisherman I interviewed told me how his supposed salary of GBP1000 per month became GBP600. When his wife confronted the management of the recruitment company, she was told firmly that the deduction would continue until the expenses incurred by the company to find him a job and send him to Scotland were fully reimbursed. However, the amount of this expense was never specified, hence the deductions continued until his contract was terminated due to some problems with his work visa. He worked for 16 months.[9] In terms of small-scale fishermen, while the abuse and exploitation associated with their experience may be less visible than in connection with their counterparts working on commercial fishing boats, their working lives are also replete with unmitigated dangers and difficulties. For example, in the fishing community that I studied, there had been a number of incidents involving men overboard. Their bodies were never recovered.

From Fishing to Seafaring

The precarious socio-economic conditions of fishing may explain the aspiration of many young Filipinos to look beyond the shore of their localities for better opportunities. Whilst many would not be able to pursue a career in seafaring due to poverty, others, whose families are not so dependent on fishing as their main source of income, but nonetheless exposed to the thrills of seafaring because they live near coastal areas, have found ways to pursue a career in the maritime industry. With a love and fascination for the sea, many young people troop to the city to further their education and obtain the credentials required of maritime professionals. In 2019, there were more than 90 accredited maritime schools and academies in the Philippines (Geguiento 2019). Maritime schools have an average annual enrolment of 71,200 students in 2006–2010, with about 16% or 11,386 students graduating after 4 years of school work (MARINA 2013). However, there is more than a desire for adventure and a better life driving many young people of the Philippines to pursue a career in the maritime industry. There are also a number of historical, economic and structural factors that have paved the way for the Philippines to become the world's crewing capital.

Thus, while I have explained in some detail the possible geographical, historical and cultural underpinnings of many Filipinos' connection with the sea, it is also necessary to highlight other factors that have helped them realise their dream to work

[9]The expenses of recruitment companies sending Filipino workers overseas varies from one place to another. However, most of the time, employers pay the recruiters for the recruits' expenses and therefore, what was done to the fisherman I interviewed was illegal.

in the world's merchant vessels. One factor that needs further elaboration here is the economic context of the 1970s which drove much migrant labour overseas.

In the 1970s, as President Ferdinand Marcos struggled to keep the Philippine economy afloat, battered from all sides by rampant corruption, the ferocious winds of high inflation, budget deficits, moribund domestic and international investment (due to the country's volatile political climate brought about by the imposition of Martial Law) and the oil crisis, the Philippine government created an environment in which it became attractive for Filipinos to seek employment overseas (Fajardo 2011; Oishi 2005; Semyonov and Gorodzeisky 2004; Tadiar 2003). Furthermore, with a shift toward agribusiness and export-oriented industrialization, the Philippine state began in the 1970s to actively encourage the export of temporary contract labour (Tyner 2002, p. 100; see also Acacio 2008; Parrenas 2015; Rodriguez 2010). For Marcos, sending Filipinos to work overseas en-masse became an economic stop-gap measure and a strategy to accumulate the foreign exchange necessary for imports and, in the long run, to keep the economy afloat. Thus, though the Philippines had been sending workers to the US for many years, providing farm workers to Hawaii's sugar and pineapple plantations (Boyd 1971) and to professional occupations such as medicine in public and private hospitals (Espiritu 2010), it was only in the late 1970s that other country-destinations opened up for Filipino workers including: the Middle East (Humphrey 1990); Singapore; Malaysia; and Hong Kong (Alburo and Abella undated). By the 1990s, other countries like Israel, Dubai, Taiwan, Qatar and a host of European countries like Italy, Iceland, the UK and Spain followed and became destinations for Filipinos wanting to work overseas (Debono and Vassallo 2019; Hoegsholm 2007; Skaptadottir 2010). In 2017, according to the Philippine Statistics Authority (PSA), there were around 2.3 million overseas Filipino workers (OFW).

The Philippines' role as a state broker (Rodriguez 2010) of labour to the world was eventually formalized in 1982 when the Philippine Overseas Employment Administration (POEA) was created. It is a government agency which oversees and facilitates the deployment of Filipino workers overseas. Other state agencies assisting the POEA in its functions include the Overseas Worker Welfare Administration (OWWA) which as the name suggests looks after the welfare of Filipino overseas workers. An important function of these government agencies is to protect Filipino workers from fraudulent employment practices by employment agencies. It is in this context that the international deployment of Filipinos to ocean-going merchant vessels and their positioning as a major global player in the crewing sector of the global maritime industry may be explained.

The growth and development of the crewing industry in the Philippine maritime industry can also be traced back to events shaping the shipping industry in the 1970s, including deregulation and the associated globalization of the industry and the labour market (Sampson 2013). More specifically, however, the dominance of the Philippines in the crewing sector of the global shipping industry started rather serendipitously in the late 1960s. As recounted by Peter Toundjis, the former manager of El Greco Shipping Enterprises:

> in 1966, a Greek ship came to Manila and requested his company to provide an emergency replacement crew. Although El Greco usually only helped restock and repair ships, it nevertheless agreed, thus sparking the first placements of Filipinos on Greek ships (McKay 2007, p. 622).

He further added:

> Word quickly spread in Piraeus, New York and other international maritime centers that Filipinos were good and dependable. El Greco thereupon launched an information campaign to sell the Filipino seaman, undertaken through brochures distributed to more than 2,000 ship-owning companies all over the world. The brochures generated inquiries from all directions and helped put the Philippine crewing industry firmly on its feet. Indeed, as the word spread, other major shipping firms that were experimenting with foreigners in their lower-rank positions began trying out Filipinos. (McKay 2007, p. 622)

Soon, local shipping owners as well as foreign ones (mostly European) saw tremendous growth potential in the business and started putting up or locating their crewing offices in Manila. In 1974, an association of crewing agencies in Manila was formed and called itself Filipino Association for Mariners' Employment (FAME), probably the first of its kind in Asia and the world. In the 1980s, an industry pioneer, Jacob Stolt Nielsen, made it possible for an all-Filipino crew to man a vessel. Economic developments on the global front also affected the growth of the crewing industry in Manila. By the late 1980s, Manila's transformation into the world's ship crewing capital was complete.

Other global developments also shaped the positioning of Manila as the global crewing capital. Until the 1970s, the international industry was regulated almost entirely along national lines: ship-owners registered or 'flagged' their vessels in their home country, requiring them to employ their own nationals and observe domestically negotiated labour regulations and wages. However, rising competitive pressures led ship-owners looking to lower their costs to 'flag' their vessels in countries that promised minimal interference and low or no taxes (McKay 2007, p. 620, see also Bergantino and O'Sullivan 1999; Bloor et al. 2000; Sampson 2013). Given that these 'open registers' did not stipulate the nationalities to be employed on board, or the terms for employment, ship operators became more autonomous in terms of their recruitment choices. In this context the Philippines was seen as an attractive recruitment base for many ship owners who wanted to save on operational costs without compromising on levels of commitment and professionalism. Filipino seafarers possessed sufficient technical skills, were 'cheap' compared to their European counterparts and they could speak English well, three vital components of a successful crewing strategy.

The positioning of Manila as the crewing hub of the global maritime industry created an add-on effect to other sectors of the industry as well. As demands for Filipino seafarers increased, more and more maritime schools opened. Prior to this, the production of Filipino merchant seafarers was monopolised by the Philippine Merchant Marine Academy (PMMA), which was established in 1963 although its foundation could be traced back to 1820 with the creation of the Escuela Notica de Manila by the Philippine colonial government. Another pioneering school, the John B Lacson Foundation Maritime University opened its doors to aspiring Filipino seafarers in 1948. Soon, many maritime schools were established, with the support of shipowners, business organisations, and seafarer unions. For example, in 1998 the Maritime Academy of Asia and the Pacific (MAAP) was set up. MAAP is a joint venture supported by some of the Philippines' most influential maritime business and labour organisations like FAME, Associated Marine Officers' and Seamen's Union of the Philippines (AMOSUP), the All Japan Seamen's Union, the Norwegian Seafarers' Union (NSU), the International Maritime Employers Committee Limited (IMEC), the Danish Shipowners Association, the Norwegian Shipowners Association (NSA), Japanese Shipowners Association (JSA), and the International Mariners Management Association of Japan (IMMAJ). Filipino students who are admitted to MAAP do not pay any matriculation fees. They are also provided with free accommodation on campus and a monthly stipend. Perhaps most significantly they are also promised jobs on board once they graduate from the school courtesy of Japanese and Norwegian sponsors.

These developments demanded action from government which responded with the creation of the Maritime Industry Authority (MARINA) in 1963. This paved the way for the further institutionalization of governmental support for Filipino seafarers. The agency, as well as looking after the development and growth of the local domestic maritime sector, assumes responsibility for managing the professionalization and welfare of Filipino seafarers deployed on board foreign merchant vessels. In 2014, to solidify the status of the Philippines as the prime hub of crewing in the world, President Benigno Aquino Jr signed into law Republic Act 10635 creating a single maritime administration to oversee the training and certification of Filipino seafarers. Prior to this, many public agencies were involved in managing the affairs of Filipino seafarers which made it a bureaucratic nightmare for many Filipinos aspiring to work in the industry. With only one government agency to deal with in relation to matters pertaining to licensing, training and certification, it was hoped that the establishment of the new 'super' agency would improve the competitive edge of Filipino seafarers over their foreign counterparts.

Financially, working as a seafarer provides Filipinos with one of the best ways out of poverty. Though the Philippines has registered one of the highest economic growth rates in Asia since 2010 (Tupaz and Wagner n.d.), the country is still mired in poverty. The Philippines has one of the highest unemployment rates in Asia, pegged at 5.8 in January 2016 (Inquirer 2016). In addition low quality jobs persist in the labour market. In 2014, just 58% of workers—in both formal and informal employment—were in paid jobs. Of the rest, 28% were self-employed, with no guaranteed income, and 11% worked on family owned farms or other businesses where they typically receive food and lodging but no actual cash (Salvosa 2015). With a basic salary of PHP10,000–20,000 (USD220440)[10] gross per month for most workers, the quality of life is relatively poor. However, amongst seafarers such problems are less pervasive. The lowest ranked seafarers—ratings—whose income per month, is tax

[10]Wages vary though. Workers living in the Metropolitan Manila area receive a higher rate compared to their compatriots living in other cities and the provinces.

free, averages USD1000. As a result, Filipino seafarers are financially better off than their land-based counterparts, including their overseas compatriots in Hong Kong, Singapore and the Middle East. In many rural areas in the country, it is not uncommon for big houses to be owned by seafarers (Acejo 2012). Such economic opportunities fuel the desire of many to work on board regardless of the emotional hardship that it entails (Sampson 2005).

Conclusion: Challenges and Opportunities for Filipino Seafarers

Fishing communities may be described as the 'staging post' for many Filipinos seeking to expand their horizons and have a better life. This is not an overstatement since as the study of Filipino seafarers by Amante (2003) tells us, some 32% of those he interviewed came from fishing families and more than 80% of respondents from the same study hailed from the Visayas and Mindanao, two major groups of islands in the Philippines known for their fishing activities. Whether the archipelagic character of the Philippines and the promise of a better life will continue to inspire many young Filipinos to seek employment in the maritime industry remains to be seen. There is a myriad of challenges ahead. As alternative careers open up to Filipinos ashore providing them with better and safer working conditions and career progression, the sea becomes a less alluring place to work. Though there are now more maritime schools than before, matriculation expenses (charged by private schools and colleges) have become even more prohibitive. In 2003, it was estimated that around 5000 USD would be needed by a Filipino seafarer to complete a maritime degree (Amante 2003). This amount has since increased significantly.[11] In addition, as more and more schools and training centres open to meet the rising demands of the domestic and global maritime markets, substandard maritime education and training have become an issue (Bloor and Sampson 2009). MARINA has the challenging task of monitoring compliance by recognised Maritime Higher Educational Institutions (MHEIs) and accredited Maritime Training Institutions (MTIs). In recent years the European Maritime Safety Agency (EMSA) has

[11] An interview with a maritime student studying in Manila in 2016 revealed the following expenses: PHP25,000 tuition fee ($\times$2 semesters per year $\times$4 years) = PHP200,000. Other expenses include monthly stipend of PHP10,000 $\times$ 10 months $\times$ 4 years = PHP400,000. So a maritime student will spend roughly P 600,000.00 to be able to complete a degree in marine transportation (deck and engine) in the Philippines. This is equivalent to USD12,500 (48 exchange rate to 1 dollar), a big leap from the estimate made by Amante in 2003. Students studying in other cities and in the provinces spend much lower than the figures provided here. Training and examinations to obtain certificates and licenses are not included in the estimates made. The last year for maritime students is spent on-board as a trainee. Some shipping companies pay them while they are on-board (usually ocean-going vessels where they 'work' as cadets) while others don't and in many cases, they have to pay the shipping company that provides them with seatime on-board (usually domestic ships).

identified serious deficiencies in the auditing of training and education in the Philippines (Inquirer 2013; Manila Bulletin 2019). To avoid sanctions MARINA has sought to address many problems but this has sometimes been challenging. Failure to address the issues identified by EMSA would have meant some 80,000 Filipino seafarers being barred from joining ships registered in the EU. Additional challenges come in the form of political interventions in running the affairs of the maritime industry. Continuity of programs to make Filipino seafarers competitive in the global market are always under threat given the ways in which every successive president appoints 'their own people' to run government agencies. As every administration comes and goes, existing programs are scrapped without due diligence to give way to new ones favoured by the incumbent. This could ultimately prove disadvantageous to the Philippines in the face of stiff competition from other seafaring countries like Poland, Ukraine, and India all of which also provide highly skilled seafarers to the global fleet. For the moment, however, the Philippines leads the way in the crewing industry and is predicted to remain as the prime crewing hub for shipping in the foreseeable future.

In spite of these challenges and others relating to global competition as the sun sets on one of the fishing communities in the Philippines, it seems for the moment that opportunities remain within the global merchant maritime sector and that for the present Filipino seafarers will continue sailing the oceans of the world.

References

Acacio, K. 2008. Managing Labor Migration: Philippine State Policy and International Migration Flows, 1969-2000. *Asian and Pacific Migration Journal* 17 (2): 103–132.

Acejo, I. 2012. Seafarers and Transnationalism: Way of Belongingness Ashore and Aboard. *Journal of Intercultural Studies* 33 (1): 69–84.

Aguilar, F. 2012. Manilamen and Seafaring: Engaging the Maritime World Beyond the Spanish Realm. *Journal of Global History* 7 (3): 364–388.

Alburo, F., and D. Abella. undated. Skilled Labour Migration from Developing Countries: Study on the Philippines. In *International Migration Papers 51*. Geneva: International Labour Office.

Amante, M. 2003. *Philippine Global Seafarers: A Profile*. Seafarers International Research Centre, Cardiff University.

Asis, M. 2017. *The Philippines: Beyond Labor Migration, Toward Development and (Possibly) Return*. Migration Policy Institute. Accessed November 23, 2019. https://www.migrationpolicy.org/article/philippines-beyond-labor-migration-toward-development-and-possibly-return

BFAR. 2014. *Philippine Fisheries Profile*. Manila. Accessed November 23, 2019. http://bfar.da.gov.ph/publication.jsp?id=2338#post

BFAR. 2015. *Philippine Fisheries Profile*. Manila. Accessed on November 23, 2019. http://bfar.da.gov.ph/publication.jsp?id=2363#post

BFAR. 2018. *Philippine Fisheries Profile*. Manila. Accessed November 23, 2019. http://bfar.da.gov.ph/publication.jsp?id=2369#post

Bergantino, A.S., and P. O'Sullivan. 1999. Flagging Out and International Registries: Main Developments and Policy Issues. *International Journal of Transport Economics* 26 (3): 447–472.

BIMCO. 2015. *Executive Summary: Manpower Report: The Global Supply and Demand for Seafarers in 2015*. Bagsvaerd: Denmark: Dearsley Maritime Consulting Ltd.

Bloor, M., and H. Sampson. 2009. Regulatory Enforcement of Labour Standards in an Outsourcing Globalized Industry: The Case of the Shipping Industry. *Work, Employment and Society* 23 (4): 711–726.

Bloor, M., et al. 2000. Health Risks in the Global Shipping Industry: An Overview. *Health, Risk and Society* 2 (3): 329–340.

Boyd, M. 1971. Oriental Immigration: The Experience of the Chinese, Japanese, and Filipino Populations in the United States. *The International Migration Review* 5 (1): 48–61.

Brown, D. 2009. Reports on the Shocking Abuses FACED by Burmese Fishers. *Transport International* 2: 16–18.

Clark, P., et al. 1993. The Butuan Two Boat Known as a Balangay in the National Museum, Manila, Philippines. *The International Journal of Nautical Archaeology* 22 (2): 143–159.

Corpuz, G.A. 2014. *Group Slams Fisheries Law: We Are 16 Years a Slave*. Bulatlat.com. Accessed November 4, 2016. https://pamalakayaweb.wordpress.com/2014/03/12/group-slams-fisheries-law-we-are-16-years-a-slave/

Corpuz, O.D. 2005. *The Roots of the Filipino Nation*. UP ed. Quezon City: University of the Philippines Press.

Couper, A., H.D. Smith, and B. Ciceri. 2015. *Fishers and Plunderers: Theft, Slavery and Violence at Sea*. London: Pluto Press.

Debono, M., and M.T. Vassallo. 2019. An Analysis of WORKING Conditions of Filipinos in Malta. *European Scientific Journal* 15 (26): 64–88.

DTI. 2019. *Gross Domestic Product (GDP)*. Accessed November 23, 2019. https://www.dti.gov.ph/resources/statistics/gross-domestic-product-gdp

Eder, J.F. 2005. Coastal Resource Management and Social Differences in Philippine FISHING Communities. *Human Ecology* 33 (2): 147–169.

Espiritu, Y.L. 2010. Colonial Oppression, Labour Importation, and Group Formation: Filipinos in the United States. *Ethnic and Racial Studies* 19 (1): 29–48.

Fajardo, K. 2011. *Filipino Crosscurrents: Oceanographies of Seafaring, Masculinities, and Globalization*. University of Minnesota Press.

FAO. 2018. *The State of World Fisheries and Aquaculture. Rome*. Accessed November 23, 2019. http://www.fao.org/3/i9540en/i9540en.pdf

Geguiento, E. 2019. *Filipino Maritime Cadets Shipboard Training: Complexities, Issues and Concerns. Understanding Seafarers: Identities, Narratives, and Contexts*. University of the Philippines. 18 November 2019.

Giraldez, A. 2015. *The Manila Galleons and the Dawn of the Global Economy: The Age of Trade*. Rowman and Littlefield Publishers.

Guevarra, R.P. 2011. Filipinos in Nueva Espana: Filipino-Mexican Relations, Mestizaje, and the Identity in Colonial and Contemporary Mexico. *Journal of Asian American Studies* 14 (3): 389–416.

Guieb, E.R. 2009. *Community, Marine Rights and Tenure: A Political Ecology of Marine Conservation in Two Bohol Villages in Central Philippines*. PhD Thesis, McGill University.

Hellenic Shipping News. 2019. Filipino seafarers send home 6.14 bln USD in 2018. Accessed November 23, 2019. https://www.hellenicshippingnews.com/filipino-seafarers-send-home-6-14-bln-usd-in-2018/

Hoegsholm, F.M., ed. 2007. *In de olde worlde: Views of Filipino Migrants in Europe*. Quezon City: Philippine Migration Research Network.

Howard, P.M. 2012. Sharing or Appropriation? Share Systems, Class and Commodity Relations in Scottish Fisheries. *Journal of Agrarian Change* 12 (2): 316–343.

Humphrey, M. 1990. *Asian Women Workers in the Middle East: Domestic Servants in Jordan*. Occasional Paper 22. The Centre for Multicultural Studies, University of Wollongong. Accessed November 2, 2016. http://ro.uow.edu.au/cgi/viewcontent.cgi?article=1019&context=cmsocpapers

Inquirer. 2013. *Blacklist of Filipino Seafarers in European Ships Feared*. Accessed November 24, 2019. http://globalnation.inquirer.net/95057/blacklist-of-filipino-seafarers-in-european-ships-feared

———. 2019. 2018 Remittances Hit All-Time High. Accessed November 23, 2019. https://business.inquirer.net/265151/2018-remittances-hit-all-time-high

Kaur, A. 2016. Rethinking Philippine Labour Export. RSIS Commentary. No 284, pp.

Kurien, J. 1998. *Small-Scale Fisheries in the Context of Globalization*. Thiruvananthapuram: Center for Development Studies.

———. 2003. The Blessings of the Commons: Small-Scale Fisheries, Community Property Rights, and Coastal Natural Assets. In *International Conference on Natural Assets*. Philippines, January: Tagaytay City.

Mangahas, M. 2000. *Managing Luck and Negotiating Change: Ethnographies of Fishing and Sharing in the Philippines*. PhD Thesis. University of Cambridge.

Mangahas, M.F. 1993. *Mataw, amung nu rayon, anitu (man, the Fish of Summer, and the spirits): an Ethnography of Mataw Fishing in Batanes*. University of the Philippines.

Manila Bulletin. 2019. *Filipino Seafarers in Trouble as PH's Maritime Education Fails to Meet Int'l Standard, EU Warns*. Accessed November 24, 2019. https://news.mb.com.ph/2019/06/04/filipino-seafarers-in-trouble-as-phs-maritime-education-fails-to-meet-intl-standard-eu-warns/

MARINA. 2013. *The Philippine Maritime Industry: Prospects and Challenges in 2013 and Beyond*. Accessed November 3, 2016. http://www.marina.gov.ph/reports/other_reports/Philippine%20Maritime%20Industry.Prospects%20and%20Challenges.pdf

———. 2015. *Maritime Philippines Agenda*. Accessed November 3, 2016. http://www.marina.gov.ph/transparency/plans&prog/Maritime%20Philippines%20Agenda.pdf

McKay, S. 2007. Filipino Sea Men: Constructing Masculinities in an Ethnic Labour Niche. *Journal of Ethnic and Migration Studies* 33 (4): 617–633.

Mercene, F.L. 2007. *Manila Men in the New World: Filipino Migration to Mexico and the Americas from the Sixteenth Century*. Quezon City: University of the Philippines Press.

Oishi, N. 2005. *Women in Motion: Globalization, State Policies, and Labour MIGRATION in Asia*. Stanford: Stanford University Press.

OXFAM. 2014. *Rebuilding Fishing Communities and Fisheries: Post-Haiyan Reconstruction in the Philippines*. Joint Agency Briefing Note. Accessed November 4, 2016. https://www.oxfam.org/sites/www.oxfam.org/files/bn-fisheries-reconstruction-philippines-recovery-1200214-en.pdf

Parrenas, R.S. 2015. *Servants of Globalization: Migration and Domestic Work*. Stanford: Stanford University Press.

Philippine Statistics Authority. 2017. *PSA Conducts Quarterly Commercial and Municipal/Inland Fisheries Surveys*. Accessed November 3, 2016. http://nap.psa.gov.ph/pressreleases/2015/PR-CTCO-SS-201507-02_fisheries.asp

Pocock, N., et al. 2018. Occupational, Physical Sexual and Mental Health and Violence Among Migrant and Trafficked Commercial Fishers and Seafarers from the Greater Mekong Subregion (GMS): Systematic Review. *Global Health Research and Policy* 3 (28): 1–13.

Rodriguez, R. 2010. *Migrants for Export: How the Philippine State Brokers LABOR to the World*. University of Minnesota Press.

Ross, N. 2015. Understanding the Fishing 'Community': The Role of Communities of the Mind. *Sociologia Ruralis* 55 (3): 309–324.

Salvosa, F. 2015. Philippine Struggles with Unemployment Despite Economic Growth. *Financial Times*. Accessed November 3, 2016. http://www.cnbc.com/2015/09/01/unemployment-in-philippines-an-issue-despite-rapid-economic-growth.html

Sampson, H. 2005. Left High and Dry? The Lives of Women Married to Seafarers in Goa and Mumbai. *Ethnography* 6 (1): 61–85.

———. 2013. *International Seafarers and Transnationalism in Twenty-First Century*. Manchester: Manchester University Press.

Schurz, W.L. 1939. The Manila Galleon. E. P. Dutton. Accessed November 4, 2016. http://www.seafish.org/media/publications/PhilippinesEthicsProfile_201509.pdf

Semyonov, M., and A. Gorodzeisky. 2004. Occupational Destinations and Economic Mobility of Filipino Overseas Workers. *International Migration Review* 38 (1): 5–25.

Simmons, G., and C. Stringer. 2014. New Zealand's Fisheries Management System: Forced Labour an Ignored or Overlooked Dimension? *Marine Policy* 50 (A): 74–80.

Skaptadottir, U.D. 2010. *Intergration and Transnational Practices of Filipinos in Scotland*, 36–45. Migrinter.

St. Martin, K.S. 2005. Mapping Economic Diversity in the First World: The Case of Fisheries. *Environment and Planning* 37: 959–979.

———. 2007. The Difference that Class Makes: Neoliberalization and Non-Capitalism in the Fishing Industry of New England. *Antipode* 34 (2): 527–549.

Stobutzki, I.C., et al. 2006. Key Issues in Coastal Fisheries in South and Southeast Asia: Outcomes of a Regional Initiative. *Fisheries Research* 78: 109–118.

Tadiar, N.X.M. 2003. *Fantasy Production: Sexual Economies and Other Philippine Consequences for the New World Order*. Hong Kong: Hong Kong University Press.

Tupaz, E., and D. Wagner n.d.. Aquino's Legacy in the Philippines. *The World Post*. Accessed January 18, 2018. https://www.huffingtonpost.com/edsel-tupaz/aquinos-legacy-in-the-phi_b_7922082.html

Turgo, N. 2010. *'Bugabug ang Dagat': The Local Life of a Fishing Community in the Philippines*. PhD Thesis, Cardiff University.

Tyner, J. 2002. The Globalization of Transnational Labor Migration and the Filipino Family: A Narrative. *Asian and Pacific Migration Journal* 11 (1): 95–116.

Ushijima, I., and C.N. Zayas, eds. 1994. *Fisheries of the Visayas*. Quezon City: CSSP Publications.

Warren, J.F. 2003. *Iranun and Balangingi: Globalization, Maritime Raiding and the Birth of Ethnicity*. National University of Singapore Press.

———. 2007. *The Sulu Zone: The Dynamics of External Trade, Slavery, and Ethnicity in the Transformation of a Southeast Asian Maritime State 1768–1898*. National University of Singapore Press.

Wozniak, A. 2015. Mutual empowerment? Examining the Power Relationship Between Overseas Filipino Workers and the Motherland. *Georgetown Journal of Asian Affairs*. Spring/Summer, pp. 98–121.

Yea, S. 2014. Trafficking on the High Seas: The Exploitation of Migrant Fishermen in Southeast Asia's Long Haul Fishing Industry. In *Trafficking in Human Beings: Learning from Asian and European experiences*, ed. W. Hofmeister and P. Rueppel, 85–96. Konrad-Adenauer Stiflung and European Union.

Chapter 3
Recruiting and Managing Labour for the Global Shipping Industry in China

Zhiwei Zhao

Introduction

China's economy has experienced dramatic growth in the last 30 years and in relation to seafaring labour supply many expected that Chinese seafarers would eventually come to dominate the world seafarers' labour market. In fact, although the number of Chinese seafarers in the international fleet has grown steadily since the 1990s, the increase has been slower than many international shipping industry commentators and academics predicted (BIMCO/ISF 1995; Li and Wonham 1999; Sharma 2002; Wu 2004; Wu et al. 2007; Zhao 2017).

This chapter aims to explain the shortfall in the anticipated export of China's seafarers by highlighting the reform and market-orientation of China's state-owned crewing agencies (SCAs). It raises questions concerning the interventions of the government and higher institutions in the SCAs and discusses how reforms have affected seafarers and seafarer labour export. It also systematically examines the employment and labour supply procedures of two SCAs and the impact of their strategies.

The Idea of 'Going Global'

Since the late 1990s, articles in trade papers for the maritime industry have reported that China's seafarer export would increase remarkably (Lloyd's Ship Manager 1999; Lloyd's List 2000, 2008, Zhao 2017). This conclusion is supported in the

Z. Zhao (✉)
Dalian Maritime University, Dalian, China

University of Southern Denmark, Esbjerg, Denmark
e-mail: zhao@health.sdu.dk

V. O. Gekara, H. Sampson (eds.), *The World of the Seafarer*, WMU Studies in Maritime Affairs 9, https://doi.org/10.1007/978-3-030-49825-2_3

academic literature and BIMCO/ISF (1995), which estimated that China's seafarer export would increase to more than 89,000 by 2000 and to 104,000 by 2005. Li and Wonham (1999) evaluated the report of BIMCO/ISF (1995) and argued that BIMCO/ISF had underestimated China's export of its seafarers in the 2000s, and that it could supplant the Philippines as the largest supplier of global seafaring labour (1999, 299).

Having evaluated the advantages (i.e. huge population of seafaring labour, good training infrastructure and the availability of alternative occupational opportunities) and the disadvantages (i.e. weak English and low occupational tenure) of China as a labour market, Sharma (2002) predicted that China would emerge as the new leader of the global seafaring labour market. Wu et al. (2006) also predicted the substantial increase of China's seafarer export after considering two issues. They deemed that the emergence of the hundreds of crewing agencies in the market would open new channels for Chinese seafarers to work on board foreign ships (Wu et al. 2007) and predicted that they would flood the world's seafarer labour market due to the attractions of working in foreign shipping companies, such as better pay (Wu 2004; Wu et al. 2006, 2007).

However, in 2000 and 2005, only 38,164 and 41,260 Chinese seafarers, respectively, worked in the global labour market, representing 42.8% and 39.7% of the numbers predicted by BIMCO/ISF (Bao and Liu 2008, p. 380). China has been ranked as the 4th/5th largest country in terms of maritime manpower supply[1] in the world since the 2000s but represented approximately one fourth/fifth of the seafarer export from the Philippines both in the 1990s and the 2000s (Bao and Liu 2008; POEA 2018). In 2013, the Philippines, exported 367,166 seafarers which was more than three times higher than the 119,316 seafarers supplied by China (MSA 2014; POEA 2018). In 2017, 378,072 seafarers were exported by the Philippines and China dispatched 138,854 seafarers, representing 36.5% of the number of the Filipino seafarers working in the global labour market (MSA 2018; POEA 2018).

In consideration of this overestimation, a few researchers incline to a cautious analysis of Chinese seafarer export. Shen et al. (2005), Zhao (2000, 2002), and Tang et al. (2016) discuss the reform of China's seafarer labour market and analyze the potential constraints on the development of seafarer export, such as the development of the social security system, the English-speaking ability of Chinese seafarers and the complex dynamics of the world seafarers' labour market.

Whatever the assumptions and expectations, previous studies have focused on the export of Chinese seafarer labour while neglecting to analyze the ways in which crewing agencies operate and the extent to which crewing agencies have reformed into market-oriented economic entities that play a central role in providing labour to the global market. This gives rise to a number of elementary questions:

[1]BIMCO/ICS 2015 Manpower Report indicates that China is the largest labour supply country, meaning that China has the largest numbers of registered seafarers, rather than China supplies the largest number of seafarers to the global labour market.

- To what extent can SCAs determine their own business strategy?
- To what extent are managers actively involved in improving and reforming management strategies?
- What specific management methods are applied by the crewing agencies?
- What are the consequent impacts on seafarers and on foreign manning businesses?

Answering these questions is critical when seeking to understand seafarer recruitment and employment in China and may contribute to a better understanding of the historic overestimates of China's seafarer export.

Given the lack of systematic evidence in the literature on these and related questions, the chapter seeks to explore the questions through an analysis of 54 semi-structured and 32 in-depth interviews conducted with 22 managers and 50 seafarers between 2008 and 2013 in two Chinese SCAs (hereinafter referred to as SA and IA; for more details please refer to Tables 3.1 and 3.2). The interview

Table 3.1 Interviews conducted between 2008 and 2013[a]

Years	2008 and 2011	2012 to 2013
Interviews taken in SA	11 interviews with managers and 23 with seafarers	4 interviews with managers and 3 with seafarers
Interviews taken in IA	11 interviews with managers and 27 with seafarers	4 interviews with managers and 3 with seafarers
Number of interviews in total	72 interviews	14 interviews
Identity and post of interviewees in SA	Director, the Chair of the Trade Union, the Training manager, the Human Research Management (HRM) manager, the Manning manager, the Vice Director of the Head Office and the Director of the parent shipping company (PSC); Seafarers of all ranks	
Identity and post of interviewees in IA	Director, the HRM manager, the Manning manager, the Chair of the trade union, the Business manager and the Training manager; Seafarers of all ranks	
	A majority of the interviews lasted at least 1 hour and was voice-recorded	

[a]The tables and figures in this chapter first appeared in Zhao et al. (2016), pp. 737–747

Table 3.2 Basic information about IA and SA

Company name	IA	SA
Category	ISCA	SSCA
Year established	1985	1995
Main client	Foreign shipping companies	PSC
The number of ships manned in total in 2013	32	43
The number of foreign ships manned in 2013	32	9
The number of staff in 2013	20	58
The number of regularly employed seafarers in 2013	722	3380
The ranks of seafarers	Mainly officer seafarers	All ranks
The number of freelance seafarers employed in 2013	387	0

Sources: The two crew agencies

questions were varied in accordance with the different positions of the interviewees. Each interview lasted at least one hour and was voice-recorded. The crewing agencies in the case studies have reformed to different degrees. They represent the largest examples of two types of Chinese crewing agency that dominate seafarer labour export. The study of the agencies allows an evaluation of the operations of the most important players in the Chinese seafaring labour market.

Before looking at the case studies, the chapter provides some macro level social and economic background by overviewing the reform of the Chinese economy, the seafarer labour market and ship crewing agencies.

China's Economic Reform, Seafarer Labour Market Reform and Ship Crewing Agencies

Before the economic reform of 1979, all political and economic activities in China were strictly planned and directly controlled by the Chinese government. Chinese enterprises were all state-owned. In 1979, in order to improve the economy, economic reform was introduced. The main focus of enterprise reform was the decentralization of power from the government. With the implementation of key reform measures, in theory, most of the state-owned enterprises (SOEs) were no longer supported by the government. They were supposed to operate independently and to be responsible for their own profits and losses. Non-state owned companies including privately-owned and foreign-backed enterprises made their first appearance in the late 1980s and have grown rapidly since the 1990s. They have contributed tremendously to the growth of China's economy (Garnaut et al. 2012).

The emergence and development of the Chinese seafaring labour market was the result of the economic reform. Before 1979, there was no labour market in China, as all workers were assigned by the government to certain work units (*danwei*) according to the government's plan. Since the 1990s, the evolution of the Chinese seafaring labour market has been driven by several main forces. Firstly, as a result of the economic reform the central government replaced the planned workers' assignment mechanism with a free, two-way selection system between employees and employers. This meant that workers could freely choose their employers, and employers were free to recruit and manage all employment issues associated with workers, without any intervention from senior government levels. Secondly, the reform of shipping companies, especially the emergence and development of privately-owned and foreign-backed companies, caused a huge demand for seafaring labour employed on fixed-term contracts. Thirdly, the implementation of the Labour Law in 1995 enabled SOEs which 'possessed' most seafaring labour to fire workers and to 'liberate' them from their traditional life-long employment status, replacing this with employment based on fixed-term contracts (Shen et al. 2005).

Hundreds of crewing agencies were set up to meet the demands of shipping companies as a result of these combined factors. However, according to the Labour

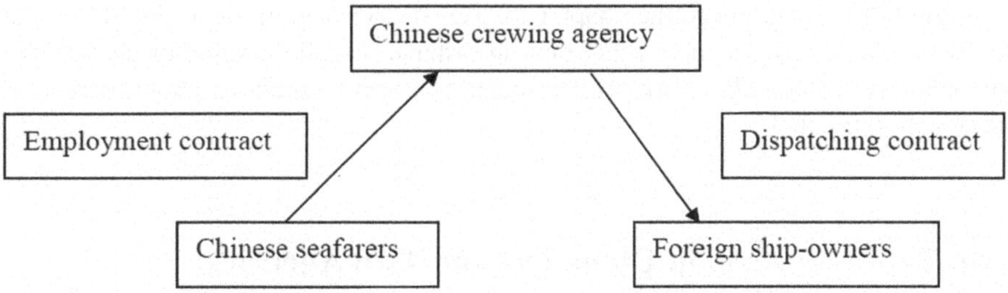

Fig. 3.1 The contract relationships in the foreign manning process

Laws of 1995 and the New Labour Contract Law of 2008, Chinese workers working overseas are not allowed to be directly employed by foreign employers but only through Chinese crewing agencies with foreign manning credentials. These serve to facilitate the participation of Chinese seafarers in the global labour market. In the crewing process, different sorts of contractual relations are involved (Fig. 3.1). Seafarers first sign an *employment contract* with a Chinese crewing agency which consequently becomes the buyer of the seafarers' labour and decides all employment issues, e.g. wages, working-hours, holidays, etc. These are based on the condition and standards of the Chinese labour market, and are lower than those of foreign shipping companies. Chinese seafarers rely directly on the Chinese agencies for employment. The crewing agency then signs a *dispatching contract* with the foreign ship-owner, the user of the seafarers' labour, who pays the agency for the labour. Chinese seafarers have no way of getting in touch with the foreign ship-owners whose ships they sail upon or to read this *dispatching contract*. They know nothing about the contents of the contract. Such a management mechanism sacrifices the interests of Chinese seafarers but protects China's shipping companies from foreign competition for labour resources.

SCAs have dominated the foreign manning business in China due to the support of the government in granting foreign manning certificates and financial subsidies. It has been reported that:

> Between 1979 and 1998, COSCOMAN [COSCO's Manning Agency] employed 150,000 Chinese seafarers for foreign ship owners and operators, enjoying the lion's share of the market (60%). MASES [a crewing agency owned by China Shipping] follows, during its ten years of business between 1988 and 1998, with a total supply of 40,000 seafarers, taking a market share of 16% (Zhao 2000, pp. 13–14).

Until the twenty-first century, the dominant position of the major SCAs was still evident. In 2012, the largest SCAs held a market share of around 65%, which in 2017 increased to about 67%. The remaining seafarers were supplied by small SCAs. Privately-owned crewing agencies played a minor role and to date only one foreign-backed crewing agency has established itself in China, making a minimal contribution to overall supply (interview with a maritime safety administrator (MSA) officer, September 4 2018).

In the following section, the chapter focuses on the operations of the SCAs that dominate the crewing business in China in order to highlight some of the reasons why Chinese seafarers have not yet dominated the world's seafarer labour market, as previously predicted.

Two Types of SCAs in China and the Two Agencies in the Case Studies

SCAs in China can be roughly divided into two types. One is an independent SCA (ISCA), which is not affiliated to any shipping company. The other is a subsidiary crewing agency of a state-owned shipping company (known, for short, as subsidiary SCA (SSCA)).

The ISCA in the case study (hereinafter referred to as Independent Agency (IA)) was set up by the municipal government. IA has cooperated with foreign shipping companies since its establishment. It is one of the crewing agencies with the longest history and also one of the most influential agencies in China. IA is not affiliated to any shipping company, but supposedly operates independently, being responsible for its own profits and losses. SSCA is another type of SCA in China. Unlike ISCAs, which are established by the government, SSCAs are set up by state-owned shipping companies following the reform aimed at 'separating the management of the seafaring labour resource from the management of ships' (*ren chuan fenli*), by the Chinese central government in the 1990s. The SSCA in the case study (hereinafter referred to as Subsidiary Agency (SA), registered in 1995, is a constituent part of the largest operator in the entire Chinese shipping industry. It is a subsidiary crewing agency of its local branch shipping company (Fig. 3.2). Before registry, SA was the Seafarers' Resource Administration Department of its parent shipping company (PSC), responsible for crewing the company fleet as well as operating a crewing business that supplying seafarers to foreign shipping companies.

At this point, it is important to understand the constraints under which Chinese SCAs operate, then look at the support provided by government and the implications

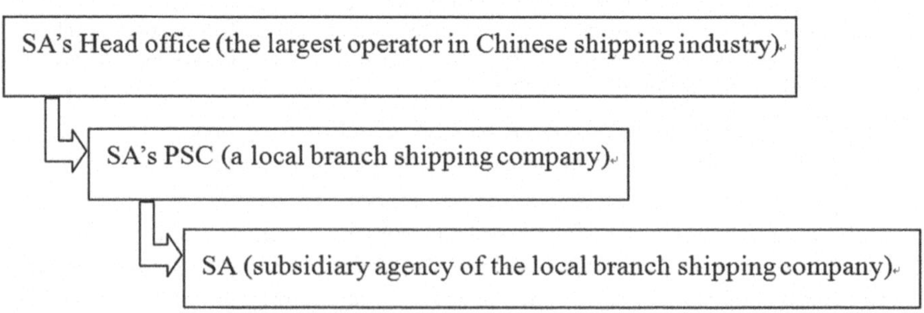

Fig. 3.2 The structure of the relationship between SA and its parent shipping company and head office

for foreign businesses. The two SCAs that are examined in the case studies represent the largest examples of the two types of Chinese crewing agencies that dominate seafarer labour export, i.e., SSCAs and ICSAs. The case studies allow us to see the operations of the most active and important players in the Chinese seafaring labour market.

The Control of the Higher Institutions

Despite registration as an independent company, at the time of the research, SA had little autonomy regarding its business operations. SA's clients and business cooperation details had to be approved by the parent shipping company (PSC) before starting the cooperation. To enjoy priority in selecting and employing high-quality seafarers, PSC defined the foremost task of SA as to offer the best crewing services to the PSC's ships, rather than enlarging the foreign manning business.

To maintain a high employment rate, the local government restricted SA in relation to sacking surplus labour (for the surplus rates please refer to Table 3.3). According to the human resources (HR) manager a vast majority of these seafarers were ratings. The Vice Director of the head office explained the reasons for employing surplus labour as follows:

> We need to maintain the stability of society by increasing employment opportunities. If surplus workers were fired, society would not be stable and the director of the PSC would be fired. It is the Party that leads the company. If you do so [fire the surplus workers], the leaders from the head office will instantly crack down on you. . .so you cannot ask SA to be market-oriented.

Concerning the specific HR management strategies, e.g. manning and promotion strategies and material support of seafarers etc., SA was also under the strict control of the PSC. Take the management of seafarers' material support for example. The gross input for the material support of seafarers and managers in SA was regulated by the head office of the PSC. When the wages of officer seafarers in the Chinese labour market increased rapidly in the mid-2000s, the wages of officer seafarers in SA did not increase much. The director of the PSC explained: 'We cannot improve

Table 3.3 The surplus rates of seafarers in some years

Year	Number of manned ships	Demand of seafarers	Number of seafarers on the books	Surplus rate %
1982	17	612	1619	62
1995	47	1692	3082	45
2006	62	2232	3003	25.7
2013	43	1548	3380	45.8

Source: SA's HRM Department

Note: With 24 seafarers on board each ship and a backup rate of 1.5, demand of seafarers equals to (number of manned ships) * 24 * 1.5

the wages of seafarers according to the situation in the labour market because the input for the wages is controlled by the head office'.

Following directives from the PSC the ratings in SA received much higher wages than the market rates in contrast to those of officer seafarers in SA. In the Chinese seafarer labour market freelance ratings were redundant, doing manual work for low wages; they were excluded from trade unions and easily exploited (Han 2008; Huang and Ning 2008; Zhang 2016). Providing ratings with high wages, permanent contracts and social insurance at the highest level was at odds with the position of ratings in the wider labour market. The HR manager explained the high material support for ratings as follows:

> Over 70% of the registered ratings are over 45 years old. We need to take care of the elder comrades. It is the tradition of SOE that the working-class is the 'elder brother'.[2] Therefore, although the wages of the ratings outside the state-owned enterprise are low, we still take care of our ratings, providing them with good wages and welfare. After all, we are all the working class.

The ratings in SA were very satisfied with their material support. However, some officer seafarers complained about management practice and considered it to be very unreasonable. A chief officer said:

> The wages of ratings in SA are high. This violates the rule in the labour market. We officer seafarers should have been given higher wages because there is a shortage of us in the market and we need much longer training and face much greater costs than ratings... But now officer seafarers' wages in SA are lower than the rates in the domestic market. But ratings' wages are higher... This is very unreasonable.

As a result many officer seafarers who were able to find jobs for higher wages in other domestic agencies and shipping companies left SA. SA suffered from a loss of high quality seafarers, which resulted in the shrinking of the number of foreign ships manned by SA, from 24 in 2006 to nine in 2013. Its profit in 2013 had decreased by 65% of the 2006 profit. In 2017, it manned 12 ships. Although the number of manned ships increased compared with 2013, because the ship-owners were small-scale, the profit levels remained similar.

Such control and intervention was not only restricted to SA. Although IA is presumed to operate independently and to be responsible for its profits and losses the case study demonstrates that there are interventions from its higher institutions (i.e. head office).

When IA was set up by the municipal government, the deputy mayor of the city at that time was elected as the first Chairman. IA merged with a SOE (which afterwards became IA's head office) in 1991 in accordance with the orders of the local government. Although IA still operated its business independently, the management

[2]In the planned economy, workers were the 'working class' and the 'masters of enterprises and the state'. Guided by this socialist ideology, workers were treated well and also as equally as possible, no matter of their skills or capability. Concerning the seafaring industry, there was no big difference in the wages of seafarers of different ranks. For instance, in 1988 a captains' wage was around 110–150 USD per month, while ratings could earn almost 90 USD.

of IA was supervised by the head office for the local government. In terms of the distribution of profits, although the head office required IA to manage its own costs, including the seafarers' and managers' wages (which are set by the head office) they were required to hand over almost all net profits. These could not be lower than a certain amount set by the head office annually. In order to fulfil these demands IA was unable to pay officer seafarers competitive wages. The Manning manager said: 'The wage of our officers is not high: it is equal to or lower than the average rate in the domestic market'. The Director of IA explained:

> We also want to increase seafarers' wages. However, the head office will not allow this. If we were to give more money to seafarers, the agency's profits would fall. In this case, how can we reach the required standard [set up by the head office]? In fact, the managers of the head office do not consider the condition of the labour market or adjust the requirements accordingly... the head office does not allow us to become independent, as it would lose the profit that we submit. So we are stuck here.

The independence of IA was still quite circumscribed by the relationship with the head office and this suggests that IA was not really independent in terms of the control that it had over its profits. This control resulted in the low wages of seafarers and a mass of officers left the agency for land-based jobs and jobs in other domestic shipping companies with higher wages. Ultimately the export of seafaring labour stagnated.

In addition to these controls and interventions, the case studies showed that SCAs received various kinds of support from their higher institutions, which resulted in managers being reluctant to carry out any reforms. This was particularly evident when looking at the case of SA.

The Support of Higher Institutions

Despite being registered as an independent company, SA still acted like an internal department of the parent shipping company (PSC). All costs of the agency were met by the PSC. Unlike IA, when SA made losses, the PSC compensated for it. Reliant on the PSC, SA did not have to be responsible for its profits and losses. The director of the PSC explained the relationship between the PSC and SA:

> The agency was registered as a company by the PSC, which means one of our departments is qualified to do business with other companies. To other companies, the agency is a company; but for the PSC, it is our department, as everything of the agency is from us.

With such support, managers in SA were not incentivized to carry out any reforms. While ignoring reforms or achieving low profits will not cause the managers problems, implementing reforms (e.g. the advancement of management strategies and improvement of market-orientation) could be complicated, risky and troublesome. The president of the Trade Union explained this in the following way:

> Everyone knows the problems of the management but no one talks about them. The reason is like this: if nobody changes the management, when problems occur, no one will be blamed.

> This is because the problems have existed for 20 years, and have not been caused by any of the current managers. But if anyone reformed any strategy, he would take the full responsibility and be blamed for any consequences. Therefore, it is safer to keep the current strategies rather than reform them.

Consequently, the managers would rather choose to stay safe than implement a potentially risky reform that might damage their personal interests. This in turn resulted in management strategies in SA lacking a market orientation in keeping with the economic reform.

Lack of Reform of Management Strategies in SA

To date, crew management and promotion policies are still based on a strategy of 'fixed ship, fixed crew' (FSFC) which can be traced back to the beginning of the 1990s. This requires seafarers assigned to a ship to work there consistently for as long as the vessel is in operation. Seafarers who have not been assigned to a particular ship get few working opportunities under this system. A HR manager said: 'In the agency, a group of seafarers are so tired because they are always called to work on board ship, while the rest have no opportunity at all'.

Lack of reform by management also resulted in the slow promotion of seafarers. The regulations implemented in 1991 required captains and manning managers to take full responsibility for any mistakes on board ships. Since newly promoted seafarers lack experience, captains and manning managers were reported to block seafarers' promotion in order to avoid potential consequences and punishment. The manning manager said:

> If there is an accident, the director of the parent shipping company or the Head Office will first ask the manning manager whether the dispatched seafarers have worked in the position before or whether the seafarers have adequate experience. If not, the leaders will ask the managers why they dispatched those new, inexperienced seafarers. There have been some bad examples when manning manager have faced serious consequences because they dispatched newly promoted seafarers. We have now learned to avoid these mistakes. This is the problem with the institutional system - seafarers' promotion is delayed.

Concerning the management of seafarers' training, managers and seafarers complained that training opportunities were not systematically planned or distributed among seafarers. As a result, some seafarers were trained repeatedly in SA while others hardly got any training. The President of Trade Union commented on the management of training:

> When there is a training opportunity, in many cases, it is the manning managers who look for training candidates, not based on any training schedule but randomly… Because of the lack of any plan, some seafarers undertake the same training several times, while others are not trained at all.

A rating who was related to a crewing manager said:

> Sometimes, when I am on leave, the manning manager calls me to take some training. I had already done those modules several times and I don't want to do them again. But considering my relationship with the manning manager and considering that he consistently gives me good working opportunities, I cannot refuse him. So I take the lessons.

The analysis shows that the reform of the management strategies was limited in SA. Seafarers experienced slow promotion, limited working opportunities and poor regulation of training. This contributed to the loss of high quality seafarers and hence limited the potential to increase seafarer export.

Conclusion

Despite 30 years of economic reform, the volume of Chinese seafarer export has grown much more slowly between 1990 and 2015 than was predicted by the international shipping industry and some academics (Li and Wonham 1999; Sharma 2002; Wu 2004; Wu et al. 2007; Zhao 2017). Though previous research mentioned some obstacles to China's seafarer export, it was taken for granted that the problems would be solved with the expansion of the economic reform and the emergence of hundreds of crewing agencies in China. The complexity of the problems and the capacity of crewing agencies to man foreign ships was not considered however. This chapter reveals the extent to which inertia prevails in the operation of Chinese manning agencies and the ways in which conservative strategies for survival block the paths to reform and the opening up of the labour market.

A few western social scientists have looked into the reform of Chinese SOEs of land-based industries. They argue that despite the dramatic growth of the Chinese economy, the reform of China's SOEs remains limited in terms of managerial autonomy due to the government restrictions (Bodmer 2002; Gu 2001; Zhang and Rasiah 2014), government's support of the SOEs (Lewis 2003; Taylor 2005; Wei et al. 2015) and the maintenance of the traditional administrative ties within the SOE system, which give parent companies strict control over their subsidiaries (Cui and Jiang 2011; Xiao et al. 2006).

So far, the SCAs dominate the foreign manning business. However, the case studies of SA and IA, two of the most influential foreign manning agencies in China, demonstrate that the SCAs may not be as reformed or market-oriented as assumed (Li and Wonham 1999; Sharma 2002; Wu 2004; Wu et al. 2007; Zhao 2017). Although the agencies were registered as independent enterprises, they received various forms of support and constraints from governmental departments and head offices. Their autonomy regarding business operations was limited and flexibility in adjusting management strategies in response to labour market conditions was constrained producing management strategies which lacked market orientation. As a result of these problems, companies faced the resignation of officers and shortfalls in high quality seafarers which consequently constrained the volume of seafarers 'exported' to the global labour market.

It seems that although economic reforms demand that the state relinquishes the control and central planning of the seafarer labour market it has nevertheless retained these by applying different control mechanisms to crewing agencies. The research underpinning this chapter indicates that that the market remains heavily government-controlled. The contradictions underlying the policy reforms explain the failure of Chinese seafarers to dominate the global market as anticipated.

To improve the competitiveness of the foreign manning business and the market orientation of Chinese SCAs, it may be necessary for the state to further relax its control over the Chinese seafarer labour market. This can be achieved by granting more autonomy and responsibility to crewing agencies enabling managers to act more effectively. This research suggests that if allowed to change then some of them are prepared for such a transition. However, there are no present indications that such changes are likely to occur.

References

Bao, J., and Z. Liu. 2008. Seafarers' Education and Training System in China. In *Shenzhen International Maritime Forum*. Shenzhen: People Communication Press.

BIMCO/ISF. 1995. *The Worldwide Demand for and Supply of Seafarers Manpower Update: Main Report*. The University of Warwick Institute for Employment Research.

Bodmer, F. 2002. The Effect of Reforms on Employment Flexibility in Chinese SOEs, 1980–1994. *Economic of Transition* 10 (3): 637–658.

Cui, L., and F. Jiang. 2011. State Ownership Effect on Firms' FDI Ownership Decisions Under Institutional Pressure: A Study of Chinese Outward-Investing Firms. *Journal of International Business Studies* 43: 264–284.

Garnaut, R., L. Song, Y. Yao, and X. Wang. 2012. *Private Enterprise in China*. Australia: ANUE Press.

Gu, E.X. 2001. Beyond the Property Right Approach: Welfare Policy and the Reform of State-Owned Enterprises in China. *Development and Change* 32 (1): 129–150.

Han, J. 2008. Providing Personnel Security for the Sustainable Development of China's Shipping Industry. In *Shenzhen International Maritime Forum*. Shenzhen: People Communication Press.

Huang, Z., and W. Ning. 2008. Study on the Necessity of Publishing Standard Contract and Auditing Regulations for Chinese Seafarers Working on Board Foreign Ships. In *Shenzhen International Maritime Forum*. Shenzhen: People Communication Press.

Lewis, P. 2003. New China-Old Ways? *Employee Relations* 25 (1): 42–60.

Li, K.X., and J. Wonham. 1999. Who Mans the World Fleet? A Follow-Up to the BIMCO/ISF Manpower Survey. *Maritime Policy & Management* 26 (3): 295–303.

Lloyd's List. 2000. Chinese crew set to increase. October 23.

———. 2008. Shanghai's surge continues apace. March 14.

Lloyd's Ship Manager. 1999. Barrier to Chinese seafarers breaking down.

MSA (Maritime Safety Administration). 2014. *Statistical Information of Seafarers*. Available at: http://xxgk.mot.gov.cn/jigou/haishi/201406/t20140626_2979758.html

———. 2018. *Statistical Information of Seafarers*. Available at: http://www.rmjtxw.com/news/yaowen/41068.html

POEA (Philippine Overseas Employment Administration) 2018. *Deployed Overseas Filipino Workers - By Type of Hiring*, 2006-2018 (1st SEM). Available at: http://www.poea.gov.ph/ofwstat/compendium/deployment%202006-2018S1.pdf.

Sharma, K.K. 2002. The Sea-Going Labour Market in the People's Republic of China and its Future. In *Shipping in China*, ed. T.W. Lee. London: Ashgate Publishing.

Shen, G., M. Zhao, L. Li, and J. Song. 2005. *Chinese Seafarer*. Shanghai: Shanghai University Press.

Tang, L., M.O.S. Llangco, and Z. Zhao. 2016. Transformations and Continuities of Issues Related to Chinese Participation in the Global Seafarers' Labour Market. *Maritime Policy and Management* 43 (3): 344–355. https://doi.org/10.1080/03088839.2015.1043751.

Taylor, R. 2005. China's Human Resource Management Strategies: The Role Enterprises and Government. *Asian Business & Management* 4 (1): 5–21.

Wei, T., J. Clegg, and L. Ma. 2015. The Conscious and Unconscious Facilitating Role of the Chinese Government in Shaping the Internationalization of Chinese MNCs. *International Business Review* 24 (2): 331–343.

Wu, B. 2004. Participation in the Global Labour Market: Experience and Responses of Chinese Seafarers. *Maritime Policy and Management* 31 (1): 69–72.

Wu, B., K.H. Lai, and T.E. Cheng. 2006. Emergence of 'New Professionalism' Among Chinese Seafarers: Empirical Evidence and Policy Implications. *Maritime Policy & Management* 33 (1): 35–48.

Wu, B., G. Shen, and L. Li. 2007. *The Transformation of the Chinese Labour Market for Seafarers*. Seafarers International Research Centre: Cardiff University. ISBN: 1-900174-33-2.

Xiao, Y., J. Morris, J. Hassard, and J. Sheehan. 2006. Downsizing The Danwei: Chinese State-Enterprise Reform and the Surplus Labour Question. *The International Journal of Human Resource Management* 17 (8): 1441–1455.

Zhang, M., and R. Rasiah. 2014. Institutional Change and State-Owned Enterprises in China's Urban Housing Market. *Habitat International* 41: 58–68.

Zhang, P. 2016. Seafarers' Rights in China: Restructuring in Legislation and Practice Under the Maritime Labour Convention 2006. In *Seafarers Rights in China: Restructuring in Legislation and Practice Under the Maritime Labour Convention 2006*. London: Routledge.

Zhao, M. 2000. Chinese Seafarers: Value for Money or Cheap Labour? In *Maritime Review*, 11–15. London: Pacific Press.

———. 2002. The Consequences of China's Socialist Market Economy for Seafarers. *Work, Employment and Society* 16 (1): 171–183.

Zhao, T. 2017. Chinese Crewing Ready for Global Shipping, Capital Link Forum, November 1, Athens. Available at: http://forums.capitallink.com/csr/2017athens/ppt/zhao.pdf

Zhao, Z., R.J. Jepsen, and L. Tang. 2016. The Reform of Chinese State-Owned Ship Crewing Agencies and Implications for China's Seafaring LABOUR Export. *Maritime Policy & Management* 43 (6): 737–747. https://doi.org/10.1080/03088839.2016.1169450.

Chapter 4
Can the UK Tonnage Tax Minimum Training Obligation Address Declining Cadet Recruitment and Training in the UK?

Victor Oyaro Gekara

Introduction

This chapter presents a critical analysis of the capacity of the nation-state to develop and implement effective policy interventions on behalf of national labour interests in highly globalized industries. This follows the consistent observation that, under neoliberal capitalism, governments have lacked the power and/or will to implement pro-labour legislation in the same way as they have done for capital (Fourcades-Gourinchas and Babb 2002; Peck 2004; Kotz 2015). This discussion is developed with reference to the Tonnage Tax policy, introduced by the UK government in 2000, as the key policy strategy to revitalize the ailing shipping industry (Department for Transport 1998). In the broadest terms, the strategy is a tax concession designed to attract British ship owners to re-flag their ships to the UK national register, retain the majority of their ship management in the UK and train British seafarer cadets (Selkou and Roe 2002; Brownrigg et al. 2001; Gekara 2010). The core of the strategy, i.e. the tax element, represents an alternative system of calculating corporation tax for shipping companies based on fixed rates and with reference to a shipping company's total operating tonnage per year rather than its total income, which represents a highly reduced rate of taxation. To specifically address the decline in the British national seafarer labour market and the supply of British officers, a Minimum Training Obligation (MTO) was included for all British-registered ships, which simultaneously incentivized and compelled shipping companies to increase their cadet recruitment and training activities (Selkou and Roe 2002).

In order to understand the developments in the British shipping industry leading to decline, one must consider the wider global-scale industrial transformations,

V. O. Gekara (✉)
School of Accounting, Information Systems and Supply Chains, RMIT University, Melbourne, VIC, Australia
e-mail: victor.gekara@rmit.edu.au

V. O. Gekara, H. Sampson (eds.), *The World of the Seafarer*, WMU Studies in Maritime Affairs 9, https://doi.org/10.1007/978-3-030-49825-2_4

involving a restructuring of global production and distribution patterns. Business liberalisation and deregulation, growing power and influence of multinational corporations, and outsourcing and offshoring of business processes are some of the key features of these changes, often generically referred to as economic globalisation (Chomsky 1999; Peck 2004). An important outcome of these transformations, particularly in advanced industrial economies, is that, key traditional local industries have declined leading to similar decline in domestic labour markets as employment opportunities are lost alongside workforce training and development opportunities. In the case of British shipping, large-scale flagging out[1] of the nationally owned and registered fleet (Kovats 2006), and consequent decline in the demand for national seafarers occurred, as globalisation opened up new cheaper international ship registers and low-cost international sources of seafarers for ship owners. It is in this context that the tonnage tax was introduced as a policy strategy for the revitalisation of the industry (Selkou and Roe 2002).

Following a qualitative social science study, in which interview data was collected from key shipping industry stakeholders between 2005 and 2007, this chapter examines the performance of the tonnage tax, with specific focus on the MTO. The discussion follows observations that, whereas the corporation tax reductions succeeded in attracting a reflagging of ships to the UK national register, as well as relocating key operations and management activities to the UK, its performance in relation to increasing cadet recruitment and training was generally poor (see e.g. Selkou and Roe 2002). Some commentators have argued that this outcome is unsurprising, considering that shipping companies clearly profited more from employing cheaper foreign seafarers (Gekara 2009, 2010; Brownrigg et al. 2001; Selkou and Roe 2002) and had little incentive to train British officers. These studies consistently conclude that the main weakness of the strategy lies in its predominantly supply-side orientation, which largely ignored the demand side of the labour market equation.

These observations and arguments will be further examined in the remaining sections of the chapter. After briefly describing the nature and extent of the decline in British shipping between mid-1975 and late 1990s, the chapter will consider the design and implementation of the UK tonnage tax. It will then examine the impact with regard to increasing training of seafarers and discuss the various inherent challenges.

[1]Flagging out is a practice by which shipowners shift the nationality of their ships from one national register to another for the purposes of benefitting from the latter's lower-operating costs, including the cost of labour, taxation as well as reduced regulatory pressures.

Globalisation and Decline in British Shipping

The shipping industry, unlike many others, is characterized by four key features, which make it susceptible to globalising processes and which make it an exemplar of industrial globalisation. Firstly, the primary shipping asset—the ship—is ordinarily globally mobile. Secondly and closely related, ship owners can switch the nationality of their ships with little national regulatory restriction, for the purposes of reducing overall operating costs, including taxes, cost of labour and regulatory costs (Metaxas 1985a; Marlow et al. 1997; Marlow 2002). Thirdly, the crews on board ships are often multinational in composition and recruited internationally on a uniquely global labour market (Wu 2003, 2004), and finally, different aspects of ship management are, more often than not, performed in different parts of the world (Klikauer 2003). For all intents and purposes, therefore, a typical international cargo ship can, without fear of contradicting any existing theories on spatiality, be described as effectively existing and operating in a regulatory space characterized by polycentric governance (Sampson 2003; Sampson and Bloor 2007; DeSombre 2006). Based on these four unique features Goss (1989, p. 75) has described shipping as:

> ... an industry which, of necessity, operates internationally, selling its services in many countries and, correspondingly, buying such factors of production as insurance, fuel and the ships themselves on a world market.

Up until the early twentieth century the shipping industry was strongly defined by the identities and national affiliations of the owners' country of citizenship, or, in many other situations by the country of registration, which often corresponded with the nationality of the owners. Thus, shipping tended to operate within strict regulatory boundaries set by nation states (Metaxas 1985b; Goss 1989). This relationship has changed over the years, following general trends of economic liberalisation, leading to a decoupling of ownership, registration and crew nationality, so that ships are no longer necessarily registered in the countries of owners' domicile, and seafaring labour is no longer nationally defined and organized but rather developed and utilized globally (Alderton et al. 2004; Sampson 2003). Consequently, between the mid-1970s and the end of the century, a lot of the countries, which previously dominated and controlled the shipping industry experienced decline, most significantly in their nationally registered fleets and national seafaring labour markets. Figure 4.1 shows the decline of the so-called traditional maritime country (TMC) national fleets as those of open registers, commonly known as flags of convenience (FoC), grew. The graph represents the yearly gross tonnage of six major open registers including Liberia, Panama, the Bahamas, Singapore, the Philippines and Cyprus (FoC curve) and six major traditional maritime countries, including USA, UK, Japan, Germany, France and Norway.

The decline in TMC fleets illustrated in Fig. 4.1 is also reflected in the national fleet of the UK, which correspondingly, experienced a significant decline in its national registered fleet, between the mid-1970s and late 1990s as shown in Fig. 4.2.

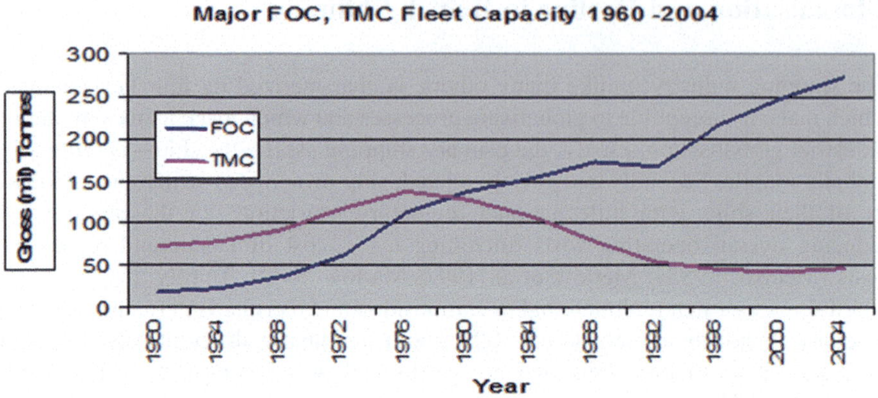

Fig. 4.1 Fleet registry trends 1960–2004. Source: Created by author from Lloyd's Register-Fairplay World Fleet Statistics, various years

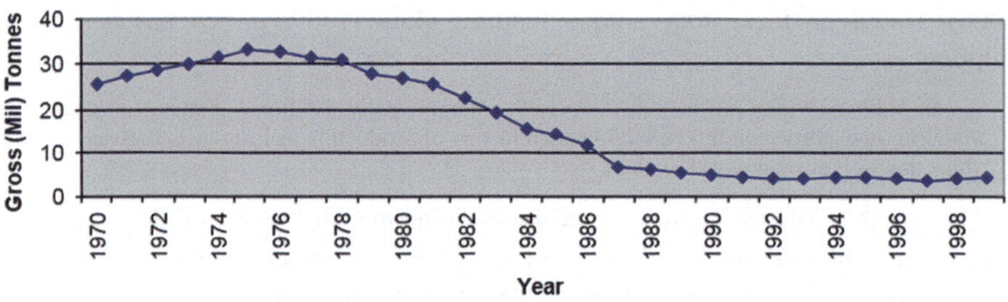

Fig. 4.2 UK Gross Registered Tonnage 1970–1999. Source: Created by author from Lloyd's Register-Fairplay World Fleet Statistics various years

From a peak of 33.1 million GT (3822) in 1975, the UK national fleet fell to 3.4 million GT (1391 ships) by 1997 (World Fleet Statistics various years). As earlier explained, the decline in the British shipping fleet inevitably caused a decline in the pool of available British seafarers.

During the same general period the number of British qualified officers dropped from 28,000 in 1980 to 17,000 in 1998 (House of Commons 1993; Obando-Rojas et al. 1999). Thus, by the mid-1990s it was clear that the entire UK maritime sector was under significant threat of irreversible demise. The shrinking national fleet, combined with a similar shrinkage in the number of qualified British officers, further threatened the shore-side maritime cluster of firms in the City of London, which relied heavily on the transfer of essential skills from the sea to fill technical positions in shore-side operations (Gardner and Pettit 1999). The possibility that some of these firms could cease operations while others relocated to emerging overseas maritime centers, as a result of critical skills shortages, became a major concern for industry and government. Furthermore, the decline in the fleet also meant that the country's training capacity was reduced since domiciled shipping companies are traditionally responsible for the recruitment and training of seafarers.

The Impact on Seafarer Training and Skills

The shrinking national seafaring skills base in the UK maritime sector happened as a direct consequence of the many years of decline in the UK national fleet and seafaring labour market. Within the wider maritime sector, the shipping industry commonly plays the role of core catalyst for all the other maritime related industries. Growth or decline in shipping activities, therefore, automatically influences similar fluctuations in the entire sector. For example, traditionally, ship-owners not only recruit cadets but also financially support their training and provide training berths for practical sea experience. The impact of the declining fleet on cadet training was, therefore, that the capacity to recruit and train cadets significantly reduced because British ship-owners operating under foreign flags were neither willing nor obliged to train British officers. As Gardner et al. (2001) observe:

> .... many British shipping companies have reduced or given up altogether their former commitment to cadet and junior officer training in order to save costs and remain competitive... (2001:353).

Accordingly Pettit et al. (2005), observe that what was happening in the UK national shipping industry and labour market were a result of wider transformations associated with economic globalization and global scale industrial restructuring. They explain that:

> As the shipping industry has adapted to the global labour market the UK has increasingly sourced its seafarers from other nations. This has in turn led to a significant decrease in the number of UK nationals training as seafarer cadets and following a career path through to Unlimited Certificates of Competence as either Masters or Chief Engineers (2005:521).

As indicated earlier, the shift towards the employment of foreign crews by British ship-operators had a knock-on effect on supply as, with the decline in employment opportunities for British seafarers, the number of young British nationals willing to train for, and follow, seafaring careers, reduced. This was confirmed in national statistics, which showed that following the decline in the UK ship register between early 1970s and late 1990s, cadet recruitment correspondingly reduced from about 4300 to about 1000 (see Gardner et al. 2001). By the 1990s the decline in the maritime skills base had become critical and required effective and immediate attention (Obando-Rojas et al. 1999; Selkou and Roe 2002). The government's view was that the decline hugely undermined the position of the City of London Maritime Cluster as the global center for shipping, as well as potentially threatening the country's strategic security interests, hence the birth of the tonnage tax and the MTO.

The Tonnage Tax Minimum Training Obligation and Its Impact

The Alexander Commission, which was set up to investigate and advise on a tonnage tax as the possible strategy for the recovery of the shipping industry, concluded that 'without a user-friendly and virtually tax-exempt environment there [was] no real prospect of achieving the aim of Government policy to revive the industry', and proceeded to recommend that 'a tonnage-based form of corporation tax [was] the means proposed to achieve this fiscal environment' [Alexander Report 1999, p. 3].

Following this strong endorsement, a multi-pronged strategy was developed with the intention of addressing all the aspects of the decline. That is, to rebuild the UK registered fleet, by creating a more predictable, business-friendly and tax exempt atmosphere for ship-owners, support the rejuvenation of the seafaring skills-base, by obliging ship-owners to invest more in the recruitment and training of British cadets, and shore up the City of London maritime cluster, through a requirement that all participating owners relocate key commercial and strategic ship management activities to the UK (see Department for Transport 1998; Brownrigg et al. 2001; Selkou and Roe 2002).

The Minimum Training Obligation (MTO), also referred to as the training link, was thus one of the key elements of the strategy by which participating companies are required to train one British cadet for every fifteen officer positions entered in the effective officer complement[2] of all participating vessels irrespective of their (officer) nationality, plus a notional 50% to cover back-up officers. This commitment is for an initial period of three years after which the ratio of cadets to officers reduces to one cadet for every five officer positions. In this way the number of cadets each company has to train per year gradually increases. In order to qualify, the company has to submit a comprehensive training plan to the Department of Transport (DfT) demonstrating their commitment to the MTO. Those companies, which, due to exceptional circumstances, are unable to directly execute their obligation, may opt to make a payment in lieu of training of a specified amount of money. At the time of introduction, this amount was £550 GBP but has been revised to £1236 per calendar month per trainee from October 2016 (Brownrigg et al. 2001; Gardner et al. 2001; Selkou and Roe 2002; Leggate and McConville 2005). In reality, although the companies pay for the recruitment and training of cadets, the arrangement amounts to a government cadet training subsidy, since they claim reimbursement for 50% on evidence that the company has met its quota in cadet recruitment. Employer buy-in into the MTO is crucial not just in the financial contribution to the training but, particularly, to provide training berths onboard their ships for practical sea training, without which cadets cannot qualify for their certificates of competence as junior officers.

[2]The effective officer complement is calculated as the number of relevant officers entered on the Safe Manning Document (SMD) for all vessels entered in the tonnage tax regime, adjusted to include back-up officer provision.

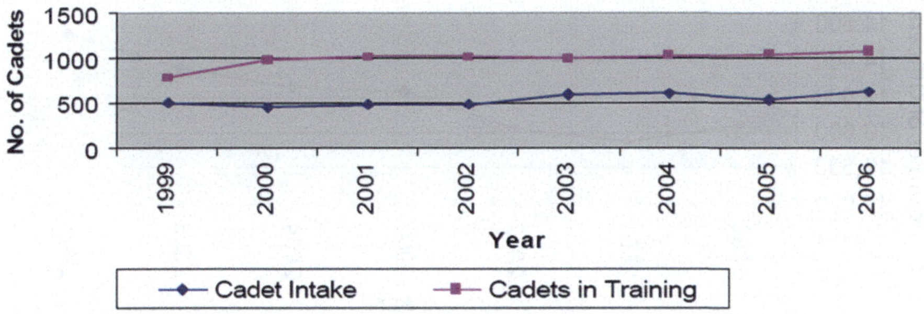

Fig. 4.3 Cadet Intake and Training Levels 1999–2006. Source: Created by author from Glen (2006), United Kingdom Seafarers Analysis, https://tinyurl.com/vx27kdd (pg 41)

In an attempt to strengthen employer obligation, the commitment is strictly implemented so that failure to fulfill the requirement will lead to expulsion from the regime and, possibly, being charged with a criminal offence for defrauding the government (HMSO 2005).

How successful this government intervention has been is subject to great academic and industry debate. On one hand, the size of the UK's registered fleet increased significantly within the first six years of its introduction, from GT 5,531,986 in 2000 to GT 12,149,988 in 2006. By 2012 it had grown to 32,185 GT, according to data from the Lloyd's Register World Fleet Statistics and UNCT AD Statistics. This is quite a remarkable positive industry response to the improved investment and tax conditions, which indicates clear success in the strategy. On the other hand, however, cadet recruitment and training did not register a similar positive response. Cadet intake showed very little recovery, remaining around the 500 to 600 level between 1999 and 2006. Similarly, the number of cadets actually in training each year grew only slightly from 981 to 1090 in the same period, according to data obtained from the Merchant Navy Training Board and the UK Seafarers Analysis for 2006 (Fig. 4.3).

According to a study conducted in the mid-1990s estimating the UK's seafaring skills requirement (Gardner and Pettit 1999), it was determined that the UK needed a yearly cadet in-take of about 1200 cadets in order to maintain the minimum maritime skills base. With the introduction of the tonnage tax it was hoped that this target would be met within the first five years but unfortunately this did not happen.

This also means that the ultimate object of revitalizing the size of the national pool of seafarers did not materialize in any significant way. As shown in Fig. 4.4, the total number of qualified British officers only increased slightly from about 13,000 to 14,500 between 2000 and 2006 according to the UK Seafarers Analysis of 2006.

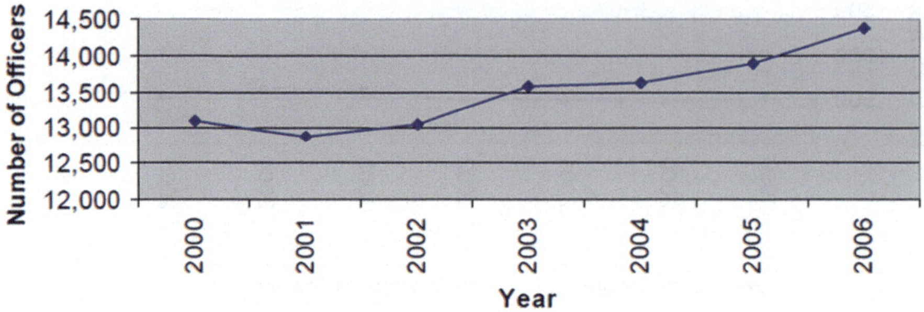

Fig. 4.4 Total Number of UK Officers 2000–2006. Source: Created by author from Glen 2006, United Kingdom Seafarers Analysis, https://tinyurl.com/vx27kdd (pg 33)

The Shortcomings of the Minimum Training Obligation

All analysis therefore seems to suggest that the MTO did not deliver the levels of cadet recruitment and training that were anticipated by the designers of the intervention in terms of raising cadet training levels. Its performance is in stark contrast to that of other aspects of the tonnage tax as illustrated by its success in the revitalization of the UK ship register, where it is viewed as achieving great success in attracting ships to the national fleet register. In order to examine why the MTO did not perform as well as intended the views of key industry stakeholders were collected via semi-structured interviews. Those interviewed included representatives of industry regulatory agencies, shipping company managers, recruitment and training company officials, industry union representatives and relevant government officials. A selection of representative interview quotes is used to illustrate the analysis of the situation in this section.

The poor performance of the MTO is clearly expressed in the majority of the interviews. For example, an official of the Merchant Navy Training Board (MNTB), which played a key role in the operationalization of the MTO, provided the following assessment:

> Clearly the training side of things has not gone as well and this is due to a combination of factors. . . we had anticipated a much better response and were hopping to hit the 1,200 mark within the first five to six years but that never happened. ... In fact we are still struggling to reach 600 even after ten odd years (MNTB Interview 2011)

With regard to the reasons, the interviewee explained that growing international competition from low cost labour supply countries and loss of competitive advantage, as a seafarer labour supply country, were the key factors:

> There are any number of reasons but mainly we are facing very strong competition from other countries internationally and, to be honest, we have lost that market and cannot expect to compete very strongly (MNTB Interview 2011)

The data however further shows that the story is a lot more complex than this. It appears that the reasons for the dismal performance of the MTO can only be understood through a complex cross perspective analysis of views and experiences. It is only by interrogating the perspectives of the different stakeholder groups that we can begin to grasp the situation. For example, employers, i.e., ship-owners and operators argue that, whereas there was an increase in the resources for training following the tonnage tax MTO, young people in Britain were no longer attracted to careers at sea. One human resource manager at one shipping company for example summed up the situation as follows.

> Our company is involved in cadet training and recruits cadets from the UK but this has been decreasing with time mainly because the number of British people wanting to go to sea seems to be drying up. Seafaring is simply not an interesting career anymore. I wouldn't go back to sea whatever it paid, and even if you paid me double what I am paid here I wouldn't consider it. There are many other better and less stressful alternatives for the young people in Britain and they are clearly taking them [Ship-owner HR Manager Interview 2006].

The unions, on the other hand, have a very different take on the issue, in as far as cause and effect go. Their view was that the MTO was inadequate as a strategy for increasing cadet training and growing the national pool of trained seafarers. The argument from the main union for merchant navy officers—National Union of Marine, Aviation and Shipping Transport Officers (NUMAST[3])—in the UK was that the strategy left out an obvious and essential element—an employment link.

> If the legislation [was] seriously aimed at the increase in UK based seafarers, there is clearly a case for establishing a method whereby these cadets are able to secure stable employment within the UK fleet [Employment Link, 2004].

The gist of this argument is that training uptake for any profession or occupation is, to a very large extent, dependent on the availability of employment opportunities in the sector. Yet, while the MTO managed to get cadets into training and whilst many completed their apprenticeships, they struggled to find a job, as ship operators preferred to employ cheaper junior officers from elsewhere and were not obliged under tonnage tax rules to retain the cadets that they trained. This argument is further illustrated in the interviews conducted with ex-cadets, i.e., cadets who, at the time of the research, had recently dropped out of training to seek career opportunities elsewhere. In these interviews, additional reasons were given for abandoning seafaring career aspirations. Some cadets described difficulties in the actual training process and content, while others talked about challenges with the environment of training, particularly on board ship and an unsupportive attitude from senior officers. Mostly, however, they described their discouragement from the knowledge that there were few job opportunities available to British seafarers, as explained by one ex-cadet:

---

[3]NUMAST has since 2006 restructured and changed its name to Nautilus International after a merger with similar maritime professionals unions in Netherlands and Switzerland.

> They say that there are no jobs for British officers, not anymore; everybody is talking about it and it is discouraging.... Companies are employing foreigners.... they claim that the British want too much money.... Too expensive....it is very discouraging.... better to find something more promising (Cadet Interview 2005)

Thus, some cadets, like the one quoted next, talked of not wanting to pursue a dead-end career while they missed out on opportunities in other sectors:

> I thought I would lose other opportunities if I waited around, so I quit and joined university instead to study engineering. Maybe I will work for a ship management company when I finish (Cadet Interview 2005)

Therefore, although many factors were given, lack of employment prospects at the end of training formed the main factor for people dropping out. In contrast to employer arguments that young British people were not interested in seafaring careers, none of the cadets interviewed thought a seafaring career was not attractive and they all seemed to have been driven by the desired to work at sea. Interviews with some of the major cadet recruitment and training agencies also contradict this popular employer view about a lack of interest in seafaring careers. As the manager of such an agency pointed out, young people were responding positively to the recently introduced cadetships under the tonnage tax:

> We get hundreds of people applying for these cadetships every time we advertise. You cannot say that they are not attractive. The problem is what happens after recruitment and placement in training.... These companies do not care about the quality of cadets admitted on their behalf, they do not care whether or not they complete the course and certainly they are not going to employ them, so they just don't care (Training Agency Interview 2006).

His conclusion therefore was that what seems to be a lack of interest in seafaring careers, was rather a response to the labour market reality that shipowners did not have jobs for British junior officers, including those that were recruiting and training them. The fact that the cadets abandoned their aspirations post recruitment, i.e., dropped out mid-training, also contradicts the lack of interest thesis. This observation concurs with previous research findings that the problem was more about cadet disillusionment with employment prospects, leading to high attrition rates, rather than a lack of general interest (Gekara 2009).

Concluding Assessment: The Peril of Supply-Side Labour Market Policies

The analysis of the data presented here points to one significant shortcoming of the tonnage tax strategy as an intervention for the British seafarer labour market. It is also illustrative of key characteristics of neoliberal state policies and affirmation of the neoliberal government's lack of capacity, and/or will, to regulate on the side of labour (Jessop 2002; Beck 2005; Peck 2004; Fourcades-Gourinchas and Babb 2002; Chomsky 1999). By availing resources, and rewarding employers, for the recruitment and training of cadets without considering the employment outcomes of the graduating junior officers, the policy ignored a major component of the equation. It is this element that NUMAST, aptly referred to as the missing link, in its campaign for the introduction of some form of employment link in the strategy, that is, an incentive or obligation for the tonnage tax participating companies to provide employment for British junior officers (NUMAST 2004). The data clearly show a number of things: first, that the failure of the strategy to increase cadet training was due to a failure in cadet retention and hence poor completion rates rather than a lack of interest in the cadetships made available under the tonnage tax, as suggested by employers. Second, that among other factors, the dominant reason for cadet drop-out was uncertainty regarding future career prospects at sea considering that most ship-owners, including training sponsors, preferred to recruit foreign seafarers from cheaper international sources. In such a situation, the implementation of a purely supply-side intervention could only be counterproductive in the long run.

A chain of events is discernible associated with the missing employment link, which confirms a vicious circle of training decline. Lack of incentive or obligation to employ British officers meant that British shipowners were not particularly keen on recruiting and training of British cadets. As one maritime academy official remarked in an interview:

> ...the training commitment is no commitment at all. It is simply a requirement for companies to fulfil so that they may benefit from the tonnage tax...

Another interviewee –a fleet manager of an old family owned shipping company in the UK was of the view that the MTO was, ‘a half-hearted and tokenistic gesture from government to placate the unions’. The training official’s observation above suggests that, in fact, many of the shipping companies which undertook to train cadets under the MTO did not get directly involved in the execution of their obligation and instead, either subcontracted the obligation entirely to third party training agencies or opted to pay the stipulated sum-in lieu of training. Interviews with some of the training agencies, as well as training academies, confirm that a large number of the companies and their training agencies failed to take proper care of the cadets during training. This is one of the causes for the reported high rates of cadet attrition. The interviews also suggest that, because the companies were not training junior officers for their own use on their ships, they were not particularly concerned with either the quality of the cadets recruited or their completion of training. Thus, there was little incentive for the shipowners to follow up on the progress of the cadets’ training or worry about whether they completed the training or not. All this, as repeatedly explained by union officials, was due to the lack of an employment commitment to give impetus to the training obligation.

In their analysis of the design and performance of the tonnage tax, (Brownrigg et al. 2001), Selkou and Roe (2002), Gardner et al. (2004) and Gekara (2010) have arrived at similar conclusions with the consistent observation that, with the blanket deregulation of the British shipping industry, removing any requirement for domicile ship-owners to employ British seafarers, a strategy such as the tonnage tax MTO would be difficult to successfully implement. These studies attribute the failure of the MTO primarily to government’s lack of capacity and/or will to legislate more assertively for labour because of its commitment to neoliberal principles. Because of the British government's commitment to the neoliberal agenda, its focus was more on supporting business, through tax cuts and labour market deregulation, than supporting the revitalisation of national labour markets, particularly in cases where it was in business's best interest to rely on cheaper foreign labour than recruit locally. Therefore, rather than a unique and isolated case, the tonnage tax strategy, in its design, implementation and overall performance, is illustrative of long-standing and broad shifts in national economic priorities under neoliberal capitalism.

References

Alderton, T., M. Bloor, E. Kahveci, T. Lane, H. Sampson, M. Thomas, N. Winchester, B. Wu, and M. Zhao. 2004. *The Global Seafarer: Living and Working Conditions in a Globalised Industry*. London: ILO.

Alexander Report. 1999. *Independent Enquiry Into a Tonnage Tax*. London: HM Treasury.

Beck, U. 2005. *Power in the Global Age: A New Global Political Economy*. Cambridge: Polity.

Brownrigg, M., G. Dawe, M. Mann, and P. Weston. 2001. Developments in UK Shipping: The Tonnage Tax. *Maritime Policy and Management* 28 (3): 213–223.

Chomsky, N. 1999. *Profit Over People: Neoliberalism and Global Order*. London: Seven Stories Press.

Department for Transport. 1998. *British Shipping: Charting a New Course*. London: http://webarchive.nationalarchives.gov.uk/20100304073751/http://www.dft.gov.uk/about/strategy/whitepapers/previous/britishshippingchartinganewc5696?page=4 [24/11/2019]

DeSombre, E.R. 2006. *Flagging Standards: Globalization and Environmental, Safety, and Labor Regulations at Sea*. London: MIT Press.

Fourcades-Gourinchas, M., and S.L. Babb. 2002. The Re-Birth of the Liberal Creed: Paths to Neoliberalism in Four Countries. *American Journal of Sociology* 108 (3): 533–579.

Gardner, B., M. Naim, B. Obando-Rojas, and S. Pettit. 2001. Maintaining the Maritime Skills Base: Does the Government Have a Realistic Strategy? *Maritime Policy and Management* 28 (4): 347–360.

Gardner, B.M., and S.J. Pettit. 1999. The Land-Based Jobs Market for Seafarers: Consequences of Market Imbalance and Policy Implications. *Marine Policy* 23 (2): 161–175.

Gardner, B.M., P.B. Marlow, M.M. Naim, R. Nair, and S.J. Pettit 2004. *The UK Economy's Requirements for People with Experience of Working at Sea 2003*. Report for the Department for Transport, the Chamber of Shipping and the Marine Society.

Gekara, V.O. 2009. Understanding Attrition in UK Maritime Education and Training. *Globalisation, Societies and Education* 7 (2): 217–232.

———. 2010. The Stamp of Neoliberalism on the UK Tonnage Tax and the Implications for British Seafaring. *Marine Policy* 34 (3): 487–494.

Glen, D. 2006. *United Kingdom Seafarers Analysis*. London: Centre for International Transport Management, London Metropolitan University. http://webarchive.nationalarchives.gov.uk/20070604212857/http://www.dft.gov.uk/162259/162469/221412/221658/223737/236072/seafarerrep2006.pdf [24/11/2019]

Goss, R. 1989. Sense and Shipping Policies. In *Shipping Policies for an Open World Economy*, ed. G.N. Yannopoulos, 61–79. London: Routledge.

HMSO. (2005). *The Finance Act. Section 93 Schedule 7*. http://www.opsi.gov.uk/ACTS/acts2005/50007-ac.htm#sch7 [24/11/2019]

House of Commons Employment Committee. 1993. *The Future of Maritime Skills and Employment in the UK*. London: HMSO.

Jessop, B. 2002. Liberalism, Neoliberalism, and Urban Governance: A State–Theoretical Perspective. *Antipode* 34 (3): 452–472.
Klikauer, T. 2003. Human Resources in German Maritime Industries: Back-Sourcing and Ship-Management. *Human Resource Management* 14 (4): 544–558.
Kotz, D.M. 2015. *The Rise and Fall of Neoliberal Capitalism*. Cambridge: Harvard University Press.
Kovats, L.J. 2006. How Flags Lost the Plot Over Shipping's Governance: Does a Ship Need a Sovereign? *Maritime Policy and Management* 33 (1): 75–81.
Leggate, H., and McConville. 2005. Tonnage Tax: Is it Working? *Maritime Policy and Management* 32 (2): 177–186.
Lloyd's Register Fairplay World Fleet Statistics (Various Years).
Marlow, P. 2002. Ships, Flags, and Taxation. In *The Handbook of Maritime Economics and Business*, ed. S. Grammenos, 512–529. London: Informa Professional.
Marlow, P., S. Pettit, and A. Bergantino. 1997. The Decision to Flag Out and Its Impact on the National Economy. In *Maritime Transport and Economic Reconstruction*, ed. K. Misztal and J. Zurek. Gdansk: University of Gdansk.
Metaxas, B.N. 1985a. *Flags of Convenience: A Study of Internationalisation*. Aldershot: Gower.
———. 1985b. *Flags of Convenience: A Study of Internationalisation*. Aldershot: Gower.
NUMAST 2004. *Employment Link. A Report on UK Seafarers, Maritime Skills & the Tonnage Tax*. June 2004.
Obando-Rojas, B., B.M. Gardner, and M.M. Naim. 1999. A System Dynamic Analysis of Officer Manpower in the Merchant Marine. *Maritime Policy and Management* 26 (1): 39–60.
Peck, J. 2004. Geography and Public Policy: Constructions of Neoliberalism. *Progress in Human Geography* 28 (3): 392–405.
Pettit, S.J., B.M. Gardner, P.B. Marlow, M.M. Naim, and R. Nair. 2005. Ex-seafarers Shore-Based Employment: The Current UK Situation. *Marine Policy* 29: 521–531.
Sampson, H. 2003. Transnational Drifters or Hyperspace Dwellers: An Exploration of the Lives of Filipino Seafarers Aboard and Ashore. *Ethnic and Racial Studies* 26 (2): 253–277.
Sampson, H., and M. Bloor. 2007. When Jack Gets Out the Box: The Problems of Regulating a Global Industry. *Sociology* 41 (3): 551–569.
Selkou, E., and M. Roe. 2002. UK Tonnage Tax: Subsidy or Special Case? *Maritime Policy and Management* 29 (4): 393–404.
Wu, B. 2003. Accession to Global Seafaring Labour Market: Principles and Application of SIRC Seafarer Database in the Cruise Sector. *WMU Journal of Maritime Affairs* 2 (1): 17–32.
———. 2004. Participation in the Global Labour Market: Experience and Responses of Chinese Seafarers. *Maritime Policy and Management* 31 (1): 69–82.

Chapter 5
Careers at Sea: Exploring Seafarer Motivations and Aspirations

Polina Baum-Talmor

Introduction

The notion of a 'career for life' in the global labour market has been under scrutiny in the last four decades or so, as flexible employment, which refers to contractual and temporary work, has become the norm in many companies worldwide (Brown 1995; Baruch 2006; Baruch and Peiperl 2000; Sampson 2013; Stone 2005). A major feature of this change has been a shift from jobs offering life-long job security to work on temporary contracts (Stone 2005; Burgess 1997). Although there are still organisations that offer long-term secure careers to their employees, it is in fact the 'norm' for most people (approximately 75% of the world population) not to have a permanent job (ILO 2015, 2019). Such a lack of permanency can result in people accepting a series of contract-based, short-term jobs which may have long-term consequences for their future career development. Consequently, some individuals are compelled to plan a skill-based career, in which their working life is constructed by way of a series of short-term positions enabling them to gain skills that they hope will assist them in finding better employment, often across different organisations and industries. This kind of career structure is referred to as a portfolio career (Cohen and Mallon 1999; Mallon 1998).

In the past, seafaring was considered to be a life-long occupation (Baum-Talmor 2018; Glen and McConville 2001; Hill 1972; Mack 2007), offering hierarchical advancement and job security Nowadays, despite the hierarchical structure of the work division and roles on board, the attitude towards the longevity of the seafaring career has shifted, and it is no longer considered to be a 'job for life' for most individuals (Alderton et al. 2004; Baum-Talmor 2018; Gould 2011; Sampson 2013).

P. Baum-Talmor (✉)
Solent University, Southampton, UK
e-mail: polina.baum-talmor@solent.ac.uk

V. O. Gekara, H. Sampson (eds.), *The World of the Seafarer*, WMU Studies in Maritime Affairs 9, https://doi.org/10.1007/978-3-030-49825-2_5

Shipping is an example of a global sector which utilises flexible employment on a regular basis. Such flexible employment is generally associated with the offshoring and outsourcing of recruitment to third-party agencies (Sampson 2013; Bloor and Sampson 2009; Fei 2011; Alderton et al. 2004; Sampson and Schroeder 2006). These modifications in industry employment and recruitment strategies have caused the origins of seafarers that join the industry to change. In the past seafarers from developed countries made up the majority of the workforce, according to BIMCO (Baltic and International Maritime Council) whereas at present the seafaring profession has become more dominated by individuals from developing countries (BIMCO 2005, 2010, 2015). The latest available manpower report (BIMCO 2015) suggests that it is anticipated that there will be a decline in officers originating from OECD countries in the next few years with a concomitant increase in seafarers from developing countries (BIMCO 2015, p. 34).

Within the context of such changes it is important to appreciate that whilst some jobs at sea are relatively unskilled (those of 'ratings') (Barnett et al. 2006; Klikauer and Morris 2002), others are highly skilled (those of 'officers') (Hill 1972; Mack 2007; Sampson 2013; Zurcher 1965). Formerly jobs with a high-skill requirement necessitated a considerable amount of training and were likely to be permanent. In contrast relatively unskilled work was more likely to be offered on a 'casual basis'. However it seems that this is no longer the case as employers are demonstrating a lesser degree of commitment to the long term training and development of their officers (Sampson and Tang 2015).

This chapter seeks to explain the attractions of seafaring which is a relatively dangerous occupation (Baum-Talmor 2018; Belousov et al. 2007; Sampson 2013), has precarious employment prospects and requires long periods of time to be spent away from home (Acejo 2012; Baum-Talmor 2012; Sampson 2013). Specifically it is of interest to consider the influences that might continue to steer individuals towards a 'career' in the modern cargo shipping industry, and to examine whether individuals nowadays perceive seafaring as a 'career' for life or a temporary job.

In order to address these issues, data that relates directly to the reasons seafarers join and stay in this occupation were collected and analysed.[1] My focus has been on current seafarers rather than retired seafarers and therefore insights into the reasons for leaving this occupation are based on seafarers' intentions as expressed during the interviews, which are complemented and enhanced by the existing literature. As part of the data collection, non-participant observation was conducted on board a cargo ship, which enabled a direct glimpse into seafarers' working routines. The use of an immersive research technique enabled a holistic view of the circumstances behind the choice of seafaring as an occupation. In addition to observation on board, in-depth interviews with key participants in the shipping industry were conducted

[1]The mentioned project is a PhD thesis at Cardiff University, funded by the Nippon Foundation and the Seafarers' International Research Centre (SIRC), entitled "Careers and Labour Market Flexibility in Global Industries: The Case of Seafarers". The thesis was published in 2018 and is available online: http://orca.cf.ac.uk/109438/.

and included interviews with seafarers, crew managers and recruiters. This provided direct input regarding seafarers' occupational choices. This chapter draws upon 56 formal interviews and 15 informal conversations. The seafarers in the research came from various backgrounds and nationalities and the categorisation used previously by the International Monetary Fund (IMF 2015, 2019) is utilised here, dividing these seafarers into those coming from developed countries (n = 11) and those from emerging nations and developing countries (n = 45).

Going to Sea: Influences on Joining

One of the common reasons for going to sea is to earn a good salary. This is seen by many individuals as adequate compensation for the hardships involved in such a career choice. In a variety of studies seafarers from countries like the Philippines, UK, Ecuador and Taiwan identify 'good pay' in the seafaring occupation as the main reason for choosing to join seafaring (Gould 2010; *Seaways* 2014; Baylon and Stevenson 2005; Østreng 2000; Calderón 2011; Guo et al. 2006). In my research both seafarers and recruitment agencies identified finance as the prime motivation for the choice of a job at sea. For example, Roslin, a crew manager from the Philippines, revealed:

> Usually, from Philippines side, [the reason to join seafaring] is always money. It is always that. [...] Well, given the economy of the Philippines, it's like there is no other option. [...] Let's talk about an OS [Ordinary Seaman], that's the entry level [of a seafarer], for a German flag, [on a] German vessel, the salary will be around $1000, which is equivalent to 50,000 pesos. If he works in the Philippines, he will most likely receive a salary of 7000 pesos. For officers, if you get paid like $4000 a month, if you work there [ashore], you can likely get 15,000-20,000 [pesos] $4000 is like 200,000 pesos a month, it's a big difference, and that's without tax. If you work at home [in the Philippines] you get taxed 25% so, the attraction is so [big]. [Roslin, Crew Manager, 38, from the Philippines, interview in English]

As a result of limited choices of alternative employment ashore Filipinos often feel pushed towards the seafaring profession. This happens in other developing countries as well (Sampson and Schroeder 2006; Dearsley 2013; IMF 2015) such as Ghana, Cape Verde, India, Russia and Ukraine. Seafarers from these countries stated that the high wages in the shipping industry meant that jobs ashore could not compete in terms of pay and the promise of a good salary was a significant reason for joining the merchant navy. Wu and Morris (2006) report that at the turn of the century the working lives of employees in China, Former Soviet Union countries and Eastern European countries were heavily affected by 'instability, job insecurity, an erosion of social welfarism and greatly differentiated wages' with the result that some individuals were compelled to join the shipping industry (Wu and Morris 2006, p. 43). Similarly, one interviewee from Ukraine revealed:

> In childhood, every person fantasises about becoming something, [...] but when you become older you start understanding that you have to choose a profession that will bring you money. For us, there are young people that don't understand that, he [a person] just goes

> and studies, and eventually, he receives a higher education in some rocket science Institute, he spent a lot of energy, wrote projects, but he works somewhere in a shop, selling cell phones. It happens. A person with higher education, in our country, Ukraine, will sell cell phones in a shop. [. . .] Because there aren't jobs. Even if there is this kind of job, there are many students. . . [. . .] You don't have places to work in. I mean, you have the qualifications but you don't have a workplace. That's why, I mean, when I was already applying [to work on board], I didn't know much about it, that's why this is not something I might have wanted in life, but I knew that I had to set myself somehow in this life, to earn [enough money]. That's why I came here [to work on board]. [Mace, Second Engineer, 26, from Ukraine, interview in Russian]

The quote indicates the lack of employment opportunities in Ukraine that can push individuals towards employment at sea. It is not exclusively for financial reasons that the choice to become a seafarer is made. Individuals' geographical origin is also mentioned as another reason for going to sea with physical proximity to the sea being cited as a reason for their career choice (Gould 2010; Østreng 2000; Barnett et al. 2006; Hill 1972). On several occasions during interviews, seafarers mentioned coming from a nautical background with pressure being exerted on them to choose this occupational path by their closest relatives. For instance, Stannis, a chief cook, mentioned:

> My family is completely seamens, they are all seafarers. So when I am in [. . .] school, I am thinking we must go to the sea, like that. That time I know. That I have to go there. Because father is a seafarer, uncle seafarer, brother seafarer, mother's father, mother's side everybody, where I live in that place, all of them seamen. [Stannis, Chief Cook, 50, from India, interview in English]

In a sense Stannis implied that he had little choice about going to sea given that this was the chosen occupation for so many family members. His career choice was almost inevitable. This emphasises the pressure individuals in sea-going societies can be under when making decisions regarding their future. Influence from families, i.e. pressure or support from partners (Barnett et al. 2006; Baylon and Stevenson 2005; Calderón 2011; Dearsley 2013; Guo et al. 2006) can be significant. For example, one seafarer revealed:

> My wife [. . .] she said 'go and earn money, we need money for the family, we need money for the baby. . .' I mean she was already used to, since my first contract, she had my card, I was receiving my salary, from the first contract [she could use my money]. And when I returned from my contract, I needed to stay at home a little bit because there weren't enough jobs, and then the complaints started. Why don't we have that, why don't we have this? And she was already used to getting everything she wanted [not denying herself from anything] and there it was. . . and is continued going downhill from there. [Will, Third Mate, 36, from Ukraine, interview in Russian]

Other seafarers report going to sea because of good career prospects (Barnett et al. 2006; Calderón 2011; De Silva et al. 2011; Baylon and Stevenson 2005; Guo et al. 2006) which may include fast-track promotion opportunities. For example, Captain Edmure described the importance of good career prospects for his choice of occupation. Throughout the interview Edmure mentioned his life-long aspirations to become a seafarer but despite his emotions he described practical motives as playing a significant role in his decision:

> When I did my [officer] license, I was still single, after that I got married, so the consideration was, instead of working in several jobs, to work in one job, hoping there was a fast promotion route, and then getting a senior position, at least first mate, and then Captain, and then to see where I can develop from there. Doors close, doors open, but this was the direction. [...] It does not mean that now, after eight years that I've reached the highest rank, that it means that I have outgrown it. In fact, now I am starting to learn, every day, in every port, you learn something that you did not know before. It is endless, this experience. To leave this area? No way. I will be doing something that relates to [the sea] for the rest of my life. [Edmure, Captain, 48, from Israel, interview in Hebrew]

In contrast to what might be termed 'aspirational reasons' for going to sea, sometimes it was the lack of an aspiration or goal that resulted in an individual joining the occupation. Many seafarers mentioned arbitrary reasons for joining seafaring, and those reasons were mostly associated with what they referred to as 'luck', 'chance', and 'fate'. Seafarers in the study mentioned that they did not have a specific plan to work at sea when they were young, but they happened to 'stumble upon' their job at some point during their lives. For instance, Renly, administrative officer, said:

> [My friend] was doing a cadet course in the [Maritime] Academy, and he told me that there is a course for the job I am doing right now, and I can apply. That is how I got to know about the seamen's life and all this. So I did four years training in the Academy. [...] [In high school] I had no idea about any kind of, like sea work, about working at sea, I had no plans like nothing, no plans for future, I just, doing my study, and whatever happens, happens. Just go with the flow, enjoy that. [Renly, Administrative Officer, 27, from India, interview in English]

Renly's work on the ship seems to be an almost coincidental occurrence, as he did not plan on becoming a seafarer before the encounter with his friend. Similar stories were uncovered by Sampson and Schroeder (2006) in their research with migrants to Germany. Others expressed the adventurous nature of working at sea as a main attraction to join and stay in this occupation (Barnett et al. 2006; Gould 2010; Hill 1972; Mack 2007; Baylon and Stevenson 2005; Dearsley 2013; *Seaways* 2014). These reasons might be interpreted as somewhat whimsical choices with seafarers describing no particular plans for a long-term future and consequently ultimately abandoning the seafaring occupation.

Leaving the Sea: Attrition Influences

Those seafarers who have no intention of staying and developing a 'career' in the shipping industry may leave the industry after several years. Some treat seafaring as a passing phase in their lives and, when they first join the occupation, their intention is to work for a short period until they have earned enough money to achieve certain set objectives (Barnett et al. 2006; Klikauer and Morris 2003; Dearsley 2013). For example, one Chief Mate revealed:

> [Seafarers] came [to work on a ship] for a short time to earn some money, like the Dutch people call it "quick money", so they joined to get "quick money". To earn money quickly and that's it, and later on, those people in the company will move forward, to something more constructive and interesting, they might open up a business, perhaps something else, but in any case, they don't return [to the company or to seafaring]. [Oberyn, Chief Mate, 40, from Ukraine, interview in Russian]

Thus, after several years during which they put aside money, they are ready to leave, to fulfil their plan to search for a different job ashore. In many cases seafarers wish to get to the 'top' of the career ladder at sea and work as a chief engineer or captain and then leave. In other cases, the opportunity to gain transferable skills that an individual can use for positions ashore is also mentioned. For instance, the prospect of a good career path was an evident attraction for Varys, a trainee cook:

> I was working in the kitchen [ashore], and I saw the chefs, how much respect they got, how [many] skills, you know, they were able to present. So, I was very, you know, fascinated about this. So when, it was a time when, [it was] hard to select a particular field, so I told my father, like okay, this is what I want to do [cooking], but, not on land, you know? Not on shore. I want to work in sea. [...] [A]shore, [in] one year I cannot become a chief cook or... you know, because there are a lot more people waiting. And here [on board] I become a chief cook in one year, even [in] less [time]. [Varys, Trainee Chief Cook, 23, from India, interview in English]

Varys perceived work at sea as his way forward to a more challenging job ashore. He regarded his work as a ship's cook as the quickest way for him to learn and gain the skills needed for opening his own restaurant ashore. In this example Varys believed that working at sea would help him develop a professional identity as a 'chef', not as a seafarer. He believed that he would be able to acquire transferable skills at sea that he would be able to apply for employment ashore, one of the characteristics of the 'portfolio career' as described by a few authors (Arthur 1994; Cohen and Mallon 1999; Mallon 1998; Platman 2004).

Another reason for leaving could be seafarers' failure to cope with the strenuous conditions of work on board. These include the cultural differences, the small crews, the constant stress and high workloads (Barnett et al. 2006; Slišković and Penezić 2017). The following example of a seafarer's intention to leave is illustrative:

> [I'm planning to work] maybe another five years more. Until I'm like 40 years old. I will stay at sea [and then leave]. [...] Because I think about the health side, this is a hectic job, especially as a marine engineer, compared to navigation side, engineering side is more tough. [...] Because we're working in heat, engine room is always above 40°C, 45°C, and the vibration, a lot of things. So it's better to quit at the age of 45, if I can make enough money, then I would think of something else. [Aegon, Second Engineer, 31, from India, interview in English]

In addition a general lack of physical and mental preparation for shipboard life (Ervin et al. 2002; Fei et al. 2012; Gekara 2009; Guo et al. 2006; Hill 1972) may cause many individuals to leave after a few contracts. Some colleges and institutions for seagoing officers still present a romanticised view of seafaring in their advertisements, promising individuals a 'unique opportunity' to 'travel the world' and develop a 'successful career' with job opportunities ashore. In reality however, seafarers are constantly pressurised to return to the ship when in port (Sampson 2013; Kahveci 2007a, b) and the number of positions available ashore for sea-going personnel are limited (Pettit et al. 2005; Barnett et al. 2006; Gardner et al. 2007). The romanticised view seems to influence some individuals since they join the shipping industry and work there for many years. Others find the reality of shipboard life negative with the romantic illusion shattered once they start working on the ship, and they are likely to leave after a short period of time.

In other cases, the influence of a seafarer's family can be behind a decision to leave the seafaring occupation. For example, some seafarers are pressurised by their families to change to a shore-based job due to the demanding nature of work at sea and the, associated, long periods of absence from their homes (Barnett et al. 2006; Calderón 2011; Ervin et al. 2002; Thomas 2003). Changes in domestic circumstances (Dearsley 2013) can also lead to a need to leave seafaring. For example, Lancel, an electrician weighing up whether to work at sea or not, predicted:

> My family, I don't know, if I get married, I will have children, yes, it will affect my decision [whether to join the shipping industry or not], [if] it will damage my family, I will be looking for something else. [Lancel, Electrician, 24, from Ukraine, interview in Russian]

Despite the fact that in many cases seafarers successfully combine their occupation and their family life (Thomas et al. 2001; Thomas 2003), it is not always perceived as possible as Lancel's example shows. For others, low pay in relation to the sacrifices they make (Dearsley 2013; Calderón 2011; Gerstenberger 2002) plays a significant part in their decision to leave and seek less demanding occupations ashore. Despite being paid much less they are able to spend more time with their families and work in less arduous conditions. Some seafarers, especially seafarers in low-demand positions like junior officers and ratings (where supply often outstrips demand), find that the lack of employment opportunities in the shipping industry causes them to search for alternative employment opportunities ashore (Barnett et al. 2006; Fei et al. 2012; Gould 2010; Mack 2007; Ervin et al. 2002; *Seaways* 2014). Many junior officers in the research complained about the lack of employment options at sea. One officer revealed:

> [Seafarers need to wait for the next contract] because there's this thing, too much of, many people are like fourth engineers, too many fourth engineers are there, so they [crewing agencies] cannot give job to everybody, too much of waiting, [for] fourth engineers especially. [Jon, Fourth Engineer, 25, from India, interview in English]

Jon indicated the difficulties he had had in securing a contract at sea due to an over-supply of seafarers holding a similar role. In the same way another officer explained:

> In my first year [of studies] we were 700 [cadets] in my university, 700 people, and we finished around 250. Most of them, they quit because they found out that there is no way to go on sea as a cadet, so no point to lose four years for nothing. Most of them they finished, but there is no chance, they didn't have any chance [to find a job at sea], so they are working either in harbour, or in [the] office, in some small companies, depends on their luck of course. [Dontos, Second Mate, 27, from Romania, interview in English]

Dontos implied that some people leave seafaring during their training because of the lack of career prospects in the industry and difficulties in finding a job. Just as good career prospects were cited as a motivation for going to sea so too were they given as a reason for staying at sea for a limited period of time (Baylon and Stevenson 2005; Calderón 2011; Barnett et al. 2006; Guo et al. 2006). When interviewed, both formally and informally, many seafarers talked about wanting to stay at sea for just a fixed length of time for example 'for ten years' or 'until I get my captain's ticket', and then continue their 'career' ashore. The following quote is illustrative:

> [Seafaring is] not a job for life. I will never work in one place for the rest of my life [laughing] [...] I don't like working in one place all the time, because after a certain time, everything repeats itself, everything will be standard, you also have to progress. [...] I want to see new things. That's what life is about, not to be stuck in the same place all the time, in the same company, in the same factory, in the same table in the same office, you always have to see new things. [Walder, Electrician, 27, from Israel, interview in Hebrew]

Nevertheless there are seafarers who continue to work at sea long-term, whether they originally planned to do so or not.

Staying at Sea: Retention Factors

Despite their intentions to leave and pursue a different career, several seafarers in my research indicated that somehow they had got 'stuck' on board. This is sometimes described as the phenomenon of 'golden handcuffs' whereby seafarers become accustomed to higher incomes that cannot usually be earnt elsewhere. One of the interviewees put it this way:

> [Being a seafarer] it's like this weakness, [...] it's like [being] a drug addict, you know? Someone who got used to drugs, and says 'well that's it, this is the last time...' and after that, 'I need to feel good', he feels the craving, he needs a particular dose of drugs to ease the craving, and once he gets off, he says 'that's it, that was the last time and I will not do that anymore'. And afterwards when he starts to feel the craving again, again he runs after this dose. The same happens with seafarers, the same. When the money finishes, do you understand? And he got used to living in luxury, he has gotten used to [spending large amounts of money], where would he go? With his education, he cannot earn anything at home, I mean what's next? You go to sea... you have to. And this way, every voyage it's like the last, that's why... I'm attracted to this profession. [...] [The seafarer] has already gotten used to not denying anything from himself, for instance he got used to, there is a new phone model that came out, he can just go and buy it. Just because he has a sufficient salary, [...] if I want to buy a phone for $400, I just go and buy it, without problems. But at home, with a salary of $200, $300, I will not be able to afford this. [Will, Third Mate, 36, from Ukraine, interview in Russian]

The difficulty in leaving the sea can also be as a result of adapting to the shipboard way of life and environment which whilst frequently disagreeable nevertheless makes settling ashore hard. For example, Tywin, motorman, describes how:

> I wake up, and after 15 minutes, I descend two levels, and I am at work already. I know that [when] I arrive [on board], I get fed, I'm always warm, I don't need to pay for water, I don't need to pay for bills, I don't need to cook. [...] But at home, [when] I come [home], I lose weight straightaway, [laughing], during the contract I always gain weight, [but when] at home I lose weight straightaway because I eat only once a day, it just happens this way. Plus, [at home] you have all these domestic problems, you need to pay for energy, for water, going there and there, you have a queue there, [stand in] a queue there, you're not used to that anymore. [Laughing] so it becomes hard in some way [to come ashore]. [Tywin, Motorman, 27, from Ukraine, interview in Russian]

Tywin describes the provision of basic needs on board that were not provided ashore, explaining how he had become too used to the institutionalised life at sea. There were similar statements from interviewees who felt unable to cope with the ship to shore transition that they had always imagined making. One Chief Engineer described how:

> If until the age of 35 a person could not separate himself from the sea, then he will not be able to do that for the rest of his life. For many reasons, I tried, about twice, once I worked for a year ashore the second time even more [...] seafarers can work only at sea. Ashore I could find a job with reasonable pay, [...] it didn't work out. I could spend time ashore, I was searching and searching and searching, but when [...] you get countless offers to work at sea, to get paid twice as much, but it is at sea, [laughing] and you also have the documents you need in order to work, to take care of all these issues, of course you will choose [seafaring], [uses an expression in Russian] "better one bird in the hand than two birds in the bush", so after that, the point of [working ashore] was lost. [...] This is it. So long as my health is good enough, I hope it is enough until retirement to continue. [Sandor, Chief Engineer, 49, from Russia, interview in Russian]

Sandor emphasized the golden handcuffs that he found himself 'wearing', however his account also endorsed the view that once acculturated to sea-life seafarers can 'only work at sea'. This resonates with accounts stressing the 'addictive' nature of working at sea, mentioned by Heen (1988) and Hill (1972), which often complicates any attempts to transfer ashore from a sea-based job and consequently transforms seafaring into a life-long occupation.

Conclusion

The nature of work at sea is different from that of employment ashore due to the intensive and all-consuming work environment on ships and the long absences from families and friends while seafarers are on board. In the light of this, this chapter focused on some of the factors which influence an individual into making seafaring a choice of occupation, on circumstances of retention that predispose a seafarer to remain and on influences of attrition that may ultimately affect a seafarer's decisions to leave the sea. The reasons behind an individual's decision to work at sea are varied. A common motivation in going to sea is money, another is the lack of local employment opportunities and a third is pressure from family and friends. In addition some seafarers may wish to develop their skills at sea, in order to pursue a 'portfolio career'. Others may plan to enter seafaring as a temporary strategy but remain because they have become institutionalised.

A challenging career development route exists. On the one hand individuals face contract-based (temporary) employment and on the other hand may have ambitions for promotion. In most cases, there is no commitment on either side (employer or employee) to remain with the same company. Despite this challenge, however, many individuals often remain and work at sea for the rest of their lives. Even though it can last over the whole period of an individual's employment, this lifelong work does not generally follow the traditional trajectory that characterises a 'career'. In bureaucratic employment practices individuals have job security and can expect employment for the rest of their lives. This is generally with a single employer. In the precarious shipping industry, seafarers' employment is not guaranteed, and they often feel that they are 'stuck' at sea with few options to work elsewhere. While some seafarers remain at sea for the rest of their working lives other seafarers develop a 'portfolio career'. They treat seafaring as a stop along the way and use it as leverage to improve their employment options in the global labour market where they intend to continue their employment across different organisations and across different industries.

By utilising flexible employment practices, shipping companies have appeared to enjoy the best of both worlds, having seafarers available for employment when required and at the same time retaining the option to shed them when it is necessary. However seafarers who develop a 'portfolio career' intend to engage with seafaring as a temporary job and are very likely to leave the sea after several years of employment. Consequently shipping companies might not be able to rely on a ready supply of seafarers. In the future the lack of commitment by both the employer and the employee to a permanent employment contract could well create supply problems across the industry.

References

Acejo, I. 2012. Seafarers and Transnationalism: Ways of Belongingness Ashore and Aboard. *Journal of Intercultural Studies* 33 (1): 69–84.

Alderton, T., M. Bloor, E. Kahveci, et al. 2004. *The Global Seafarer: Living and Working Conditions in a Globalized Industry*. Geneve: International Labour Office.

Arthur, M.B. 1994. The Boundaryless Career: A New Perspective for Organizational Inquiry. *Journal of Organizational Behavior* 15 (4): 295–306.

Barnett, M., D. Gatfield, B. Overgaard, et al. 2006. Barriers to Progress or Windows of Opportunity? A Study in Career Path Mapping in the Maritime Industries. *WMU Journal of Maritime Affairs* 5 (2): 127–142.

Baruch, Y. 2006. Career Development in Organizations and Beyond: Balancing Traditional and Contemporary Viewpoints. *Human Resource Management Review* 16 (2): 125–138.

Baruch, Y., and M. Peiperl. 2000. Career Management Practices: An Empirical Survey and Implications. *Human Resource Management* 39 (4): 347–366.

Baum-Talmor, P. 2012. *From Sea to Shore: An Ethnographic Account of Seafaring Experience* (in Hebrew). M.A. Dissertation [Unpublished], Department of Sociology and Anthropology, University of Haifa.

———. 2018. *Careers and Labour Market Flexibility in Global Industries: The Case of Seafarers.* PhD Thesis, SIRC, Cardiff University.

Baylon, A.M., and C. Stevenson. 2005. Aspirations of Filipino Cadets vis-à-vis UK Cadets. *Proceedings of the 6th LSM Conference*. Manila, Philippines.

Belousov, K., T. Horlick-Jones, M. Bloor, et al. 2007. Any Port in a Storm: Fieldwork Difficulties in Dangerous and Crisis-Ridden Settings. *Qualitative Research* 7 (2): 155–175.

BIMCO. 2005. *Manpower 2005 Update: The Worldwide Demand for and Supply of Seafarers.* Warwick: Warwick Institute for Employment Research.

———. 2010. *Manpower 2010 Update: The Worldwide Demand for and Supply of Seafarers.* Warwick: Warwick Institute for Employment Research.

———. 2015. *Manpower 2015 Update: The Worldwide Demand for and Supply of Seafarers.* London: Maritime International Secretariat Services Limited.

Bloor, M., and H. Sampson. 2009. Regulatory Enforcement of Labour Standards in an Outsourcing Globalized Industry the Case of the Shipping Industry. *Work, Employment & Society* 23 (4): 711–726.

Brown, P. 1995. Cultural Capital and Social Exclusion: Some Observations on Recent Trends in Education, Employment and the Labour Market. *Work, Employment & Society* 9 (1): 29–51.

Burgess, J. 1997. The Flexible Firm and the Growth of Non-standard Employment. *Labour and Industry: A Journal of the Social and Economic Relations of Work* 7 (3): 85–102.

Calderón, M.V. 2011. *Seafarers in Ecuador: A Labour Market Study (A Labour Market Project Undertaken by the Seafarers International Research Centre (SIRC) in Collaboration with the Pontificia Javeriana University of Colombia).* Cardiff: SIRC.

Cohen, L., and M. Mallon. 1999. The Transition from Organisational Employment to Portfolio Working: Perceptions of Boundarylessness'. *Work, Employment & Society* 13 (2): 329–352.

De Silva, R., P. Stanton, and J. Stanton. 2011. Determinants of Indian Sub-Continent Officer-Seafarer Retention in the Shipping Industry. *Maritime Policy & Management* 38 (6): 633–644.

Dearsley, D. 2013. *Maritime Career Path Mapping 2013 Update*. Europe: European Community Shipowners' Associations (ECSA) and the European Transport Workers' Federation (ETF).

Ervin, A., G. Flores-Macias, H. Lee, et al. 2002. *Reducing Attrition at the Cadet Training Academy.* Durham: Terry Sanford Institute of Public Policy, Duke University.

Fei, J. 2011. An Empirical Study of the Role of Information Technology in Effective Knowledge Transfer in the Shipping Industry. *Maritime Policy & Management* 38 (4): 347–367.

Fei, J., J. Lu, and F. Kow. 2012. Identifying the Factors Affecting Active Seafaring Career. *1st Annual World Congress of Ocean 2012.* Dalian, China, 1.

Gardner, B., P. Marlow, M. Naim, et al. 2007. The Policy Implications of Market Failure for the Land-Based Jobs Market for British Seafarers. *Marine Policy* 31 (2): 117–124.

Gekara, V. 2009. Understanding Attrition in UK Maritime Education and Training. *Globalisation, Societies and Education* 7 (2): 217–232.

Gerstenberger, H. 2002. Cost Elements with a Soul. *Proceedings of International Association of Maritime Economists-International Conference,* Panama, 13–15 November.

Glen, D., and J. McConville. 2001. Employment Characteristics of UK Seafaring Officers in 1999. *Marine Policy* 25 (3): 215–221.

Gould, E.A. 2010. *Towards a Total Occupation: A Study of UK Merchant Navy Officer Cadetship.* PhD Thesis, SIRC, Cardiff University.

———. 2011. Personalities, Policies, and the Training of Officer Cadets. *SIRC Symposium Proceedings*, Cardiff University.

Guo, J.L., G.S. Liang, and K.D. Ye. 2006. An Influence Model in Seafaring Choice for Taiwan Navigation Students. *Maritime Policy & Management* 33 (4): 403–421.

Heen, K. 1988. Norwegian Fishermen: Labour Market Behaviour and Analysis. *Marine Policy* 12 (4): 396–407.

Hill, J.M.M. 1972. *The Seafaring Career: A Study of the Forces Affecting Joining, Serving and Leaving the Merchant Navy*. London: Tavistock Institute of Human Relations.
ILO. 2015. *World Employment and Social Outlook: The Changing Nature of Jobs*. Geneva: International Labour Office.
———. 2019. *World Employment and Social Outlook*. Geneva: International Labour Office.
IMF. 2015. *World Economic Outlook: Uneven Growth Short- and Long-Term Factors (A Report by the International Monetary Fund)*. Washington: International Monetary Fund.
———. 2019. *World Economic Outlook, October 2019: Global Manufacturing Downturn, Rising Trade Barriers*. Washington: International Monetary Fund.
Kahveci, E. 2007a. Reviewing Seafarers' Welfare at Sea and Ashore. *The Sea, London: Mission to Seafarers* (186 Mar/Apr), p. 4.
———. 2007b. Welfare Services for Seafarers. *SIRC Symposium Proceedings*., Cardiff University, p. 10, ISBN 1-900174-31-6.
Klikauer, T., and R. Morris. 2002. Kiribati Seafarers and German Container Shipping. *Maritime Policy & Management* 29 (1): 93–101.
———. 2003. Human Resources in the German Maritime Industries: 'Back-Sourcing' and Ship Management. *The International Journal of Human Resource Management* 14 (4): 544–558.
Mack, K. 2007. When Seafaring Is (Or Was) a Calling: Norwegian Seafarers' Career Experiences. *Maritime Policy & Management* 34 (4): 347–358.
Mallon, M. 1998. The Portfolio Career: Pushed or Pulled to it? *Personnel Review* 27 (5): 361–377.
Østreng, D. 2000. Sailors - Cosmopolitans or Locals? Occupational Identity of Sailors on Ships in International Trade. *Vestfold College Publication Series/Paper*: 1–20.
Pettit, S.J., B.M. Gardner, P.B. Marlow, et al. 2005. Ex-seafarers Shore-Based Employment: The Current UK Situation. *Marine Policy* 29 (6): 521–531.
Platman, K. 2004. 'Portfolio Careers' and the Search for Flexibility in Later Life. *Work, Employment & Society* 18 (3): 573–599.
Sampson, H. 2013. *International Seafarers and Transnationalism in the Twenty-First Century*. Manchester: Manchester University Press.
Sampson, H., and T. Schroeder. 2006. In the Wake of the Wave: Globalization, Networks, and the Experiences of Transmigrant Seafarers in Northern Germany. *Global Networks* 6 (1): 61–80.
Sampson, H., and L. Tang. 2015. Strange Things Happen at Sea: Training and New Technology in a Multi-Billion Global Industry. *Journal of Education and Work* 29 (8): 1–15.
Seaways. 2014. Seafarer Survey - Why Sail? *Seaways - The Nautical Institute Magazine*, March 2014 Issue, p. 10.
Slišković, A., and Z. Penezić. 2017. Lifestyle Factors in Croatian Seafarers as Relating to Health and Stress on Board. *Work* 56 (3): 371–380.
Stone, K.V.W. 2005. Flexibilization, Globalization, and Privatization: The Three Challenges to Labor Rights in Our Time. *Osgoode Hall Law Journal* UCLA School of Law Research Paper No. 05–19: Public Law & Legal Theory Research Paper Series.
Thomas, M. 2003. *Lost at Sea and Lost at Home: The Predicament of Seafaring Families*. Cardiff: SIRC.
Thomas, M., H. Sampson, and M. Zhao. 2001. *Behind the Scenes: Seafaring and Family Life. SIRC Symposium Proceedings,* Cardiff University, June, ISBN 1-900174-16-2.
Wu, B., and J. Morris. 2006. 'A Life on the Ocean Wave': The 'Post-socialist' Careers of Chinese, Russian and Eastern European Seafarers. *The International Journal of Human Resource Management* 17 (1): 25–48.
Zurcher, L.A. 1965. The Sailor Aboard Ship: A Study of Role Behavior in a Total Institution. *Social Forces* 43 (3): 389–400.

Chapter 6
Women Seafarers: An Analysis of Barriers to Their Employment

Momoko Kitada

Introduction

Historically, men have been the predominant gender in seafaring. Political debates regarding the need to empower women in the maritime sector are strengthened by the economic projection that in the future there will be a shortage of maritime officers. Seafarers are a long-term investment, particularly because under the International Convention on Standards of Training, Certification and Watchkeeping for Seafarers (STCW), 1978 as Amended, they are required to spend at least 12-months on board prior to being issued with a licence. In 2016, the International Chamber of Shipping (ICS) and the Baltic and International Maritime Council (BIMCO) reported that an additional 16,500 officers would be needed worldwide to meet anticipated future demand (BIMCO and ICS 2016). In this context it would be unwise for shipping companies to discount the potential of women in mitigating crew shortages.

Notwithstanding labour market imperatives, the development of gender equality in the maritime sector is currently slow. Some efforts have been made to promote the recruitment of women seafarers in the last couple of decades but these have not had a significant impact on the overall numbers of women seafarers employed at sea. For the purposes of this chapter women seafarers are classified as those women who work in the operational section of cargo ships as deck officers and engineers. Where they are employed at all, these women are usually assigned as a lone female to a vessel which typically accommodates 18 seafarers. This chapter examines the barriers to the employment of women seafarers and identifies problems in the current attempts at addressing the gender imbalance in the maritime industry.

Three impediments to female employment will be discussed in the context of modern shipping: occupational cultural barriers; lack of awareness and knowledge

M. Kitada (✉)
World Maritime University, Malmö, Sweden
e-mail: mk@wmu.se

V. O. Gekara, H. Sampson (eds.), *The World of the Seafarer*, WMU Studies in Maritime Affairs 9, https://doi.org/10.1007/978-3-030-49825-2_6

about women at sea; and the slow development of effective policies and strategies aimed at recruiting and retaining women seafarers. It draws the conclusion that the employment of women seafarers should be more focused and that the engagement of employers, including shipping companies and crewing agencies, is necessary to improve the situation of women seafarers.

Gender Segregation in Seafaring Occupations

Transport businesses, including road, rail, and air (ITF 2014) are generally male-dominated. Similarly, shipping is known worldwide as an extremely male-dominated industry. Accurate numbers of female maritime transport workers are difficult to obtain especially in the private sector, including merchant shipping and the fishing industry. However, it has been reported that the percentage of women seafarers in 1998 was approximately 2% according to the International Maritime Organization (IMO) (Belcher et al. 2003). This figure included women in non-operational sections of vessels such as hotel and catering. Female deck officers and engineers are present in much smaller numbers on cargo ships, and are estimated to constitute 0.12% of the total seafaring population (Drewry, ILO and ITF 2009).

The latest manpower report estimates that women seafarers represent only 1% of all seafarers (BIMCO and ICS 2016). This seems to imply a 1% decrease in the number of women seafarers over 15 years. However, this figure includes women in ship operational sections only. Nevertheless, approximately a half of this figure comes from female cadets and trainees who have not yet completed their 12-month sea time in order to obtain a license. Therefore, fully qualified women seafarers in ship operational sections would be considered to number only 0.5%. Women officers are sometimes observed in passenger ship sectors, such as cruise ships, passenger ships, and small ferry boats. If these numbers were contributing to a part of this 0.5 percent, the earlier figure of 0.12% of women seafarers on cargo ships would still be a realistic picture.

Gender segregation in seafaring occupations is even more significant in the engine department. Most women choose to study nautical sciences rather than marine engineering in school. According to the study conducted by the Women in Maritime Association, Philippines (WIMA-Phil) from 2008 to 2011, among 30 maritime education and training institutions in the country, the numbers of female graduates were five (0.56%) in marine engineering courses and 123 (0.94%) in marine transportation courses (Limcaoco 2013). Women's participation rates in both navigation and engineering courses are reflected in the actual proportion of women in deck and engine departments where female deck officers outnumber female engineers (Belcher et al. 2003; Chan 2019).

It is clear that there has not been much progress made in terms of increasing overall numbers of women seafarers. This begs the questions:

- Have there been any efforts made to encourage women to go to sea?

- Who participated in these efforts and who did not?

Why Are Women Seafarers Still a Minority?

It has been only in the last few decades that women have emerged as an important element of the workforce in seafaring. There have been a small number of female pioneers who proved themselves to be competent seafarers and most of these hailed from Europe, in particular, Scandinavian countries (Belcher et al. 2003; Kaijser 2005; Kitada and Langåker 2016).

In response to the poor representation of women, the IMO has launched several campaigns to promote women in the maritime sector. During the period 1988–1996, the IMO focused on the development of a gender strategy to establish formal institutional structures to include gender balance in their strategic goals. From 1997 to 2004, the programme entered a sensitisation phase with campaigns across the regions. Since 2004, the IMO has engaged in the strategic development of regional associations for women maritime professionals (Tansey 2015) and in April 2013 the IMO hosted a regional conference relating to the development of a global strategy for women seafarers in Busan, South Korea. This concluded with the Busan Declaration,[1] which refers to the promotion of women seafarers around the world.

An important milestone was the recognition of women seafarers at the level of international conventions which was achieved in 2010. The so-called, 'Manila Amendment' of the STCW, included 'Resolution 14: Promotion of the participation of women in the maritime industry' which was adopted in the Final Act of the Conference of Parties to STCW (IMO 2010). While the STCW convention focuses on the education and training of seafarers, another convention specifies the rights of seafarers, including women.

The International Labour Organization (ILO) provided some support to women seafarers in the drafting of the Maritime Labour Convention (MLC) 2006, by including specific requirements to ensure the conditions of shipboard facilities for women. Those conditions include separate sleeping rooms and separate sanitary facilities for men and women (ILO 2006). The MLC 2006 specifies the minimum living standards for seafarers, including women, and defines the responsibilities of flag states in responding to the needs of seafarers (Kitada 2015b). The 2016 amendment of the MLC, 2006, included the Guideline B4.3.1 at paragraph 4 with the addition of a new subparagraph (d) harassment and bullying. This was a specific reference to the Guidance on eliminating shipboard harassment and bullying, jointly published by the International Chamber of Shipping (ICS) and the International Transport Workers' Federation (ITF) (ICS and ITF 2016). Other organisations who

[1]http://www.imo.org/en/MediaCentre/HotTopics/women/Documents/BUSAN%20DECLARATION(Revised1)%20(3).pdf (Accessed on 21 July 2020).

support women seafarers are the Women's International Shipping and Trading Association (WISTA), and the International Seafarers' Welfare and Assistance Network (ISWAN) who actively advocate the rights of women seafarers.

As discussed earlier, various reports indicate a negligible increase in the number of women seafarers, however the efforts made by international associations seem to have contributed to the advancement of women seafarers to some extent. The following section looks more closely at the evidence.

Advancements in the Promotion of Women Seafarers

Thanks to the international campaigns, including the United Nations (UN) Millennium Development Goals (MDGs) in 2000 followed by the Sustainable Development Goals (SDGs) in 2015, the importance of encouraging women to work in the maritime sector has been generally acknowledged across countries. Despite the fact that women are seemingly welcomed into the shipping industry, the actual progress in encouraging women seafarers seems to be limited. There are still some shipping companies which are reluctant to employ women seafarers and some which openly refuse to consider female applicants because of their gender. This problem was widely acknowledged by the participants at the IMO's regional conference on the development of a global strategy for women seafarers, held in Busan, in 2013. The IMO launched a publicity video to promote positive change for women seafarers, called 'Women at the Helm',[2] and the Busan Declaration was adopted as a conclusion to the conference, requiring a further advancement of unified efforts to support women seafarers. Such efforts were followed up by the IMO's World Maritime Day (WMD) 2019 theme: 'Empowering women in the maritime community' by corresponding to SDG 5 (Achieve gender equality and empower all women and girls). The World Maritime University (WMU), which was established by the IMO in 1983, hosted the Third WMU International Women's Conference on Empowering Women in the Maritime Community, and adopted a set of conclusions, calling for actions to increase the visibility and employment opportunities of women maritime professionals (IMO 2019a; WMU 2019). These conference conclusions were further emphasised by the adoption of the IMO resolution A.1147(31) at the 31st session of the IMO Assemby, recalling for the roles and responsibilities of various maritime stakeholders to promote gender equality in the sector (IMO 2019b).

In recent years, more Maritime Education and Training (MET) institutions have opened their doors to women for enrolment in navigation and marine engineering courses. For example, the Arab Academy for Science Technology & Maritime Transport (AASTMT) in Egypt accepted the first female student in the College of

---

[2]http://www.imo.org/en/MediaCentre/PressBriefings/Pages/10-women-film.aspx#.Vom6qZOLTVo (Accessed on 21 July 2020).

Maritime Studies in 2007 (Saeed 2015) while the Bangladesh Maritime Academy (BMA) recruited 16 female cadets in 2012 and increased its intake to 20 in 2013 (Hussain 2014a). Among these women, 13 female cadets were accepted as on board trainees by the Bangladesh Shipping Corporation (BSC) (Hussain 2014b). These examples are often initiated by a few champions who act as change makers. However, unless they continue to advocate and reach out at the industry level, there may be a limited impact on the encouragement of women seafarers.

In China, the Shanghai Maritime University (SMU) accepted female students into nautical studies from the year 2000 onwards. While SMU is still the only university in China to offer a nautical study course to women, they seem to controversially discourage their female students from becoming seafarers. According to the Gender, Empowerment and Multicultural Crews (GEM) project conference in 2016,[3] female nautical students at SMU are required to take an additional course on 'ship management', because it is believed that women are most unlikely to be employed as seafarers. It is common practice for SMU to convince female students to 'backup' their future. The SMU female nautical students, therefore, have the double burden of studying two courses for the same duration and are expected to perform well. In addition, they have a higher financial burden of paying for double courses at the cost of 50,000 Chinese yuan while male students pay 25,000 yuan for their navigation courses. These male students are further entitled to receive a 50% subsidiary from the government with an expectation of going to sea. Female students are not eligible because they are not expected to gain employment as seafarers.

This example clearly shows the gap between the education and the employment of women seafarers. The problem is, although more women have been receiving education and training as seafarers, they face barriers in relation to getting jobs at sea. Despite the successful efforts to increase female students in MET in line with global initiatives, (for example, 'Education for All (EFA)' (UNESCO 2015) and 'Ensure inclusive and equitable quality education and promote lifelong learning opportunities for all' as SDG 4 (UN 2015), few women succeed in gaining their licences. One barrier relates to the completion of their required 'sea-time' as cadets. Unless MET institutions have access to training ships, it is entirely up to female cadets to find a company with which to complete their 12-month sea-time and obtain their licence (See for example, Tifuh 2014).

Consequently the advancement of women seafarers is slow and it seems that the many initiatives have failed to facilitate the engagement of the industry. In order to further understand this gap in encouraging women seafarers, three aspects of the barriers to women seafarers will be discussed based on the literature: the occupational culture of seafaring; lack of awareness and knowledge; and slow development of effective policies and strategies.

[3]https://www.solent.ac.uk/research/current-projects/gem-project.

Occupational Culture and Barriers for Women Seafarers

Seafaring has been a male-dominated occupation from the Age of the Sail. An assumption that seafarers are men can be found in a number of documents referring to seafarers as 'he', 'his' and 'him' (Kitada 2013). Researchers describe how rarely women have participated in seafaring and how their presence has been substantially overlooked within accounts of the male-oriented culture of the seas (Cordingly 2002; Bin Ahmad Ong 2019; Chan 2019).

The first barrier for women seafarers is culture embedded in occupation. Kitada (2010, 2011) studied the occupational culture of seafaring and concluded that masculine norms and values are reflected in the work culture on board ships. Seafaring jobs are often assumed to require muscles to operate equipment on board. According to the research (Kitada 2010; Chan 2019), women seafarers noted that even though technology is advanced, using muscle power demonstrates the traditional masculine value of labour and privileges the employment of strong and tough men. The idea of masculinity embraced in the occupational culture of seafaring is not limited to physical aspects but also to mental aspects. The idea that women tend to be emotional and cry promotes a negative image about women's capacity to work at sea (Kitada 2010, 2013). Leadership and teamwork skills have been formally recognised as part of seafarers' competences in the STCW convention (IMO 2011). In one institution, their course material on leadership and managerial skills defines 'determination and drive' as one of the leadership qualities and describes 'masculinity' to be important for seafarers:

> DETERMINATION AND DRIVE - include traits such as *initiative, energy, assertiveness, perseverance,* ***masculinity****, and sometimes, dominance.* People with these traits often tend to overheartedly pursue their goals, work long hours, are ambitious, and often are very competitive with others. [emphasis added by the author][4]

This example reflects an expectation about leadership in the maritime industry in the context of the STCW convention. Kitada's research (2010, 2013) reveals that as a result of these stereotyped expectations many women seafarers attempt to conceal feminine characteristics using various identity management strategies, including avoiding tight clothes and choosing loose and baggy garments to hide their bodies, trying not to show their emotions and feelings, and/or smiling less. Some women used swear words to behave in a similar manner to their male colleagues. Such gender identity management strategies help women to make themselves look less feminine and/or more masculine in male-dominated workplaces like ships. Stapleton (2003) also pointed out in her study on gender and swearing that strong language is habitually deployed by both women and men in the context of shared group enterprises.

---

[4]It was reported on the Facebook group, 'Coastal Beauties' which comprises of primarily women at the US Coast Guards.

The masculine tone of seafaring work culture is significant. It encourages minority groups of workers, such as women seafarers, to adapt to masculine norms in order to be part of the team. Unless women modify their behaviour to meet the expectations of masculinity embraced within the occupational culture of seafaring, many of them will not succeed or survive. Some women suffer from gender stereotypes implying that women cannot perform as competently as men at sea and others experience overt and covert discrimination while on board (Belcher et al. 2003; Kitada 2010; WMU 2019). The burden of such gender-related challenges often falls onto women. Changing the attitude of the industry towards female maritime professionals is not always a priority, because employers have not yet come to fully appreciate that recruiting women seafarers may be their best available option in the face of a shortage of officers. The major seafaring supply nations, such as China, Philippines, Russia, Ukraine, and India, are currently regarded as able to maintain their capacity to supply seafarers (BIMCO and ICS 2016) whilst shipowners can easily explore the male labour markets in other emerging economies, such as Myanmar, Vietnam, Brazil, and South Africa.

A Lack of Awareness and Knowledge About Women at Sea

The second barrier for women seafarers is the misconception that women are not suitable for seafaring jobs and this is a common prejudice worldwide (Kitada 2010). Basak (2015) highlights that such prejudice is often proved wrong and many Turkish women seafarers have proved to be capable in their jobs at sea. In addition a widely held old myth in Europe is that women bring bad luck at sea when they are on board (Cordingly 2002).

The main challenge for women seafarers is a common problem in general for women workers in male-dominated occupations: a lack of awareness and stereotyping about women's ability to work. A gendered division of labour is still common in many parts of the world (Walby 1988; Cunningham 2007; Kring 2017). Women tend to be perceived as suitable for 'caring' jobs while men are likely to fit to muscle-required or managerial jobs. Stereotypes for both masculine and feminine types of jobs are culturally and socio-economically constructed and hinder the opposite gender from entering a gender-segregated industry (e.g. the ideas of seafaring being unsuitable for women; and nursing not suitable for men). An overall development plan of gender equality by reducing a bias against women in general would affect the ways in which women seafarers are perceived and accepted on board as well as in shore communities. Hence, the integration of women into seafaring jobs should be a long-term strategic objective for the industry.

A limited amount of research about women seafarers is available on a variety of topics, such as sexual harassment and discrimination (Belcher et al. 2003; Thomas 2006; Raun 2019; Piñeiro and Kitada 2020), perceptions (Dragomir and Surugiu 2013; Theotokas and Tsalichi 2013), gender identity management (Kitada 2010, 2013), work-life balance in relation to marriage and family (Kitada 2009, 2015a), leadership (Fjærli 2015; Ortega et al. 2015; Kitada 2016), religious influence (Bin Ahmad Ong 2019), and health issues (Hansen and Jensen 1998; IMHA, ISWAN, ITF and SHS 2015). Such a pool of research-based knowledge is useful and constant efforts to do research should be encouraged.

Nevertheless the necessary information for women who are considering seafaring jobs is not easy to obtain or may simply be lacking. For example, a company's policy about the security and health issues of women on board is of the utmost importance to women seafarers and those who are contemplating a career at sea. However the way a company deals with such critical issues is often unclear. Consequently this lack of transparency may in itself present a further barrier to women who are considering work at sea.

Slow Development of Effective Policies and Strategies for Women Seafarers

The development of effective policies and strategies for women seafarers seems to have been rather slow in the past couple of decades. At an international level, MLC 2006 specifies a minimum level of work conditions for women seafarers and is the only legal instrument to enforce its implementation, although it is limited to the ratifying countries—95 nations as of November 2019. International laws, including the Convention on the Elimination of All Forms of Discrimination against Women (CEDAW) by UN, and the Maternity Protection Convention (C183) by ILO, have an upper level of priorities applicable to all human beings on earth. Such international agreements are effective only when each country adopts them into their national laws. These national laws regulate shipowners and other stakeholders, prohibiting discrimination against women (Piñeiro and Kitada 2020).

While such laws need to be strengthened at a national level, a wide range of instruments, including guidelines and codes of conducts, can be developed. ITF has developed a guideline for the cruise sector, so-called 'ITF Miami Guidelines Policy'[5] which includes rules against discrimination. Some shipping companies proactively promote women to seafaring positions as part of their corporate social responsibility (CSR). CSR is indicated in the ISO 26000[6] as a marketable element of corporations. Yet, industry engagement, including knowledge sharing of business strategies and best practices for women seafarers, is limited. To respond to this concern, the ILO hosted the Sectoral Meeting on the Recruitment and Retention of Seafarers and the Promotion of Opportunities for Women Seafarers in Geneva from 25 February to 1 March 2019. The conclusions identified several priority areas, including cadet and trainee berths, equal opportunities and treatment of seafarers, and combatting harassment and bullying. It also reminded stakeholders that

[5]The full name of the document is called 'Policy Guidelines Governing the Approval of ITF acceptable CBAs for Cruise Ships flying Flags of Convenience'.

[6]International Organization for Standardization 26000 – Social responsibility.

'mandatory pregnancy testing shall not be used to discriminate against women as this would violate the Discrimination (Employment and Occupation) Convention, 1958 (No.111), and the Maternity Protection Convention, 2000 (No.183) (ILO 2019).

A lack of gender policies in shipping companies has been addressed in various literatures. For example, the survey of shipping companies conducted by Belcher et al. (2003) shows that very few companies have specific policies regarding women. In 2019, Bin Ahmad Ong collected data from 15 Malaysian shipping companies, only two of which had a gender equal employment policy, and three of which actually employed women seafarers. While some shipping companies were positive about recruiting women seafarers, even to senior positions like Captains, it was also reported that quite a few European and Asian shipping firms had a negative image of women seafarers and they had never employed women (Belcher et al. 2003; Bin Ahmad Ong 2019). The main concern of shipping companies, relates to the safe operation of ships, with any human element, including seafarers' rights and gender issues tending to be overlooked. The priorities are operational costs, safety and security (Couper 1999; Fitzpatrick and Anderson 2005; Kitada and Langåker 2017). After many years, it is still the case that a large number of shipping companies do not have gender-related work policies; or even if they have one, they may not necessarily have a mechanism to effectively implement such a policy and fail to communicate it with their (potential) employees.

It may be also worth noting that the distance between a manager and employees also creates a further complication in the effective implementation of gender equality policies. Kitada and Ölçer (2015) explain that the shipping industry tends to be hybrid at inter-organisational levels in terms of regulated/unregulated, or in-house/ outsourced workplaces, which can pose a challenge. If the employer of seafarers is a third party crew agent to whom responsibility for crewing has been outsourced it may be difficult for a distant manager further up the supply chain to ensure gender equality in place and know whether there is a problem and how the problem is solved. Detailed reporting may be replaced with simplified checklists relating to compliance with gender-related issues and these may not be adequate. In the end, no one may be interested in gender-related policies unless a problem is raised externally with implications for public image and reputation.

Conclusion

The efforts to promote women seafarers in the past decades have focused on MET which has appeared to be successful to some extent in opening doors for more female students to enrol into seafarer training around the world. However, not as much progress as expected has occurred because there has been a missing link between this vocational education and actual employment practices. No matter how many female cadets are trained, unless shipping companies or crewing agencies employ them, those human resources are simply wasted and unwanted in the labour market.

The recruitment practices in the maritime sector still favour men over women. This chapter has outlined three barriers to the employment of women seafarers. Firstly, masculine values and norms are evident in the occupational culture of seafaring where gender discrimination or sexual harassment can be triggered towards a lone woman seafarer. In the globalised nature of shipping, many ocean-going vessels accommodate multi-national crew who bring various gender norms that may include different interpretations and expectations of women working at sea. Secondly, although awareness and knowledge regarding women seafarers are generally growing, the critical information needed for women to be employed as seafarers, such as security and health issues, is often unavailable. It is notable that very little research has been conducted in the area of employment policies for women seafarers. This should be a focus of future research, which would combat the third barrier: the slow development of effective policies and strategies for women seafarers. Greater engagement with shipping companies and crewing agencies should be promoted in terms of the development and implementation of gender-related policies and strategies for seafarers. Were more companies to employ women seafarers effectively the promotion of women seafarers would be facilitated.

References

Basak, A.A. 2015. Women's Role in the Turkish and Global Maritime Industry. In *Maritime Women: Global Leadership*, edited by M. Kitada et al. WMU Studies in Maritime Affairs 3. https://doi.org/10.1007/978-3-662-45385-8_8.

Belcher, P., H. Sampson, M. Thomas, J. Veiga, and M. Zhao. 2003. *Women Seafarers: Global Employment Policies and Practices*. Geneva: International Labour Office.

BIMCO and ICS. 2016. *Manpower Report: The Global Supply and Demand for Seafarers in 2015*. London: Maritime International Secretariat Services Limited.

Bin Ahmad Ong, H. 2019. *Gender Equality in the Malaysian Maritime Sector: Religious Influence on Empowering Women at Sea*. MSc dissertation. Malmö: World Maritime University.

Chan, F.M. 2019. *Female Engineer Officers – Breaking the Glass Ceiling*. MSc dissertation. Malmö: World Maritime University.

Cordingly, D. 2002. *Heroines & Harlots: Women at Sea in the Great Age of Sail*. London: Pan Books.

Couper, A.D. 1999. *Voyages of Abuse: Seafarers, Human Rights and International Shipping*. Pluto Press.

Cunningham, M. 2007. Influences of Women's Employment on the Gendered Division of Household Labor Over the Life Course: Evidence From a 31-Year Panel Study. *Journal of Family Issues* 28 (3): 422–444.

Dragomir, C., and F. Surugiu. 2013. *Seafarer Women - Perception of the Seafaring Career*. Advances in Fiscal, Political and Law Science. ISBN: 978-1-61804-191-3.

Drewry, ILO, and ITF. 2009. *Manning 2009*. London: Drewry.

Fitzpatrick, D., and M. Anderson. 2005. International Standards. In *Seafarers' Rights. Seafarers' Rights International*, ed. D. Fitzpatrick and M. Anderson. Oxford: Oxford University Press.

Fjærli, B.A.B. 2015. *Differences in Perception of Male and Female Leaders*. Master's dissertation, Faculty of Technology and Maritime Sciences, Buskerud and Vestfold University College.

Hansen, H.L., and J. Jensen. 1998. Female Seafarers Adopt the High Risk Lifestyle of Male Seafarers. *Occupational Environment Medicine* 55: 49–51.

Hussain, S. 2014a. Young Bangladeshi Women Embarking on Blue Highways! Paper presented at the *2nd International Conference on Maritime Women: Global Leadership*. Malmö, Sweden. 31 March–1 April.

———. 2014b. *Young Bangladeshi Women on the Blue Highway*. http://www.eduicon.com/News/Details/4741.html. Accessed 26 November 2019.

ICS and ITF. 2016. *Guidance on Eliminating Shipboard Harassment and Bullying*. London: The International Chamber of Shipping and The International Transport Workers' Federation. http://www.ics-shipping.org/docs/default-source/Other-documents/guidance-on-eliminating-shipboard-harassment-and-bullying.pdf?sfvrsn=4. Accessed 25 November 2019.

ILO. 2006. *The Maritime Labour Convention, 2006*. Geneva: ILO.

———. 2019. *Conclusions on the Recruitment and Retention of Seafarers and the Promotion of Opportunities for Women Seafarers (SMSWS/2019/9)*, The Sectoral Meeting on the Recruitment and Retention of Seafarers and the Promotion of Opportunities for Women Seafarers. Geneva: International Labour Organization. https://www.ilo.org/wcmsp5/groups/public/%2D%2D-ed_dialogue/%2D%2D-sector/documents/meetingdocument/wcms_674553.pdf. Accessed 26 November 2019.

IMHA, ISWAN, ITF and SHS. 2015. *Women Seafarers' Health and Welfare Survey*. A Joint Initiative of the International Maritime Health Association (IMHA), International Seafarers' Welfare and Assistance Network (ISWAN), International Transport Workers' Federation (ITF) & Seafarers Hospital Society (SHS). https://www.seafarerswelfare.org/assets/documents/resources/women-seafarers-health-and-welfare-survey.pdf. Accessed 26 November 2019.

IMO. 2010. Adoption of the Final Act and any instruments, resolutions and recommendations resulting from the work of the Conference. I:\CONF\STCW\2\32.doc https://www.gc.noaa.gov/documents/afs-convention.pdf. Accessed 26 November 2019.

———. 2011. The International Convention on Standards of Training, Certification and Watchkeeping for Seafarers STCW), 1978 as Amended. 2011 Edition. ISBN: 978-92-801-1528-4.

———. 2019a. *Capacity-Building: Strengthening the Impact of Women in the Maritime Sector: Report of the Third WMU International Conference: Empowering Women in the Maritime Community held in Malmö, Sweden, from 4 to 5 April 2019 (TC 69/10/2)*. The 69th Technical Cooperation Committee, Agenda item 10. London: International Maritime Organization.

———. 2019b. *Preserving the legacy of the World Maritime Theme for 2019 and achieving a barrier-free working environment for women in the maritime sector. (A 31/Res. 1147)*. The 31st IMO Assembly, Agenda item 19(d). London: International Maritime Organization.

ITF. 2014. *Making a Difference - Women Transport Workers in the 21st Century*. Report on Activities 2010-2014. (14/WConf/Ag1/RoA). London: ITF.

Kaijser, I. 2005. *Kvinnliga sjömän – finns dom?* Stockholm: Statens Maritima Museer.

Kitada, M. 2009. Risking Marriage and Family: Maintaining Seafarers' Gender Identities. Maritime Matters in the 21st Century, *The 1st SIRC-Nippon Fellow Maritime Conference*. Cardiff University, 22 January. ISBN: 1-900174-36-7.

———. 2010. *Women Seafarers and Their Identities*. PhD thesis, Cardiff University.

———. 2011. Rethinking the Occupational Culture of Seafaring: Challenges in the New Era of Cultural Diversities. *Ocean Law, Society and Management* 3. Qingdao: Ocean University of China. ISBN: 978-7-5027-8187-3.

———. 2013. Code of Behaviour at Sea: Women Seafarers' Shipboard Identity Management. *WMU Journal of Maritime Affairs* 12: 213–227. https://doi.org/10.1007/s13437-013-0044-7.

———. 2015a. Absent Mother Sailors: How Possible Is It to Do the Impossible? In *Maritime Women: Global Leadership*, edited by M. Kitada et al. WMU Studies in Maritime Affairs 3. https://doi.org/10.1007/978-3-662-45385-8_9.

———. 2015b. A Prospect for Women Seafarers. *The Mariners' Digest* 39: 18–21.

———. 2016. Female Captains and Their Leadership: Human Factors in the Shipping Industry. In *Advances in Human Factors, Business Management, Training and Education*, 1265–1273. https://doi.org/10.1007/978-3-319-42070-7_114.

Kitada, M., and L. Langåker. 2016. *Women Seafarers as Minority Organizational Members*. International Association of Maritime Universities (IAMU) Conference. 26–29 Oct, Haiphong, ISBN: 978-604-937-120-2.

———. 2017. *"The Body" Matters in Maritime Employment Contracts*. International Association of Maritime Universities (IAMU) General Assembly. 11–14 Oct, Varna.

Kitada, M., and A. Ölçer. 2015. Managing People and Technology: The Challenges in CSR and Energy Efficient Shipping. *Research in Transportation Business & Management*. https://doi.org/10.1016/j.rtbm.2015.10.002.

Kring, S.A. 2017. Gender in Employment Policies and Programmes: What Works for Women? Working Paper No. 235. Geneva: International Labour Organization (ILO). https://www.ilo.org/wcmsp5/groups/public/%2D%2D-ed_emp/documents/publication/wcms_613536.pdf. Accessed 26 November 2019.

Limcaoco, C. 2013. Women in Maritime Philippines. A paper presented at the *IMO's Regional Conference on the Development of a Global Strategy for Women Seafarers*. Busan, 16–19 April.

Ortega, O.D., K.I. Øvergård, and V. Henden. 2015. Women Are Better Leaders Than They Think: Gender Differences in the Self-Assessment of Leadership Skills in the Maritime Industry. In *Maritime Women: Global Leadership*, edited by M. Kitada et al. WMU Studies in Maritime Affairs 3. https://doi.org/10.1007/978-3-662-45385-8_15.

Piñeiro, L.C., and M. Kitada. 2020. Sexual harassment and women seafarers: The role of laws and policies to ensure occupational safety & health. *Marine Policy* 117:103938.

Raun, K.G. 2019. *Over 1000 Women Seafarers Share Sexual Harassment Experiences*. Shipping Watch. https://shippingwatch.com/carriers/article10219785.ece. Accessed 26 November 2019.

Saeed, L.E. 2015. Maritime Education and Training: A Gender Perspective. Paper presented at the International Women's Day event, *The Maritime World We Want*. Malmö, 13 March.

Stapleton, K. 2003. Gender and Swearing: A Community Practice. *Women and Language* 26 (2): 22–33.

Tansey, P. 2015. Women at the Helm: 25 Years of IMO's Gender Programme. In *Maritime Women: Global Leadership*, edited by M. Kitada et al. WMU Studies in Maritime Affairs 3. https://doi.org/10.1007/978-3-662-45385-8_2.

Theotokas, I., and C. Tsalichi. 2013. Employment of Women at Sea. Perceptions, Attitudes and Experiences of Male Seafarers in the Greek Context. Proceedings of the *IAME 2013 Conference*, Marseille, 3–5 July.

Thomas, A.M. 2006. Sexual Harassment in a Residential Occupation: The Experiences of Women Seafarers. *Health Education Journal* 65 (2): 170–179.

Tifuh, A.N. 2014. *Women Merchant Mariners: Empowering West African Women*. Master's dissertation, Malmö: World Maritime University.

UN. 2015. *Sustainable Development Goals*. New York: United Nations.

UNESCO. 2015. *Education for All 2000-2015: Achievements and Challenges*. Paris: UNESCO.

Walby, S., ed. 1988. *Gender Segregation at Work*. Milton Keynes: Open University Press.

WMU. 2019. Third WMU International Women's Conference on Empowering Women in the Maritime Community: Conference Report. Malmö: World Maritime University. https://commons.wmu.se/lib_reports/62/. Accessed 26 November 2019.

Part II
Being at Sea

Chapter 7
Transitions and Adjustments Made by Seafarers Whilst at Sea

Helen Devereux

Introduction

In this chapter some of the issues surrounding seafarers' experiences of transition, readjustment and change during a tour are presented. The voices of seafarers are heard through the inclusion of verbatim quotes from interviews conducted on board ships.

Seafarers' experiences of life at sea encompass two distinct phases: being on board a ship and being at home. As such the life of a seafarer is somewhat cyclical with change, readjustment and transition between the two phases occurring. For some seafarers this circular routine of employment-related mobility is regular with periods of time on board and at home remaining relatively consistent. These seafarers tend to be from economically developed countries. However seafarers from less economically developed countries experience sporadic employment-related mobility with their periods of time at sea occurring on a generally more ad hoc basis (Sampson 2013).

This chapter aims to give a flavour of a seafarer's cyclical lifestyle and considers themes regarding change and transition throughout an entire tour. These themes are discussed in chronological order moving from the start, to the middle and concluding with a consideration of the end of a tour.

It is important to note that these three concepts of start, middle and end of time into tour mean different things to each individual seafarer and as such it is not possible to quantify them. These concepts have been used as a device in order to examine seafarers' perceptions of the nature of their work and to make sense of their experiences. Bailey et al. (2007) used similar concepts of 'the beginning and end of a seafarer's time on board' to consider seafarers' perceptions of risk.

H. Devereux (✉)
Solent University, Warsash School of Maritime Science and Engineering, Southampton, UK
e-mail: helen.devereux@solent.ac.uk

V. O. Gekara, H. Sampson (eds.), *The World of the Seafarer*, WMU Studies in Maritime Affairs 9, https://doi.org/10.1007/978-3-030-49825-2_7

In order to appreciate the somewhat unique aspects seafarers experience in relation to change, readjustment and transition throughout a tour it is firstly important to understand some of the peculiarities of being a seafarer.

Life as a Seafarer

One such peculiarity of life at sea relates to the number of seafarers on board a ship. Long gone are the days of hundreds of individuals employed on board a single ship, sailing from their home port around the world for vast periods of time before returning to their home port and 'paying off' with the wages they have earned.

In today's seafaring industry the number of seafarers on board can vary with the number of seafarers decided by the vessel's flag state in accordance with safe manning regulations (ILO 2006). Winchester et al. (2006) state the average crew size of dry cargo vessels to be between ten and twenty-five people (depending on various factors including ship size). On board a single ship there are likely to be crew members of numerous nationalities, all of whom are subject to different pay scales. Furthermore, the length of time a seafarer spends on board a ship per assignment is subject not only to the type of ship they are sailing on but also to factors such as rank, nationality and which crewing agency recruited them. It is not uncommon to find two seafarers on board the same ship, working at the same rank but having completely different tour lengths. As one seafarer described:

> There's a Polish guy and a Croatian. The Croatian he has I think 3 months and the Polish I don't remember but they have a much longer contract than we have Second Officer.

To give a further example, Oldenburg et al. (2009) found the average contract duration for Europeans to be between three and six months and for non-Europeans between six and nine months.

Inevitably, the differences in tour lengths between seafarers working on board the same ship can lead to issues which can include resentment as well as a lack of understanding of the amount of time some individuals spend on board in comparison to those from more economically developed countries.

Perhaps the main reason why differences in terms of employment for seafarers exist is the issue of widespread precarious employment prevailing throughout the seafaring industry. Bloor and Sampson (2009, p. 713) explain:

> [...] contractual arrangements for outsourced labour vary between ship operators and between ship sectors (ferry, cruise, bulk carriers, container ships, oil tankers, gas carriers, etc.) but typically only senior officers will be employed on permanent contracts if permanent contracts are in place at all: junior officers (frequently) and crew (almost invariably) will be employed on short-term contracts of a year or less, but will remain 'on the books' of the crewing agency.

It is necessary to understand how issues regarding precarious employment relate to a seafarer's familiarity with both their workplace and their colleagues in order to appreciate the concept of transition, readjustment and change throughout a tour.

Therefore, in terms of familiarity with colleagues and their vessel seafarers can be broadly categorized into the following three categories:

1. Seafarers who return to the same vessel and work alongside familiar colleagues.
2. Seafarers who return to the same vessel and work alongside unfamiliar colleagues.
3. Seafarers who join an unfamiliar vessel and work alongside unfamiliar colleagues.

A seafarer who returns to the same vessel for subsequent tours is generally employed on a back-to-back schedule. 'Back-to-back' is a term used to describe a situation where an individual is 'paired' with another seafarer of the same rank. These two individuals return to the same vessel for consecutive tours, with one individual on leave whilst the other is on board and as such the position on board is consistently filled by these two seafarers. These seafarers tend to be senior officers from more developed countries and the back-to-back working arrangement facilitates a number of advantages when compared to other seafarers' working schedules. Back-to-back seafarers enjoy greater flexibility regarding when they join and leave the vessel, and they are to some extent able to determine their tour length. This is because back-to-back seafarers tend to arrange relieving each other between themselves with little input from shore side manning. As one explained:

> I could just email [seafarer's name] and say can you join now and he would just say yes or no and then that's how we do it. We arrange our reliefs and then I just go and see the captain and say [seafarer's name] is coming this port (Second Engineer).

Other seafarers however are granted little, if any, flexibility regarding when they join the vessel. For some seafarers the notice they are given prior to joining is particularly short. One complained that:

> They [crewing department of shipping company] tried 12 hours once and I said no way Able Seaman (AB).

The AB's comment gives rise to an interesting issue as it suggests that some seafarers may begin a tour with little or no time to begin to process the transition between life at home and life at sea.

The Beginning of a Tour

The idea of transition between life at home and life on board suggests that a seafarer's use of time immediately prior to joining a ship is of particular interest. In addition, the change, readjustment and transition is further complicated by the fact that not all seafarers travel directly from home to the ship. Some seafarers, particularly those from developing countries, first attend a manning agency to complete paperwork and other formalities prior to joining. This situation exists in the Philippines whereby a seafarer must travel to Manila, regardless of the distance from their home prior to joining a vessel. Other seafarers attend International Convention on Standards of Certification and Watchkeeping (STCW) or company training immediately before going to a ship. In addition some seafarers may transfer from one ship directly to another according to company requirements.

Even when travelling directly from home a seafarer may travel for a considerable period of time in order to reach a ship. The journey may involve any number of connecting flights and then numerous hours travelling in a helicopter or taxi before arriving at the ship. The following example is illustrative:

> We usually take the [Swedish term] flight in the morning, 6 o'clock in the morning from the airport, you arrive at the ship, if you go to Pembroke you arrive at the ship 3 o'clock in the afternoon and then you have your reliever standing there and he want to go also (Chief Engineer).

This increasingly international nature of joining a ship means that many seafarers arrive at a vessel weary from travel and jet lagged, a result of the time zones crossed during the journey. Cleary this is not an ideal situation as jet lag can cause effects such as difficulties with sleeping and decreased performance (Waterhouse et al. 2007). These effects are likely to hinder a seafarer's ability to transition to life on board at the early stage of time into tour.

To put this issue into perspective Wadsworth et al. (2006) utilized questionnaires and identified that 66% of respondents had no opportunity to sleep between travelling to a ship and beginning their first work shift. Of particular concern is the fact that 47% of this group had travelled in excess of six hours and 19% had travelled for 12 hours or more (Wadsworth et al. 2006).

In addition to tiredness from travelling, seafarers may well be joining a vessel they are completely unfamiliar with and sailing with colleagues they have not met previously. For some seafarers, particularly those with little experience of the lifestyle, it can be somewhat overwhelming. One told me that:

> The first week I don't know my way around, I don't know the people, I'm jet lagged, I'm tired, I hate it, I want to go home, I want to cry, it's just the worst experience ever (Deck Cadet).

Furthermore, even with experience of life at sea, a lack of familiarity with their vessel can cause additional stresses to individuals. One seafarer described how:

> I haven't even done any bridge equipment familiarization yet. I mean cos tomorrow morning I'm going to get a pilotage on the way out, you know I might have to set up the bridge and of course I can't do the AIS or any of that shit yet because I haven't even been shown it, different radar systems, different ECDIS systems (Third Officer).

The issues regarding familiarity are not so apparent for those seafarers working a back-to-back schedule however the process of readjusting to the generality of sea-life can still be challenging as a bosun stated:

> You're just getting back into it, you've had 5 weeks off of possibly doing nothing, playing golf, getting drunk and then you're back to no alcohol, no free time as such and that's it so you're well, I would liken it to prison but it's not, you've gone from being able to do anything you want to this is what you've got to do so yeah probably say 3 or 4 days to a week to sort of get into it (Bosun).

Readjusting to life on board can take different seafarers different periods of time. Therefore to appreciate the concept of the beginning of a tour it is important to understand that the seafarers interviewed suggested the beginning was until they felt settled on board with any time after this being considered either the middle or the end of the tour.

The Middle of a Tour

Regardless of when within a tour they are, seafarers work fixed routines whilst at sea and in port and these routines last for the entire duration of their time on board. As such, daily life at sea has a rhythm as regular as clockwork, marked by recurring events such as meal times and watch changes (Knudsen 2009). For some seafarers the routine can be an issue, particularly during the middle of a tour when they look back at the length of time they have already followed the routine for and also look forward to how much longer they must continue to do so. One explained how:

> The middle of the trip is quite tough because you are feeling little bit tired, the routine you know like the well every day's the same, every day you are eating on the same time, every day you are starting the day from the same things (First Officer).

This mid-tour feeling of monotony could be compared to workers in shore-based occupations who work a traditional pattern of Monday to Friday and refer to Wednesday as 'hump day', meaning 'the middle of a work week; used in the context of climbing a proverbial hill' (Urban dictionary 2019) [online].

Unlike workers in shore-based occupations however seafarers experience a lack of traditional temporal markers such as weekends. For this reason seafarers devise concepts to observe the passage of time spent on board. One described how:

> I start counting down, I work on ports I might say I've got 3 ports to go, 2 ports to go, 1 port to go, if it's a long trip then. No say 3 weeks, I'm counting down now I'm thinking I've only got 3 weeks (Deck Cadet).

There is however an interesting variation regarding the routine of life on board between officers and ratings. The routine of ratings on board is controlled by the officers and generally, tasks are set each day by those seafarers sailing in management positions. The tasks are set according to the planned maintenance system and prevailing weather conditions. In contrast those in management positions plan their own work day and many reported doing different tasks depending on how they felt. One explained that:

> Sometimes you have harder day but the next day you can compensate it a little bit do different kind of work but my job you know I do different things every day I have some routine jobs but I can plan for myself (Chief Cook).

In addition to controlling the tasks carried out on board each day, senior officers also control the working hours of each individual seafarer on board. This power held by senior officers and lack of oversight from shore-side however is not always a positive aspect for seafarers. One suggested that:

> When I was with [company name] I was doing sixes[1] all the time cos we had this lazy Chief Officer (Third Officer).

In this quote the third officer illustrates how senior officers can utilize their ability to dictate the working routine of another seafarer in order to work less hours themselves. Clearly such a senior officer would be unpopular on board due to what would be seen by many as an abuse of power but there would be little the junior officers could officially do in such a situation unless they were breaking any rest hour regulation.

Working such a demanding routine of successive shifts with no days of rest in a demanding physical and psychosocial environment invariably impacts upon seafarers and for many the end of a tour is eagerly anticipated.

The End of a Tour

Inevitably, it is during the time period at the end of a tour that seafarers may begin to focus on the transition between leaving the vessel and returning home and for some seafarers this process of adjustment involves a change in working practices. One suggested that one way in which working practices change at the end of a seafarer's time into tour is a reduction in the amount of work undertaken. He said that:

> I try and do as little as possible towards the end, seriously. I'd say a week before I go home or anyone goes home my opinion is you shouldn't be undertaking anything new you should just be repairing stuff and preparing for your handover (Second Engineer).

This reduction in work at the end of a tour is sometimes a pre-planned alteration in working practices as illustrated by a first officer who explained that:

> I did everything ahead, looking ahead to be prepared to not leave too much work on my last days, to get proper rest before home (First Officer).

Other seafarers however suggested that whilst they worked the same number of hours the work at the end of their time into tour involved more paperwork and less manual labour than at other periods of time during their tour. In contrast some seafarers reported that they did more work at the end of their tour in order to ensure they left their responsibilities fully discharged for the person relieving them.

In addition, this process of change towards the end of a tour is further complicated by the fact that only rarely do some seafarers know the exact date on which they are going home and mandatory extensions of time on board are common. The reason for this is that for many seafarers their employment contract permits the shipping company to keep the seafarer on board for a predetermined time in addition to that

[1]Sixes is a common term used to refer to a shift pattern of six hours work followed by six hours rest.

stated in the contract. A seafarer having to remain on board may be due to the lack of available relieving seafarers. In some countries crew members may be unable to leave the vessel due to visa requirements; such is the situation in China for British seafarers. Additionally, the vessel may be sailing on a long ocean passage and the next port of call may be a number of weeks' away.

In some shipping companies managers are reluctant to let seafarers leave the vessel in expensive countries and try to minimize repatriation costs by waiting for the vessel to call at cheaper ports. Repatriation costs can be further reduced by only allowing seafarers to be repatriated in small groups and some seafarers may then be required to wait until such a group can be formed. These mandatory tour extensions can impact upon a seafarer's transition, readjustment and change. One described how:

> When you came and you know you need to do 6 weeks it's you know you prepare yourself looking for the calendar, that okay end of the month you will be at home yeah but other things you are coming and middle of the month you will be at home and then someone is telling you you need to stay longer. Then you are not thinking about the job you are thinking only to finish your trip and not that the job needs to be done. Of course you are doing everything but the way of the thinking has changed rapidly (First Officer).

In some circumstances mandatory tour extensions can therefore be a cause of additional anxiety and worry for seafarers who are anticipating returning home and impact upon the transition process. It is important to consider that there are few other industries whereby it is compulsory for workers to remain at work for weeks or even months longer than they anticipated.

Conclusion

This chapter has illustrated how the transition, change and readjustment process which seafarers experience is a complex process and not one which can be quantified. Seafarers' lives are characterized by different temporal rhythms and two locations, one being home and the other being a ship. Whilst parallels can be drawn with other occupations which require an individual's intermittent absence from home the transition, readjustment and change process undergone by seafarers is somewhat unique. The transition process varies at different points within a tour, with an early stage and a late stage of a tour proving to be the most demanding for many seafarers.

Upon joining a vessel readjustment must occur quickly and in many cases alongside recovery from long distance travelling and jet lag. It is also important to acknowledge that many seafarers do not know when they will be returning home, an issue which affects not only themselves but also those individuals who are waiting at home for the seafarer to return.

References

Bailey, N., N. Ellis, and H. Sampson. 2007. *Perceptions of Risk in the Maritime Industry: Personal Injury*. Seafarers International Research Centre (SIRC), Cardiff University.

Bloor, M., and H. Sampson. 2009. Regulatory Enforcement of Labour Standards in an Outsourcing Globalized Industry the Case of the Shipping Industry. *Work, Employment & Society* 23 (4): 711–726.

ILO. 2006. Maritime Labour Convention [Accessed on 23rd November 2019]. Available at http://www.ilo.org/wcmsp5/groups/public/@ed_norm/@normes/documents/normativeinstrument/wcms_090250.pdf.

Knudsen, F. 2009. Paperwork at the Service of Safety? Workers' Reluctance Against Written Procedures Exemplified by the Concept of 'Seamanship'. *Safety Science* 47 (2): 295–303.

Oldenburg, M., H.J. Jensen, U. Latza, and X. Baur. 2009. Seafaring Stressors Aboard Merchant and Passenger Ships. *International Journal of Public Health* 54 (2): 96–105.

Sampson, H. 2013. *International Seafarers and Transnationalism in the Twenty-first Century*. Manchester: Manchester University Press.

Urban dictionary. 2019. Hump Day. http://www.urbandictionary.com/define.php?term=hump+day [Accessed on 23rd November 2019].

Wadsworth, E.J., P.H. Allen, B.T. Wellens, R.L. McNamara, and A.P. Smith. 2006. Patterns of Fatigue Among Seafarers During a Tour of Duty. *American Journal of Industrial Medicine* 49 (10): 836–844.

Waterhouse, J., T. Reilly, G. Atkinson, and B. Edwards. 2007. Jet Lag: Trends and Coping Strategies. *The Lancet* 369 (9567): 1117–1112.

Winchester, N., H.A. Sampson, and T. Shelly. 2006. *An Analysis of Crewing Levels: Findings from the SIRC Global Labour Market Study*. Seafarers International Research Centre (SIRC), Cardiff University.

Chapter 8
The Rhythms of Shipboard Life: Work, Hierarchy, Occupational Culture and Multinational Crews

Helen Sampson

Introduction

Several words repeatedly crop up when you ask a seafarer working in the international cargo fleet to describe a life at sea: 'boring', is one; 'lonely' is another; and the word 'sacrifice' is used very frequently as well. Most contemporary seafarers are recruited from developing economies where well-paid opportunities for work ashore are scarce and, if they can be found at all, are only available to highly skilled or qualified personnel. As a result, the money that can be earned at sea by both officers and ratings is often unparalleled and this encourages people to seek work as a seafarer when they are young. It also keeps many of them coming back to sea as they get older (as described so vividly by Baum-Talmor in Chap. 5) despite having come to grips with some of the rather unglamorous aspects of the job.

However, from the outset some people can't cope with the conditions found on board. Many leave after their first or second experiences of 'sea-time' as cadets (Gould 2010). They speak of the institutionalized regimes, the bullying, the monotony, and the isolation, as 'intolerable'. As the observations of Hill (1972) attest, this is not a new phenomenon. However, as modern life and the expectations of young people have changed it is likely that some of the disadvantages of a life at sea have come to be even less acceptable to contemporary seafarers than they once were to their predecessors. In 2010, some of Gould's young interviewees struggled with captains who bullied them, physical abuse, loneliness, and depression. One described his experiences of a ship from which he was hugely relieved to ultimately 'escape'. He told Gould that:

> [The cook] threatened me with a knife, he was absolutely blind drunk. When he was cooking he used to drink, it was awful really. So after that episode I, well, after that incident I just

H. Sampson (✉)
Seafarers International Research Centre, School of Social Sciences, Cardiff University, Cardiff, Wales, UK
e-mail: sampsonh@cf.ac.uk

V. O. Gekara, H. Sampson (eds.), *The World of the Seafarer*, WMU Studies in Maritime Affairs 9, https://doi.org/10.1007/978-3-030-49825-2_8

> went to my room and cried. And I've never, I've never actually cried in my life, I was just so, so scared and so, so lonely. And my company couldn't care less, they didn't even phone in, or send anything. [. . .] Well I, I just could not wait to leave the ship, I could not wait to get off that, off that ship. No one was there to say, you know good luck and see you later, or anything. So, I got off the ship and then I got back home. I was so glad to be home. (Sam quoted in Gould 2010, p. 174).

The institutionalized nature of the ship, its isolation, the occupational culture on board and the complexities of legal jurisdiction, all combine to make ships unique workplace settings which carry both threats and opportunities for seafarers. They are first and foremost workplace settings where work dominates almost all other concerns. However, they are also spaces where strong hierarchies determine all activities (work-based and leisure-based) and where occupational cultures and multinational crewing practices have a strong influence on behaviour. This chapter describes some of these features of contemporary ships and provides a sense of the context of daily shipboard life. It is based upon the insight that has been acquired as the result of ethnographic work undertaken over a period of 21 years.

The Dominance of Work

One of the central reasons why many seafarers describe life on board as 'boring' is because it is overwhelmingly dominated by work. Work is 'what the ship does' and an idle ship 'haemorrhages' cash at a phenomenal rate. Ship operators are driven to maximize the productivity of their vessels which essentially means keeping them at sea, and on the move, for as much of their time as possible (Sampson and Wu 2003). They are driven by financial imperatives to keep the ships loaded and in transit and this, in turn, causes them to maintain pressure on their seafarers to keep to schedules, load and off-load cargoes as swiftly as possible, and maintain vessels in seaworthy condition.

For seafarers this essentially means that: they get very little leisure time ashore; that they may be at work at any time of the day or night; and that the majority of them work seven days a week (Ellis et al. 2012). In 2016, the average number of days spent in port (this means within port limits and not necessarily on a berth) was reported by Marine Traffic to be 1.37 days across all vessel types. The average for container vessels was lower with an average of just 0.87 days in port (UNCTAD 2017). Given that this is an average and that many ships will arrive in a port during the hours of darkness it is evident that many seafarers have little, if any, opportunity for shore-leave. Once their vessel is berthed the port-based duties of seafarers are onerous with a requirement for some of them to work six hours on and six hours off in shifts that involve duties relating to cargo, stores, maintenance and security. In general, seafarers work above average hours with a normal working day described as just over ten hours long once berthed in port and almost nine and a half hours long when at sea (Ellis et al. 2012). Much of the remainder of a seafarers' time is spent eating, sleeping and undertaking domestic chores such as laundry. If there is an email or internet connection on board (which is frequently **not** the case) then some of their non-working time is also spent 'chatting' with family or friends via email, SMS, and (more rarely) video link. Otherwise, seafarers may socialize intermittently whilst watching a DVD, or they may engage in physical activity if there is gym equipment on board (usually in the form of a fixed cycle, weights or a treadmill). This generally represents the extent of their non-work shipboard life.

In terms of work, the vessel is divided into three 'departments' namely the 'deck' department, the 'engine' department and the 'galley'. On most contemporary vessels, the galley crew is skeletal in nature and consists of just two crew members—a chief cook and a messman. Between them these two people cook for the whole crew, keep the galley and the food storage spaces clean, manage the garbage, order provisions and maintain cleanliness in communal spaces (messrooms and alleyways) and sometimes the cabins of senior officers. They are amongst the hardest working of all the seafarers on board, working split shifts seven days a week for months at a time.

The remaining crew are fairly evenly divided between the deck and engine departments. On the 'deck side' the officers are generally involved in navigating the vessel, maintaining stability, and stowing and offloading the cargo. The captain is the highest ranking officer and beneath him there is usually a chief officer, a second officer, and a third officer. There may also be a cadet. The bosun occupies a position in the hierarchy that is sandwiched between the officers and the ratings. The bosun and deck ratings are mainly involved in vessel maintenance and cleaning. The bosun usually meets with the chief officer each morning to report back on the tasks that have been accomplished by his team and to receive instructions relating to new ones. He then goes on to assign jobs to the ratings who work with him on maintenance jobs such as washing decks, chipping and painting.

In the engine room, a chief engineer oversees operations and undertakes administration and 'paperwork'. The second engineer is usually the overall supervisor and each engineer has responsibility for different pieces of engine equipment (generators or purifiers, for example, or the main engine itself). Ratings assist the engineering officers and as such there is usually at least one wiper and one motorman. Fitters may also be attached to the engine department and, as with the deck department, there may be one or more cadets at any given time.

There are other positions that are associated with very particular kinds of ship. On a tanker a pumpman is employed, and on a refrigerated cargo ship there is normally a specialist 'reefer' engineer who takes care of the refrigeration systems. On container vessels, when large numbers of refrigerated containers are on board, there may be several electrical engineers monitoring and maintaining them to ensure that valuable cargoes are not damaged as a result of the malfunction of cooling systems. These officers are part of the regular crew, however, from time to time so-called 'riding crew' may work on board for limited periods of time to accomplish specific maintenance tasks which are too time consuming for the usual crew to take care of. These additional members of the crew are often quite segregated from the other seafarers on board. This is partly a consequence of their transient presence and partly due to the fact that there are normally at least two of them and they are usually of the same nationality as each other and may regularly work together. From time to time a company may also provide additional support in the form of an extra third officer to assist officers with arduous navigational schedules where it has been demonstrated that it is not possible to meet the requirements for work-rest hours without additional resources.

All seafarers understand the primacy of work on board and all have generally joined the vessel to make money. Ratings welcome overtime if it will attract extra pay and resent officers who restrict their hours in ways that limit their capacity to earn extra cash on board. Officers are concerned to get good reports from their seniors and to achieve promotion and therefore put in any extra hours which they feel are necessary to achieve this and senior officers (captains and chief engineers) are frequently paid bonuses that are linked to key performance indicators (KPIs). They are also subject to a great deal of pressure from ashore if, and when, things go wrong in terms of damage to machinery, delays to port schedules, accidents, or detentions by inspectors in ports. Many seafarers also find that keeping themselves busy with work on board is a good way of staving off the boredom which is associated with their very limited and institutionalized experience. When combined, these factors generally produce an attitude to work that was nicely summed up by a seafarer posting to a public web forum about life at sea in the 'old' days. He wrote:

> We were trained at sea by our superiors that it didn't matter if you were sick or dying on your feet. It didn't matter if you were injured or genuinely ill. 'get your **** down below. You have a watch to keep. Your god is 'the job' [sic]. http://www.shipsnostalgia.com/showthread.php?t=48587 (accessed 24/11/19)

Whilst this engineer felt that 'times' had 'changed' this attitude is still hugely pervasive on board (Sampson 2013). 'Your God is the job!' nicely sums it up.

Hierarchies and the Social Order

Not only do work activities dominate the lives of seafarers on board but occupational rank dominates all aspects of the shipboard social order and all the interactions between seafarers on board. The captain makes every decision pertaining to social matters such as 'parties', 'shore leave' and access to the ship's 'shop' known as the 'bond' or 'slop chest'. Many also liaise a great deal with the galley staff, setting the overall 'policy' for meals on board and deciding on provisioning—what should be bought and where. Some captains consult with chief engineers on such matters and some have a less collaborative approach. However, everyone is very clear that ultimately the captain is 'king': that what the captain says goes (Sampson 2013).

Chief engineers are also socially powerful figures on board as they are of the same 'rank' as the captain, carrying the same number of 'stripes', but they do not have the same overall responsibility for the vessel and its activities. Seafarers defer to chief engineers and to captains in similar ways but recognize that it is the captain who 'rules the roost' at the end of the day. On a recent voyage I witnessed a clear example of this understanding in action. The captain and chief engineer did not enjoy a close relationship and they were quite often seen to be at odds with each other. On one occasion, the air-conditioning was switched off by the chief engineer to allow for a procedure to take place in the engine room. As a result, the chief engineer ordered all the outer doors of the accommodation block to be left open so that there was adequate ventilation. The captain did not agree with this and was particularly concerned to ensure that the outer doors (which were watertight and as such played an integral part in the ship's safety design) were closed at night. I was on the bridge when the officer on watch instructed the watchman to go around the vessel and to close all of the outer doors on every deck. He went further telling him that if the chief engineer saw him and said anything about his actions he must reply that it was 'captain's orders' and must continue to close all doors. The seafarers in this situation displayed their understanding of the fact that the captain and chief engineer were in disagreement about the best course of action but they were concomitantly in no doubt at all over whose orders must be obeyed.

In general, chief engineers and captains do their best to get along together and the happiest ships are usually those where the senior officers enjoy a good rapport with each other as well as with other crew members. However, rapport with crew members is usually seen by officers as something which must be constrained and kept within certain limits. Officers are acutely aware of the need to maintain their authority on board so that their orders will be unquestioningly followed. Whilst the personal management style of captains varies considerably, there is nonetheless a strongly shared understanding amongst them of the need for captains to maintain a social distance between themselves and the remainder of the crew. Chief engineers and more junior officers also share this view—but usually to a lesser extent. Generally speaking, the most junior of the officers on board (particularly cadets) feel the most at liberty to freely socialize with ratings. In this context, it is interesting that many senior officers feel that it is much easier for them to preserve the necessary social distance with more junior ranks when they do not share a nationality. For this reason, multinational crews are often preferred over single nationality crews (Sampson 2013). Once again this emphasizes the primacy of work on board as it is precisely because social relationships are less easy-going (and enjoyable) amongst multinational crews that seafarers regard these contexts as the easiest ones within which to maintain a 'suitable' professional distance.

Regardless of the precise nature of the relationships between the individuals on board, the social life that is possible is, in any case, very limited. There are a variety of reasons for this. Firstly crews are very small and many crewmembers work split shifts. The galley crew wake up early each morning to prepare breakfast. They then clear up and prepare lunch. After lunch they may take a short break before preparing dinner and they are usually the first crewmembers to go to bed. Deck officers work on shifts (08.00–12.00, 12.00–16.00, and 16.00–20.00 repeating the same hours again through the night and morning respectively—20.00–00.00, 00.00–04.00, 04.00–08.00) and they are accompanied by watchmen (particularly in the hours of darkness and periods of poor visibility) in the form of able seamen (ABs) who may alternate the additional night shifts that are required. Engineering officers on vessels with so-called 'unmanned' engine rooms (which do not require constant overnight attendance) nevertheless rotate night watches. In the course of these they are tasked with visiting the engine room and carrying out any necessary activity whenever an engine alarm sounds (this can be expected to happen several times a night even on well-maintained modern vessels). Finally, the senior officers may all be called upon to work late hours at any time in response to urgent tasks such as demands for information from shore-side managers (Sampson et al. 2016). Consequently the opportunity for social activities is constrained from the outset by the rhythms of work. However there are also other factors which contribute to the extent to which modern vessels are 'all about work'. They include: company rules pertaining to social activities such as sports, barbecues and alcohol consumption; the limited space that is provided for leisure activities; seafarers' fears about accidents; and (relatedly) the extent to which seafarers are constantly aware of the need to stave off the effects of fatigue.

Alcohol consumption on board is restricted by international law. The 2010 Manila Amendments to the International Convention on Standards of Training, Certification and Watchkeeping, (STCW) 1978 establish limits on permitted levels of blood alcohol for any seafarers while 'performing designated safety, security and marine environmental duties' (Spark 2016). Prosecution for contravention in the UK (for example) may result in fines and/or prison sentences of up to two years. For many companies, however, such limits are insufficient. In response to fears about accidents at sea resulting in costly pollution incidents and damage to infrastructure/vessels many companies have introduced 'no alcohol' policies on board what are known as 'dry ships'. Large companies such as Maersk have banned alcohol on all of their vessels (Karstensen 2016) and many tanker and gas carriers are also designated by companies as 'dry' in line with charter party agreements imposed by cargo owners and/or their own requirements. The findings from a questionnaire survey undertaken in 2016 indicate that 58% of contemporary cargo ships are 'dry' (Sampson et al. 2017). This represents a significant change from the past.

For crew members who are culturally inclined towards an association between alcohol and relaxation these limits have had a profound impact on the social life on board. This is perhaps summed up best by seafarers themselves and one posting to a public online forum for merchant seafarers just before Christmas in 2012 put it like this:

> Present company went [to a daily limit of] four beers, then reduced to two then this year went dry. What limited social scene there was given the multinational demographic, it has virtually disappeared now. Our non-alcoholic beer and soft drinks are free, but that's little compensation. Happy feckin Christmas! (sic). (http://www.shipsnostalgia.com/showthread.php?t=48587 accessed 29/01/2018)

However it is not only the absence of a 'bar' and the chance of a 'chinwag' over a cold beer that has killed much of the social life that once existed on board. There are other rules that have been introduced by companies which have had an impact too. It was formerly commonplace for seafarers to enjoy the ritual of a barbecue on deck if, and when, a weekend fell in the midst of an ocean passage. Today many companies have banned the barbecue in line with their safety policies much to the chagrin of seafarers. I sailed with one such company in 2000. The captain on board was generally a great supporter of his company but when he described the barbecue ban to me, and the fears underpinning it (largely—fire risk due to potential flying sparks), he laughed bitterly and contemptuously whilst gesturing upwards towards the smoke stack 'haven't they seen what comes out of the funnel' he exclaimed. I looked upwards and sure enough witnessed a stream of small glowing particles rising into the air from the ships' 'exhaust'. Some sports have also been banned alongside the barbecue. Basketball was banned on a tanker I sailed with in 2006 because too many seafarers were adjudged to have sustained finger injuries whilst playing. More pervasively, other facilities, such as swimming pools, have just been removed from ships and have thereby been 'designed out' of seafarers' shipboard lives (Sampson and Ellis 2019).

A further constraint on the shipboard social lives' of seafarers is the very basic matter of physical space. The prioritization of cargo space over accommodation block space has led to a squeeze on communal spaces on board. Messrooms which were once large enough to accommodate whole crews for social events are now too small to do so. Indeed the last vessel I sailed with did not have a room which was large enough to accommodate the whole crew for a first aid training drill or for debriefings following training. The crew squeezed into the deck office as best they could but some were forced to sit in the alley way, such was the limited space. This is not untypical in the modern fleet.

Finally, seafarers themselves may limit their own social lives on board as a result of their need to protect themselves from fatigue. The shipboard motion, disturbance from vibration, uncomfortable mattresses, light 'pollution', and shift work all combine to make sleep on board a precious commodity. Many seafarers recognize the critical importance of achieving adequate levels of rest and spend their free time trying to sleep or undertaking domestic tasks. They may also attempt to preserve their physical health by using weight machines, fixed cycles or other 'gym' equipment where this is provided. Most of these activities are inherently solitary and militate against the development of any kind of vibrant shipboard social life.

Within this constrained context it is still possible for particular ships to be characterized as 'happy' ships by seafarers. These are usually vessels where the captain permits and encourages social activities such as bingo, 'horse racing', and similar 'games'. In general, and perhaps universally, the shipboard occupational hierarchy is such that without the captain's encouragement and endorsement such activities do not occur. The same applies to the scheduling of social events such as 'parties' to mark birthdays on board or significant cultural occasions such as Christmas. It also applies to barbecues where these remain permitted by companies and to the filling and use of swimming pools where these exist. Captains may even determine use of gym equipment by having some of it moved to areas where it may be exclusively used by themselves or perhaps by other officers.

For many seafarers the captain is only one of a relatively long list of people who hold a position of authority over them on board. Deck ratings are subject to the authority of the bosun, the junior officers (deck and engine), the chief officer, the captain and the chief engineer. This means that the majority of their crewmates are in fact their superiors in rank and authority. For them, socialising in the presence of seniors is inevitably constrained and it may be avoided by some seafarers altogether for fear of attracting criticism. Hierarchy is also an issue when seafarers have the opportunity to enjoy shore-leave, as senior ranks do not cease to exercise their authority once ashore. This results in some seafarers choosing to go ashore alone rather than in company, simply to have a few brief hours when they feel free of 'surveillance' from managers and supervisors.

Occupational Culture and Multinational Crews

As previously noted, truly multinational crews are often popular amongst seafarers. However some crewing patterns are less effective than others in terms of both the work and the social life on board. Generally speaking where there are just two or three nationalities present on a ship there are associated challenges. These are considerably exacerbated when there is only a small group of people from a particular country. On the vessel *Pollyanna,* which I joined in 2013, I found that almost the entire crew was from India with just the chief engineer from elsewhere. In this instance, given the professional distance that he preferred to keep between himself and lower ranking seafarers, and his long experience at sea, the chief engineer was not unduly perturbed. Nevertheless for lower ranking seafarers, and particularly cadets, such skewed patterns of crewing can be highly unsatisfactory and associated with an extreme degree of social isolation.

Ships carrying only two or three nationalities may be characterized by strong divisions. Sometimes officers are all from one country and ratings are from another. However, in many cases the divide between nationalities does not match perfectly with the occupational divide between ratings and officers. In such circumstances ratings who share the same nationality as all the officers on board (but not the other ratings) may be accorded the temporary social status of officers (eating in the officers' mess etc.). By the same token on other vessels, where the demarcation between nationalities takes place further 'up' the hierarchical ladder, some officers may be 'demoted' to ratings' status in relation to social activities and life on board (Sampson 2013). This can have significant operational as well as social consequences, as it may often be in 'off-duty' time (e.g. during a lunch or coffee break) that significant information and knowledge is shared amongst officers. Junior officers who are relegated to the 'crew mess' as a result of their shared nationality with ratings will not be party to such information and as a result will not be as effective in contributing to the officer team as they could otherwise be. Equally, they may be encouraged to relate more to the ratings of their nationality than to the officers from whom they are socially excluded. This could result in the inappropriate sharing of confidential information which could contribute to undermining officer authority and/or respect and trust. Such practices are exacerbated by the tendency of crews, made up of just two or three nationalities, to frequently speak in their own languages rather than in the commonly understood international language of the sea—English. This can create a range of misunderstandings, a strong sense of suspicion and a crew which lacks a sense of solidarity and motivation (Sampson and Zhao 2003).

Mixed nationality crews may also be associated with discrimination and bullying, although bullying is by no means unique to multinational ships and is described by some seafarers as part of the overall occupational culture on board any ship. As one seafarer responding to a survey by the trade union *Nautilus* put it 'I think it will be nearly impossible to change the attitudes in the industry. Traditionally seafarers should be 'made of stern stuff' so we are almost expected to take a degree of bullying from superiors.' (Nautilus International 2010). Another suggested that 'Bullying, discrimination and harassment at sea has always been a problem in my experience even with all British crews' (Nautilus International 2010). Some seafarers go further in identifying single nationality crews as actually **more** prone to bullying or to its corollary—favouritism—than others (Sampson 2013) and it is revealing that in a study of stowaways and their strategies (Senu 2018) single nationality crews were often regarded as higher risk than mixed nationality crews. Some stowaways described how they felt that a single nationality crew was more prone to stick together in covering up abuses (of them) making violent treatment towards them more likely to occur. On the other hand, they felt that the slight mistrust between individual members of multinational crews was likely to protect them from maltreatment given that seafarers did not feel entirely confident about their crewmates' loyalty and the likelihood that such abuses would remain un-reported. This could imply that seafarers in genuinely mixed nationality crews receive a degree of protection resulting from a pervasive lack of certainty that the actions of potential bullies will be covered up by crewmates.

Whether it is more likely that bullying will take place on board a multinational vessel or a single nationality ship is a matter of debate. The pervasiveness of bullying reflects the degree to which it is embedded in the occupational culture of the sea. In such a culture, any individuals who are not well-established in the crew hierarchy by dint of their age/rank, gender or nationality are all potential objects of abuse and bullying. In this context, both women and cadets report a considerable amount of harassment, assault and abusive behaviour (Gould 2010; Belcher et al. 2003; Nautilus International 2010) which would not generally be tolerated in shore-based corporations. The shipboard occupational culture may exacerbate such behaviour as it discourages the telling of 'tales' about the misdemeanours of colleagues to managers and those ashore. On board my first vessel, I was instructed by a Swedish chief officer that 'what happens on the ship stays on the ship'—a lesson that is starkly brought home when reading the reports of incidents where seafarers have endured significant physical abuse from others but have chosen to remain silent about it. One telling example can be found in the case of the vessel *Karin Schepers*. The vessel grounded off Cornwall with the drunk captain at the helm. She was relatively quickly re-floated and sailed to her next port (Rotterdam) where she was met by MAIB inspectors. The inspectors removed her voice data recorder and retrieved recordings of activity on the bridge which had been deliberately left 'un-saved' by the captain. The recordings suggested that, prior to the grounding, the

Ukrainian master had physically assaulted the Filipino second officer on the bridge punching him and causing him to audibly cry. Despite this, the MAIB report notes that:

> When interviewed by MAIB inspectors, the second officer had bruises and marks on his face and body that appeared to have been recently sustained. Subsequent analysis of the audio recordings from the VDR indicated an assault could have taken place on the bridge in the period before the grounding. In subsequent interviews, the second officer was unwilling to account for his injuries, and consequently this aspect of the events of the midnight to 0400 watch on 3 August remains unresolved (MAIB 2012, p. 17)

Other aspects of occupational culture are less overtly unpleasant. Seafarers have a very strong 'work ethic' and there is little patience exercised with suspected malingerers (and indeed oftentimes with those in genuine distress). This results in a very strong sense of seafarers 'pulling together' on board with each individual fulfilling his or her duty to the best of their ability. In a crisis or emergency there is a culture of 'can do' on a ship which is frequently one of the characteristics which renders seafarers attractive to employers ashore (once their seagoing career is over). The occupational culture encourages seafarers to look favourably on colleagues who 'step up to the plate' in terms of effort, ingenuity and inventiveness when it comes to any operational matters. It also encourages stoicism, humour, and emotional toughness.

Many of these qualities are entwined with traditional European notions of masculinity and to that extent they doubtless reflect the historical roots of the merchant navy and the current European and OECD dominance of ownership of the global merchant fleet. Despite the move to developing countries in relation to labour supply, and the rampant surge of shipping in Asia, the shipping industry remains dominated by European/Russian and US owners. Notwithstanding the challenges of the Greek economy, Greece retains its longstanding position as the largest shipowning nation by deadweight tonnage and twelve of the top twenty ship owner countries are from Europe/USA/Russia (UNCTAD 2017). Germany dominates container shipping with a market share of 21% and Greece and Denmark occupy third and fourth positions respectively (China holds a market share of 9% and lies in second place). European norms associated with traditional forms of masculinity remain pervasive in this context, as the mostly male workforce moves from ship to ship carrying with it a widely shared idea of appropriate shipboard behaviour. These norms determine how seafarers live and work alongside each other despite having little personal knowledge of one and other. They are inculcated into cadets and constitute an important part of the 'apprenticeships' which nascent seafarers undergo (Gould 2010).

Conclusion

There is little doubt that life for seafarers working in the 'deep-sea' cargo fleet is challenging. They endure physically difficult shipboard conditions for months on end: sacrificing sleep; being subject to continual vibration and noise; and existing in constrained physical spaces. They face dangerous weather conditions and a hazardous working environment. At regular, if not frequent, intervals seafarers are killed at sea aboard vessels which founder too quickly for safe evacuation (see for example the MAIB 2016 report on the loss *Cemfjord* with all hands) or explode (such as the case of the *Sanchi* an Iranian and Bangladeshi-crewed tanker which exploded and was lost with all hands off the coast of Shanghai in early 2018). In an article focussing on the environmental impact of the explosion of *Sanchi,* the *Guardian* newspaper correspondent Benjamin Haas marked its final disappearance with the following text:

> The Iranian oil tanker Sanchi sank off the coast of Shanghai on Sunday, after a week of burning and sending plumes of smoke hundreds of metres into the air. Only three bodies of the 32 sailors were recovered. The ship was carrying 136,000 tons, or about 1 million barrels, of oil, that now threatens to pollute some of China's most important fishing waters. (Haas 2018)

Most seafarers prefer not to dwell on such tragic events. However, they rarely hesitate to suggest that being on board a ship is like being in a 'prison' frequently adding 'only worse' to their descriptions. They point to: the limited access to entertainment, recreation, and communication; the hierarchy and institutionalisation; the homesickness; and the constrained relationships between colleagues (Sampson and Ellis 2019). However, the challenges for some seafarers are more difficult than for others and this is an environment where it can be particularly difficult to be in a minority as either a woman, a cadet, or a sole representative of a particular nationality. Cargo ships in the international fleet are not suitable workplaces for the feint-hearted. To withstand a life on board, seafarers require mental resilience, strong coping mechanisms, and a capacity to endure privation of both a physical and emotional nature.

References

Belcher, P., H. Sampson, M. Thomas, J. Veiga, and M. Zhao. 2003. *Women Seafarers: Global Employment Policies and Practices*. Geneva: International Labour Office. ISBN 92-2-113491-1.

Ellis, N., H. Sampson, I. Acejo, L. Tang, N. Turgo, and Z. Zhao. 2012. *Seafarer Accommodation on Contemporary Cargo Ships*. Cardiff: SIRC, December. ISBN: 1-900174-43-X.

Gould, E. 2010. *Towards a Total Occupation: A Study of UK Merchant Navy Officer Cadetship*. PhD Thesis, Cardiff University and online at http://orca.cf.ac.uk/55023/1/U585412.pdf (accessed 24/11/2019).

Haas, B. 2018. 'East China Sea oil tanker disaster: what it means for the environment' *The Guardian*. https://www.theguardian.com/world/2018/jan/16/east-china-sea-oil-tanker-disaster-what-it-means-for-the-environment (accessed 5/2/18).

Hill, J. 1972. *The Seafaring Career: A Study of the Forces Affecting Joining, Serving and Leaving the Merchant Navy*. London: Centre for Applied Social Research, Tavistock Institute of Human Relations.

Karstensen, S. 2016. *Policy Statements*. Maersk Supply Services published online at http://www.maersksupplyservice.com/Lists/HSEQ/Attachments/2/Policy%20UK.pdf (accessed 29/01/18).

MAIB. 2012. *Report on the investigation of the grounding of Karin Schepers at Pendeen, Cornwall, UK on 2 August 2011* report No. 10/2012, May. Available on line at https://assets.publishing.service.gov.uk/media/547c6f83e5274a4290000033/KarinSchepers.pdf (accessed 24/11/2019).

———. 2016. *Report on the capsize and sinking of cement carrier Cemfjord in the Pentland Firth, Scotland with the loss of all eight crew on 2 and 3rd January 2015* report No. 8/2016, April. Available on line at https://assets.publishing.service.gov.uk/media/571760fee5274a22d300001e/MAIBInvReport_8_2016.pdf (accessed 24/11/2019).

Nautilus International. 2010. *Report: Bullying, Discrimination& Harassment Survey*. London: Nautilus and on line at https://m.nautilusint.org/media/169246/Bullying-Discrimination-Harassment-survey-2010.pdf (accessed 24/11/2019).

Sampson, H. 2013. *International Seafarers and Transnationalism in the Twenty-First Century*. Manchester: Manchester University Press.

Sampson, H., I. Acejo, N. Ellis, L. Tang, and N. Turgo. 2016. *The Relationships Between Seafarers and Shore-Side Personnel: An Outline Report Based on Research Undertaken in the Period 2012-2016*. Cardiff: SIRC, April. ISBN: 1-900174-48-0. On line at www.sirc.cf.ac.uk (accessed 24/11/2019).

Sampson, H., and N. Ellis. 2019. *Seafarers' Mental Health and Wellbeing*. Institution of Occupational Safety and Health (IOSH). https://www.iosh.com/media/6306/seafarers-mental-health-wellbeing-full-report.pdf (accessed 24/11/2019).

Sampson, H., N. Ellis, A. Acejo, and N. Turgo. 2017. *Changes in Seafarers' Health 2011-2016: A Summary Report*. Cardiff: SIRC, July. ISBN: 1-900174-49-9.

Sampson, H., and B. Wu. 2003. Compressing Time and Constraining Space: The Contradictory Effects of ICT and Containerization on International Shipping Labour. *International Review of Social History* 48 (S11): 123–152. https://doi.org/10.1017/S0020859003001299.

Sampson, H., and M. Zhao. 2003. Multilingual Crews: Communication and the Operation of Ships. *World Englishes* 22 (1): 31–45. https://doi.org/10.1111/1467-971X.00270.

Senu, A. 2018. *The Global Assemblage of Multi-centred Stowaway Governance*. PhD thesis, Cardiff University.

Spark, S. 2016. Safety feature: Why alcohol and ship crews don't mix. *Fairplay* January 29th 2018. https://fairplay.ihs.com/safety-regulation/article/4261711/safety-feature-why-alcohol-and-ship-crews-don-t-mix (accessed 30/1/2018).

UNCTAD. 2017. *Review of Maritime Transport 2017*. Geneva: UNCTAD. Available on line at http://unctad.org/en/PublicationsLibrary/rmt2017_en.pdf (accessed 24/11/2019).

Chapter 9
The Experience of Being a Filipino Seafarer on a Multinationally Crewed Ship

Iris Acejo

Introduction

The globalised labour market for seafarers has led to multinationally crewed vessels. According to a study conducted by Seafarers International Research Centre in 2003, about 60% of ships have multinational crews (Ellis and Sampson 2003). A more recent study showed that 85% of vessels that call in ports in Finland have multinational crew mix and that two and three nationalities are the most prevalent crewing pattern (Storgård et al. 2013). The Philippines, is one of the world's biggest source of seafarers, as such it is worth considering the lived experiences of Filipino seafarers on multinationally crewed vessels.

It is common for Filipino seafarers to work on board under temporary contractual arrangements between 6 and 12 months, with 8 to 12 hour work days. Watchkeeping deck officers work 7 days a week, on a 'week in and week out' basis. Seafarers in other positions may have an occasional Sunday off when their vessel is not in port. Reduced opportunities for shore leave make the ship ever more confining in what is already a risky and uncomfortable environment. Accounts of how Filipino seafarers grapple with these contemporary realities can provide an insight into their day-to-day lives. This chapter explores the nature of Filipino seafarers' relationships within a multi-ethnic crew under temporary, fixed-wage employment and the strategies they adopt on board to survive in such working conditions. The results presented here consider the ways in which Filipino seafarers engage with, and assert themselves in, restrictive social spaces given the inter-workings of routines, hierarchies and nationalities on board. The way in which Filipino seafarers interact within a closely controlled environment reflects how the present structure of the shipping industry

I. Acejo (✉)
Cardiff University, Seafarers International Research Centre, School of Social Sciences, Wales Cardiff, UK
e-mail: acejoi@cf.ac.uk

V. O. Gekara, H. Sampson (eds.), *The World of the Seafarer*, WMU Studies in Maritime Affairs 9, https://doi.org/10.1007/978-3-030-49825-2_9

has evolved. The challenges impinging on meaningful shipboard experiences for Filipino seafarers are discussed.

Filipino seafarers currently estimated at around 215,500 comprise the second largest share in the global maritime industry (BIMCO 2015). Bangko Sentral ng Pilipinas (2016) estimates that 21% of the annual total cash remittances received from abroad, comprising US$ 5.572 billion, is contributed to the nation by seafarers. As international seaborne shipments remain an important force for most economies worldwide, the significance of Filipino seafarers, both globally and locally, grows. Filipino seafarers' representation in the seafaring workforce is roughly divided into officers (34%) and ratings (66%) (BIMCO 2015). In today's merchant fleet, multinational crewing has become the norm and English is recognised as the language of the sea. In the Philippines where the system of education utilizes English as a medium of instruction, Filipino seafarers are better positioned to capture opportunities in the seafaring profession than their counterparts in China and Russia, for example. The active participation of the Philippine government in terms of promoting seafaring as a career likewise helps bolster Filipino seafarers' dominance in the sea-going labour market.

Trends in Seafaring in the Philippines

In the 1960s the number of Filipino seafarers working on board international vessels was estimated to be around 2000 and by 1975 this had jumped to 23,534 and continued to show a steady increase (McKay 2007) with an upsurge in the number of seafarers occurring in the late 1980s indicating a sixfold increase (see Table 9.1). Since 1987, the Philippines has consistently been the leading supplier of seafarers worldwide.[1] In the 2003 Global Labour Market Survey by the Seafarers International Research Centre, about 28.1% of seafarers are Filipinos, comprising the highest proportion, according to nationality. In the survey, 72% worked as ratings and the rest were senior (9%) and junior officers (19%).

The global presence of Filipino seafarers has to be understood in an historical context and this includes the migration processes that have characterized Filipino society and helped constitute migration and working abroad as an accepted part of life. The development of international labour migration in the Philippines started during the Spanish era, was ingrained during US rule, and was institutionalised from the 1970s onwards. Crucial contributory factors were the American legacy such as the opportunity for seafaring work in the US fleet, the emergence of English as a widely-spoken language following the American occupation together with the development of a relatively advanced educational system; the role of the

---

[1]As quoted in http://www.ilo.org/global/about-the-ilo/newsroom/features/WCMS_219974/lang%2D%2Den/index.htm.

Table 9.1 Number of Filipino seafarers, 1960–2013

Year	Number
1960	2000
1975	23,534
1980	57,000
1984	50,604
1985	52,290
1986	54,697
1987	67,042
1988	85,913
1989	103,280
1990	111,212
1995	165,401
2000	198,324
2005	306,297
2010	347,150
2013	367,166
2014	401,826
2015	406,531
2016	442,820

Sources: Adapted from McKay (2007), POEA various years

government; the economic downturn due to the world oil crisis in the 1970s, and the subsequent deregulation of the shipping industry.

The Rise of Contractual Work and Developments in the Shipping Industry

The emergence of a global demand for labour encouraged the development of temporary and contract-based migration flows. The initially opportunistic response of the Philippine government in the 1970s to ease local economic pressures and adapt to the global changes became a long-term strategy for development and growth. Structural changes in the shipping industry also made it suitable as an alternative source of overseas employment for Filipino workers. Developments in sea trade, such as the growth of open registers from around the 1950s (Alderton and Winchester 2002) emphasised seafaring's potential as an income source. Under the open register system, nationally registered ships could be registered or re-flagged in another country. Such registers are commonly known as Flags of Convenience (FOC) (Lillie 2004; Stopford 2008). The global oil crisis of the 1970s led to more FOC-registered ships, which allowed for the development of multinational crewing (Sampson 2013). Consequently a global labour market for seafarers emerged (Winchester et al. 2006) and the shipping industry has emerged as the most globalised of all economic activities. (Couper et al. 1999, p. 9).

In such a deregulated, globalised environment, it became more cost-effective for ships to recruit seafarers from different parts of the world. The Filipinos, whose primary exposure to this trade had been through the US Navy, were now able to work beyond military-related operations and in the merchant fleet. As Filipino seafarers continue to face complex issues concerning their position, participation and prospects, understanding their shipboard lives will illuminate the many ways they grapple with changes occurring not only at the global scale but also at the level of day to day operations on board.

The seafarers in this study were interviewed in two primary sites: in a town in the province of Iloilo and on board a container ship. In the community of Sta. Ana, Iloilo, a total of 49 seafarers' wives were interviewed of whom ten were with their partners as couples. The community in Iloilo was chosen because of its high number of seafaring households. The shipboard fieldwork aboard a container ship, *Manuelita*, lasted for 41 days (i.e. 30 March to 10 May 2009). All 25 seafarers on the ship participated in the study. There were three nationalities on board: Filipino, Indian and Sri Lankan. Out of 25 seafarers, there were 14 Filipinos, ten Indians and one Sri Lankan. In terms of rank, among the 12 officers, there was one Filipino second mate, a Sri Lankan third mate and a Filipino electro cadet while the rest were Indians. Of the 13 ratings, one was Indian while the rest were Filipinos.

Shipboard Life

Life on the ship can be likened to life within a total institution to the extent that there is an overlap between life and work and the ship is isolated from the wider society. Shipboard life embodies a strongly routinized occupational culture. According to Lane (2002, p. 101), such characteristics of seagoing vessels' provides the necessary, but not sufficient, conditions for a high level of social cohesiveness and professional competence'. While this allows the shipboard society to operationally function, seafarers' social and domestic life remains subject to a bureaucratic authority. Such restrictions mean that learning to cope with isolation and confinement as part of 'the everyday' constitutes the totalness of the shipboard routine (Gould 2010).

The occupational hierarchy on board defines work roles within a time-conscious and fast-paced work flow. The captain's authority and power allows him/her[2] direct control of the ship's operations including the living conditions of the crew. Although the chief engineer has the same rank, his/her role mainly revolves around engine concerns. The highest authority in the shipboard chain of command is the captain, also known as the ship's 'master' who oversees various departments (deck, engine and catering). The quality of work dynamics and socialization among crew members is largely influenced by the captain's manner of exercising authority as he is in charge overall (Sampson 2013).

[2]Seafarers are overwhelmingly men (see Kitada's discussion in Chap. 6).

As a result of various developments in the shipping industry and the pursuit of cost cutting, there has been a reduction in the numbers of crew on ships to such an extent that 'crew sizes at the turn of the century were reduced from approximately 40–50 per ship to 20–30' for the same sized vessels (Couper et al. 1999, p. 11). The recent technological innovations, in terms of containerisation and fast vessel turn-around, can be seen to have negatively affected the ratings more than the officers. For example in their study of a modern container terminal Sampson and Wu (2003) describe how reduced time in port and remote ports locations have the overall effect of confining ratings to the ship in both physical and social terms. The ship that I sailed on stayed in port no more than 2 days. The combined effects of reduced turnaround times and the smaller numbers of seafarers may be said to have contributed to job enlargement and the imposition of relentless routines which see seafarers being increasingly bound to the work role on board, with little time for a social life or leisure.

Language and Communication

As mentioned earlier, it has become increasingly common to find seafarers of different national backgrounds working together. Within the diversity found in present-day merchant vessels, English is recognised as the language of the sea and is an essential requirement for seafarers. This entails having communicative competence, using the appropriate vocabulary, phrases and intonation in operational and social contexts found on board. Sampson and Zhao (2003), in considering data from 14 multilingual ships, highlight the need for English proficiency in crew members. A variety of issues relating to the importance of communication to the working environment have been raised in other studies on board multicultural ships such as effective implementation of health and safety on board (Kahveci et al. 2002; Bhattacharya 2009) and social involvement relating to satisfaction and morale on the ship (Sampson and Thomas 2003).

Overall, on board *Manuelita*, seafarers reported being able to interact effectively however they identified certain challenges pertaining to safety-critical operations. A second engineer recalled how he would ensure that commands issued to engine trainees were properly followed:

> He is a bit new. So whenever I use certain terms, maybe he is not able to understand so I repeat it for two or three times more. When he says 'okay, I know now', that is when I know he understood me. But, I would still send fourth engineer to go and see what he is doing. (Second Engineer, Interview 155)

In adopting the standards of the current ship, the trainee's knowledge and techniques had to conform to specific performance measures. Part of learning by experience involved being able to display a functional proficiency in clarifying procedures involved in a particular task. While using a shared language was critical for coordinating tasks, the acquisition of a variety of communication strategies (such as repetition of instructions and sign language) helped avoid misunderstandings and ensured that work was carried out properly.

In adapting to the work environment, professionally and personally, willingness to learn cut across nationality. Being aware of such dynamics, seafarers modified their manner of communicating and often avoided a polarised view of certain nationalities' work ethics. In this way they were able to concentrate on creating working relationships that accepted and valued diversity. Such awareness is crucial because not only does it influence how people are perceived but also the extent to which they are treated with respect, support and self-reflection. Adopting a more sensitive approach than that which relies on stereotypical assumptions enabled seafarers to be more effective, particularly in supervising ratings from different nationality backgrounds. A conscious choice to avoid the labelling of a particular nationality group facilitated good interactions.

For newcomers on the ship, learning the 'communication' ropes may not be straightforward owing to the fact that they encounter different accents and ways of speaking. Aboard *Manuelita*, there were two seafarers who were relatively new to working on board ships. One of them was having difficulty in understanding the job orders issued by the second engineer, who was an Indian officer. He mentioned that in trying to grasp some of the words spoken to him, he had to rely on context clues in carrying out tasks. He stressed that:

> It's hard if you are new or if you come from a different ship type as you have to adjust to words you have never heard before in your line of work. (Engine Trainee, Ship, Interview 136)

Experience has shown that it is especially important for new crew members to make initial connections with others on board so as to become familiar with the language of the ship. Given the work-focused setting on board, the language used is primarily to convey information and issue commands. In dealing with communication breakdowns, most of the ratings on board the ship resort to what Kahveci and Sampson (2001) refer to as pidgin English which is stylistically consistent with other seafarers' patterns of speech. As one Filipino rating recounted:

> When you speak using grammatically constructed English, it becomes difficult for them to be understood. So they learn how to break it up so others get what they mean. (Fieldnotes 5 April 2009)

In this case, the rating's adaptation of his language to his work environment necessitated learning how to vary speech patterns and hence 'speak' like the others. Observing conventional manners in speaking involves not only technical know-how but also the 'ability to penetrate accents and indeed to understand new and particular forms of English' (Kahveci and Sampson 2001, p. 51 in citing Butler 1999). Knowledge of this kind of maritime English allows seafarers to strengthen their work involvement, integrate with others on board and avoid isolation.

Because the learning process takes time, new recruits often struggle with understanding and adapting to seafaring jargon.

> I feel different. Various people that you see, languages that you use. There are times you don't understand each other. Really need to adjust. (OS, Interview 139 Julius)

The multinational context within which seafarers self-consciously operate requires a firm grasp of the language since communication is quite crucial on board in both operational and social contexts. An effective grasp of the English language accompanied with technical knowledge was considered very relevant to work performance. While this may indeed be true, Sampson and Zhao (2003) have shown that proficiency in standardised Maritime English is, to some degree, insufficient as it focuses on resolving job-related issues rather than facilitating informal interactions. The work-centred use of English may have social consequences such as engendering feelings of social estrangement amongst seafarers.

Coping and Enduring: Socialization on Board

Hierarchy determines not only the structure of roles but also the social order on board. While its organizational function creates conditions of responsibility and compliance, its social currency in terms of developing smooth relations among seafarers poses a barrier. High-ranking seafarers, whether senior or junior officers, seldom mingle with ratings except during informal occasions. Social breaks in the routine of the voyage usually depend on the master's initiative due to the dominance of work schedules. Crewing patterns on a ship also exert an influence on whether social interaction is encouraged or restrained. Sampson (2013) has described how vessels crewed by two or three nationalities may be more socially divided than those with multiple nationalities on board. This was the experience of the seafarers aboard *Manuelita* with interaction becoming confined according to nationality. In this case numerous ways of coping or 'making do' were employed to ease the socially restrictive environment on board. One of these was humour.

In the stressful, busy situation characteristically found on a ship, humour can be effective in lightening the atmosphere. An exchange of witticisms allows seafarers to cope with daily monotony and job tensions. This makes a difference to how others get through their work, as one rating stated:

> It makes the work more bearable. You don't suffer and you get through it happily. (Able-bodied seaman, Ship, Interview 145)

He mentioned that he and the Indian deck cadet had been ordered to wash the bridge floor thoroughly by the chief mate and while they were cleaning the bridge he teased the deck cadet about whether he could do it faster than usual. The ability to make such jokes breaks the ice with other seafarers and is a sign of adaptability towards workmates. It becomes an effective tool in establishing a seafarer's presence on board as it conveys the idea of a crew member attuned to the ship's internal workings. In the process, it also becomes part of the natural coping mechanism that connects crew members when on board.

When there was conflict amongst the Filipino ratings regarding the kind of 'bossy' management style practised by the bosun, he was called *lolo* or grandfather as a reference to his old age.

> Sometimes in the morning you can hear not so nice words from him. We just smile. Then call him lolo. He doesn't know that. (Ordinary Seaman, Ship, Interview 140)

Of course, they all refrained from insulting the bosun when he was around. For instance, when the bosun was a few minutes late one of the ratings asked, '*Where is lolo*?' The collective manner in which the other Filipino seafarers connected with this joke could be seen at the moment when the bosun appeared—all of them automatically changed the topic and discussed something else. Even the engine ratings at the table nearby took the cue and immediately discussed other topics. The use of the word 'lolo' became a way for the ratings to express contempt without being judged as insubordinate. This was what Noon and Blyton (1997) described as the 'informal triumphing over the formal' (Douglas 1975). The same situation was identified by Collinson (2002, p. 270) among shop floor workers. In that case, joking was the manual workers' way of 'coping with deskilled, high pressure and/or physically dangerous work'. As the bosun decided to stand by his way of instilling discipline, the tensions that remained were ameliorated through humour in order to emphasize tacitly his unfair approach.

This strategy enabled all the ratings to share some form of connection with each other. Although the ratings from the engine department did not usually work under the direction of the bosun, their annoyance about the bosun's tendency to monitor their beer consumption when in the lounge was a source of tension. Hence, the act of joining in the laughing whenever a 'grandfather' joke was brought up revealed their agreement with its accompanying undertones as they shared and empathized with the group's general feeling. Although laughing with the group indicates one form of subtle resistance to domination and control, it also reinforces the sense of belonging amongst the ratings. The entertaining critical look at the bosun, albeit momentary, provided a way to enact social cohesion. As succinctly expressed by Noon and Blyton (1997, pp. 159–160): 'joking at work plays an important regulatory function by providing a means of expression that assists group cohesion, deflects attention from the dehumanizing aspects of work and acts to preserve the existing power hierarchy'.

Although humour can be useful in forming cohesion in a group, it can have the opposite effect when not properly executed. Newcomers on board learned that funny stories were only amusing when used in a particular context or when expressed according to accepted boundaries. An electro-cadet shared his story on how he sensed a negative reaction from a joke he made about stray dogs with one of his superiors:

> I mentioned how in our area, if your dog gets into the neighbours' place then it is no longer yours. (Electro-cadet, Ship, Interview 134)

The awkward silence following the supposedly witty remark hinted that such an attitude towards eating dogs was not considered funny. Using humour in the workplace required a broad perspective that takes into consideration the position of those at the receiving end. On a ship with different nationalities, funny remarks required sensitivity towards the others' beliefs, traditions and practices. Otherwise, the inappropriate use of humour could further widen and reinforce the isolating conditions on board. Nevertheless, the capacity of humour to bring nationalities together was also manifested:

> The Filipino messman acted gay when he saw the Indian engineer and put his arm around him. The other seafarers in the corridor laughed and teased him about it. (Ship Fieldnotes April 2009)

Joking has its risks, especially among multinational crews, but if properly executed can bring seafarers together (Kahveci et al. 2002).

Forming Names

Just as nationality may create social divisions, it also becomes a way for seafarers of the same nationality to come together using a common language. Amongst Filipino seafarers for instance, the use of localised names for the officers bonded them together. For instance, the captain was called 'tatay' (father) or 'apat' (which means four, and is a reference to the four stripes on his shoulders), the chief engineer was called 'hepe' (chief) while the chief officer, 'kamote' (a pun on scratching the head). Using a different language allowed ratings the freedom to express their viewpoints and to critically discuss certain behaviours of the officers. This was shown in the following instance:

> The ship had just left the port and the Filipino ratings were having their dinner. They were chatting freely about the second engineer whom they call *hepe*. Then suddenly that person passed by the mess hall door. Everyone shared a laugh and someone said out loud, "good thing he can't understand us!" (Fieldnotes 24 April 2009)

The use of Filipino names enabled the Filipino seafarers to freely express their opinions. They could, for instance, criticise the Indian officers without the threat of being reported by the only Indian rating. This was akin to hidden transcripts whereby 'every subordinate group creates...a hidden transcript that represents a critique of power spoken behind the back of the dominant' (Scott 1985).

More often than not, this strategy was used when gossiping about the officers' peculiarities. The messman for instance revealed that:

> We talk about this officer on board who went on a shore leave and stayed out for a long time. We thought, he couldn't be just by himself! (Fieldnotes 7 May 2009)

> There was this engine officer who requested rolls of tissue paper so many times per month that he exceeded what is allowed. We think that he might have taken some of that home...or maybe used them for something else. We talk about that. (Fieldnotes 7 May 2009)

Through this mechanism they developed and sustained strategic acts of resistance. The use of a common language gave them the chance to refer to those in power without fear of risking their position. Lawrence and Robinson (2007) refer to the 'disparity between need for autonomy and an experienced loss of freedom' as a potential contributor to frustration in the workplace. Use of the Filipino language gave them a sense of privacy so that:

> They wouldn't know they are being talked about. (Ordinary Seaman, Ship, Interview 140).

It made for them an avenue to vent their disappointments about work or share stories about past seafaring experiences or even refer to current news about the Philippine government or their families in a relaxed atmosphere. The versatility of using the local language somehow recouped some of the curtailed freedom on board.

Tales of Threats and Revenge

Most of the stories of threats and revenge by Filipino seafarers are surrounded by myths on exacting well-deserved vengeance on abusive officers. These are passed on from one seafarer to another and from one ship to another and often come to the fore in threatening situations. When asked about the desirable qualities of an officer at work, most of them referred to respect as very important in their work environment. Lack of respect, they said, could actually push them to commit extreme actions. One deck rating cited the situation that occurred in the engine department when the engine ratings were not granted their holiday entitlements. He empathized by referring to possible ways in which he could inflict revenge if pushed to extremes:

> If you are really angry at one person then you can create trouble for him. For me, say I am angry at the chief mate, I can go to the ballast room and just push on those buttons that can create trouble. Say, nobody saw me, then who will be blamed? Him! Or his computer, I can destroy all his files. Right? I can get back at him. (Able-bodied Seaman, Ship, Interview 142)

Conveying their grievance by referring to their capacity for sabotage not only highlighted the importance of the holiday entitlement but also underscored the need to retain their sense of worth when unfairly treated. In addition, given the large number of Filipino seafarers on board, this also underlined the potential for such events to happen.

Consequently, they would occasionally refer to myths regarding revenge successfully achieved by others, such as:

> There is one crew member who got some mighty adhesive and glued the lock in the captain's suitcase so it couldn't be opened. There is also one who was thrown overboard with stones on his body... (Able-bodied Seaman, Ship, Interview 142)

By diminishing the inherent power of those in position, seafarers were able to reassure themselves that not only was this done on board the ship but that others have gone through it and therefore shared the same view. The perspective put forward by Morrill, Zald and Rao regarding social spaces in organisations aptly referred to the creation of an autonomous social space in which 'subordinates spin tales of revenge, celebrate hero myths of those who stood up to exploitive superiors and engage in discourses that underscore the inherent dignity of subordinates' (2003, p. 398) Moderating the degree of dominance by their superiors through the act of sharing stories of revenge creates a way for them to reinforce their common view and re-establish their potential for togetherness in unfavourable situations.

Overall, resistant strategies show how group cohesion is reinforced while at the same time emphasising how Filipino seafarers develop awareness of themselves functioning as one nationality. The potentiality for divisiveness reveals how it can be isolating for all crew members if social togetherness becomes constrained according to nationality. By simultaneously consenting to and resisting authority, Filipino ratings adjust the boundaries of their social space on board in order to cope with the tensions arising from such conditions.

Conclusion

As a result of the shipping industry becoming internationalized, globalized and deregulated, Filipino seafarers aboard merchant vessels increasingly find themselves working alongside those from different nationalities. In achieving cooperation, team effort and socially fulfilling relationships are highlighted as crucial to seafarers' daily shipboard life and having a good command of the English language provides confidence in interacting with the crew, suggesting a good capacity for teamwork. This however comes with various challenges such as communicating effectively within a multicultural environment and avoiding stereotype-based biases in dealing with other nationalities. Fluency in the English language including maritime jargons and phrases help seafarers, particularly the new ones, integrate within the strong occupational context of the ship. Officers tasked with managing the crew are better able to adopt management practices that value diversity at work and avoid stereotyping certain nationalities. Such a level of cultural awareness is helpful in integrating seafarers in the ship in terms of re-establishing and strengthening their work involvement and avoiding isolation.

The nationality mix on a ship affects the social order on board. For ships with two nationalities where officers belong to one nationality and ratings belong to another, it may become more difficult for the crew to get together informally. The nationality-divide and the division by hierarchy can be seen as mutually reinforcing. As the ratings' feelings of being overpowered are magnified, the seafarers form small groups (according to their nationality) to dissipate such threats. Conjuring a resistant space by way of humour and tales can serve to circumvent the resulting labour insecurities. As recounted previously, without the support of certain key officers, achieving genuine inclusion on board, in the sense of having a 'happy ship', presents a challenge.

References

Alderton, T., and N. Winchester. 2002. Globalisaton and De-Regulation in the Maritime Industry. *Marine Policy* 26: 35–43.

Bangko Sentral ng Pilipinas. 2016. Overseas Filipinos' Remittances [online] URL: Accessed February 18, 2018. [www.bsp.gov.ph/statistics/keystat/ofw2.htm]

Bhattacharya, S. 2009. The Impact of the ISM Code on the Management of Occupational Health and Safety in the Maritime Industry. PhD Thesis, Cardiff University.

BIMCO. 2015. *Manpower Report The global Supply and Demand for Seafarers in 2015 International Chamber of Shipping*. London: Maritime International Secretariat Services Limited.

Butler, S. 1999. A View on Standards in South-East Asia. *World Englishes* 18 (2): 187–198.

Collinson, D. 2002. Managing Humour. *Journal of Management Studies* 39 (3).

Couper, A., et al. 1999. *Voyages of Abuse: Seafarers, Human Rights and International Shipping*. London: Pluto.

Douglas, M. 1975. *Implicit Meanings. Essays in Anthropology*. London: Routledge.

Ellis, N., and H. Sampson. 2003. *The Global Labour Market for Seafarers Working Aboard Merchant Cargo Ships 2003*. Cardiff: SIRC.

Gould, E. 2010. Towards a Total Occupation: A Study of UK Merchant Navy Officer Cadetship. PhD Thesis, Cardiff University.

Kahveci, E., and H. Sampson. 2001. Findings from the Shipboard Based Study of Mixed Nationality Crews. In SIRC, Seafarers International Research Centre Symposium 2001: Proceedings of SIRC'S second symposium held at Cardiff University. [Online] [Accessed September 24, 2016] Cardiff, Seafarers International Research Centre (SIRC) Cardiff University.

Kahveci, E., T. Lane, and H. Sampson. 2002. *Transnational Seafarer Communities*. Cardiff: Seafarers International Research Centre.

Lane, T. 2002. Social Order of the Ship in a Globalised Labour Market for Seafarers. In *Changing Forms of Employment: Organisations, Skills and Gender*, ed. Rosemary Crompton, Duncan Gallie, and Kate Purcell. London, New York: Routledge.

Lawrence, T., and S. Robinson. 2007. Ain't Misbehavin: Workplace Deviance as Organizational Resistance. *Journal of Management* 33 (3): 378–394.

Lillie, N. 2004. Global Collective Bargaining on Flag of Convenience Shipping. *British Journal of Industrial Relations* 42 (1): 47–67.

McKay, S. 2007. Filipino Sea Men: Identity and Masculinity in a Global Labor Niche. In *Asian Diasporas: New Formations, New Conceptions*, ed. R. Parrenas and L.C.D. Siu, 61–83. Stanford: Stanford University Press.

Morrill, C., M.N. Zald, and H. Rao. 2003. Covert Political Conflict in Organizations: Challenges from Below. *Annual Review of Sociology* 29: 391–415.

Noon, P., and M. Blyton. 1997. *The Realities of Work*. Basingstoke, Hampshire: Macmillan Press Houndmills.

Sampson, H. 2013. *International Seafarers and Transnationalism in Twenty-First Century*. Manchester: Manchester University Press.

Sampson, H., and M. Thomas. 2003. Lone Researchers at Sea: Gender, Risk and Responsibility. *Qualitative Research* 3 (2): 165–189.

Sampson, H., and B. Wu. 2003. Compressing Time and Constraining Space: The Contradictory Effects of ICT and Containerisation on International Shipping Labour. *International Review of Social History* 48: 123–152.

Sampson, H., and M. Zhao. 2003. Multilingual Crews: Communication and the Operation of ships. *World Englishes* 22 (1): 31–43. ISSN 0883 2919.

Scott, J. 1985. *Weapons of the Weak: Everyday Forms of Peasant Resistance*. Yale University Press.

Stopford, M. 2008. *Maritime Economics*. 3rd ed. London: Routledge.

Storgård, J., N. Berg, and O-P. Brunila. 2013. Insight in Ships Crews. Multiculturalism and Maritime Safety. Proceedings of the International Scientific Meeting on Corporate Social

Responsibility (CSR) in Shipping. ed. V. Kunnaala, and J. Viertola. 2nd International Maritime Incident and Near Miss Reporting Conference (IMISS 2013). 11–12 June 2013, Kotka, Finland. Publications of the Centre for Maritime Studies University of Turku, A71.
Winchester, N., H. Sampson, and T. Shelly. 2006. *An Analysis of Crewing Levels: Findings from the SIRC Global Labour Market Study*. SIRC: Cardiff University. ISBN: 1-900174-27-8.

Chapter 10
Environmental Management at Sea: What Being 'Green' Means for Seafarers

Ngwatung Akamangwa

In this chapter the practice of complying with pollution regulations at sea is examined in relation to how work on board ships is affected. The central argument made is that while seafarers mostly perceive pro-environmental practices as morally correct and therefore worthwhile, a number of them believe that being 'green' makes great demands on their time and upon the quality of work and life on board the ship.

Some form of waste and garbage management has historically been required aboard most merchant ships. However, in response to global concerns about the need to preserve the environment, regulatory requirements in this area have become increasingly stringent. The transnational nature of commercial shipping activity and the industry's continued expansion has prompted port states to enforce higher regulatory standards than those prescribed under international law, particularly in instances where there are significant risks to public health and the environment. Pollution from ships has been linked to adverse public health, and socio-economic, impacts including cancer-related mortality, seafood contamination and a decline in the number of recreationally and commercially important fish species. The need to regulate the sector is widely acknowledged today but little is known about how environmental-protection-related tasks are implemented on board because it is an activity which is often hidden from public sight.

Ship staff, play a pivotal role in 'greening' the industry yet little is known of the difficulties with which they are often confronted whilst endeavouring to fulfil the requirements of ecological protection. In discussing the understandings that seafarers have of green practices on the ship, reference will be made to the management of specific waste streams (including garbage, sewage, ballast water and oily wastes) on board, as well as to the control of atmospheric emissions.

One of the earliest attempts to regulate pollution at sea was through the enactment of the IMO's international convention for the prevention of pollution

N. Akamangwa (✉)
New Mexico State University, Department of Sociology, Las Cruces, NM, USA

V. O. Gekara, H. Sampson (eds.), *The World of the Seafarer*, WMU Studies in Maritime Affairs 9, https://doi.org/10.1007/978-3-030-49825-2_10

from ships (MARPOL) on 2 November 1973. Today, this international treaty addresses almost every aspect of pollution, covering oil, harmful substances, garbage, sewage and atmospheric emissions. It is not only the shipping industry which has evidenced concern. Pressure has come from other quarters too with environmental groups and individual customers making growing demands for greater environmental sustainability in shipping activities (Sampson 2016).

The enforcement of environmental standards in the shipping sector, be they legal or commercial, is complicated by the nature of the business itself. Ships trade at sea and are often far away from those countries exercising authority over them. The vessels and their crews are managed remotely by their employers, consequently it is difficult to keep track of everyday occurrences or to resolve practical difficulties relating to the work on board. Nevertheless, despite these limitations, organisations in the shipping sector have generally upheld environmental standards, arguably because of the international practice of subjecting ships to regulatory inspections when in foreign ports. A report by the International Maritime Organization (IMO 2012) shows a downward trend in the number of ships detained globally in the last decade after undergoing a regulatory inspection. The report also indicates that there has been only a small increase in the number of vessels found to be non-compliant during the same period.

The enforcement of legal requirements for preserving the environment both locally and across borders has been successful in increasing awareness and global recognition regarding the environmental impact of shipping. Strict enforcement of these requirements has also led to a reduction in the number of shipping incidents over the past decade. The circumstances underlying the improvement in compliance levels and the issues that ship crews may have to face up to are not immediately apparent unless examined at the shipboard level of the industry. Seafarers interact with a broad mix of complex legal requirements as they traverse the world's oceans calling at one port after another. It is the difficulties faced by ship staff when fulfilling these different requirements that can shape their interpretation of pollution prevention measures.

The following describes the practical implications of pollution prevention at sea and examines the legitimacy of the practices employed by ship crews.

The Regulatory Framework for Reducing Atmospheric and Marine Pollution from Ships

Legal requirements for protecting the environment from ship-source pollution are embedded in international law and conventions. The international convention for the prevention of pollution from ships, also known as MARPOL, and the ballast water convention are among the most common of those applying to everyday operations on board merchant ships today.

Nation states are required to provide the necessary support to help seafarers comply with the requirements of implementing pollution regulations. However concern is mounting regarding the inadequacy, and in some cases the absence, of provisions for the reception of ship's waste in many ports worldwide. Wastes cannot be retained on board indefinitely, both for operational safety and for legal reasons, consequently the lack of port facilities places great demands upon seafarers tasked with finding solutions. These may include the risky practice of dumping waste overboard or seeking alternatives outside the guidelines.

Seafarers are aware that a range of sanctions is applicable when violations are detected. In Northern Europe, where strict requirements are in operation, vessels can be fined for not complying with pollution control measures. For example, in the UK the master and ship owners can be fined up to £250,000 for illegal discharge of oil and up to £5000 and/or 6 months imprisonment for falsifying entries in the ship's oil record book. Across the EU the penalties are generally capped at between EUR 150,000 and EUR 300,000 for minor offences; and between EUR 750,000 and EUR 1,500,000 in the most serious cases, including intentional infringements.[1] In the US the sanctions are much more severe and individual crew members can be personally fined or even imprisoned (Mukherjee 2006). While these punitive measures should serve to deter any acts of infringement, critics have argued that the measures also undermine the welfare (Mitropoulos 2004) of today's 1.5 million seafarers who work to support the flow of international trade.

Ship operators have developed standard procedures for seafarers to follow on board to ensure that seafarers follow international regulations and also to avoid being fined. In addition, individual customers hiring the company's ships (commonly referred to as charterers), trade associations such as the Oil Companies International Marine Forum (OCIMF) and the Chemical Distribution Institute (CDI), and organisations certifying quality management systems used by shipping companies to help reduce their environmental impact, provide best management practice guidelines for preserving the environment. These supply chain influences and economic considerations have come about because in the current global economic climate many firms are seeking to secure a competitive edge, especially in the tanker sector of the industry where strict requirements are in operation (Walters and James 2009). They are also, to some extent, prompted by the shipping industry's own desire to promote a positive image.[2] Such voluntary initiatives make a worthwhile contribution to the environment but their implementation on board ships places demands on seafarers that add to those they are already dealing with in the psychosocial setting of work at sea.

[1]Council Framework Decision 2005/667/JHA of 12 July 2005 to strengthen the criminal-law framework for the enforcement of the law against ship-source pollution [2005] OJ L255/164.

[2]See, for example, the Sustainable Shipping Initiative's (SSI) Case for Action white paper which can be downloaded at https://www.ssi2040.org/wp-content/uploads/2017/01/SSI_fullreport.pdf.

Greening the Shipping Industry: Seafarers' Practices and Perceptions

The following account is based on qualitative interviews conducted by the author as part of a wider study as to how environmental governance affects seafarers (Akamangwa 2013, 2014). In the interviews, seafarers talk about green practices on board the ship and the benefits. They speak about the experience of fulfilling the requirements at work, about the prospect of criminalisation and about regulatory enforcement practices in EU and US ports. They also speak about their greatest concern: the fear of going to jail.

The original 34 interviewees were from Asia, Europe and the Pacific, and were working and living aboard two OECD-registered container ships, some trading between North Europe and the Mediterranean and others between Central and South America and the Caribbean. They were working to earn a living to support their families and to develop their careers. They are not statistically representative of the world's more than one and a half million seafarers but their views provide a sense of what it might mean for a seafarer to be 'green'.

The first thing to note is that in terms of environmental protection, many seafarers express a genuine commitment to pollution control despite the demands that international regulations place on them. One of my interviewees from the Philippines explained that: 'It's good for us so that the nature is good'. His colleague, a second officer, also from the Philippines, held a long-term perspective arguing that 'If everybody is not caring for the environment then it's very bad future for the next generation'. The case for preserving the environment in the interest of posterity was echoed by a Russian chief officer who warned against the potential socio-economic and ecological impacts in the next 5–10 decades:

> You just imagine if nobody will follow; nobody will take care about the environment. So what will we get in the next 50 years? No white sand, no cold beer, no sunshine, no clear water [. . .] yeah. You just come to the beach and plastic around you. No fish, no animals, no birds, no anything. It will come shortly. Ok let's give it another 50-100 years. Three to four generations and it's no more green world.

Time on the planet and the natural balance of the ecosystem were also among some of the arguments advanced by seafarers for protecting the environment, as expressed in the following view by a trainee deck officer from Scotland:

> I guess it's necessary to manage the environment because global warming is honestly a big issue. If somebody doesn't manage it then who knows how long we would be here for. The [rules] are important for keeping the life at sea like dolphins [laughs], try not to affect their populations, and the sharks. They all need to be present; the ecosystem needs to be present for us to function as well.

Arguing that the planet was the only home to mankind, a ship's captain from Russia believed that it was imperative to safeguard the environment for future generations:

> We must save our earth; our planet. So that is why for my opinion we must have control; we must have special organisations; and we must have these rules and we must follow these rules. We must be thinking about our children, our future. Who knows how long we can stay in this planet. Everybody is dreaming that they will stay forever. How to stay forever if you are damaging this: our air, our water, our earth?

Other seafarers found a moral argument to comply with green practices on board ships. An able-bodied seaman from the Philippines was convinced that even without penalties, perpetrators of pollution will ultimately be punished by God. He explained:

> You throw it yourself and nobody sees but someone will see – God. So I think you cannot escape from this because God created the world, the oceans. So from the Christian or Catholics they say that: 'Protect our globe earth'.

The AB went further to describe the act of wilfully polluting the environment as a boomerang, recounting his experience of growing up in the Philippines:

> The Philippines now is crowded by garbage every time because some people are throwing everywhere and when bad weather comes, strong rains and the rivers flood, the garbage is coming. And they say in Tagalog: 'Basura mo itanpon ay babalik din sayo...' [If you throw garbage, it will come back to you. (Adapted from local religious song)]

Ship crews' environmental practices at sea also appeared to be linked to their environmental behaviours at home, suggesting that the company message about sustainability was attractive. A junior engineer who was using the knowledge of recycling in his private life confirmed this, remarking that he had carried the message into his community:

> I have a small beach resort in Manila. So during summer time plenty [customers] coming. I instruct my [staff] that you must segregate. This is ship's instruction [laughs]: bottles, metals, cartons, paper and food waste.

Notwithstanding these views, tensions were also mounting among seafarers in this study about the practices of land-based dwellers. Ship crews appeared to be assessing green practices at sea against similar requirements to protect the environment ashore. In the view of one chief officer, the rules were somewhat disproportionate because 'nobody' was 'interested' in the environmental impact of land-based activities, and perhaps because acts of pollution on land were less noticeable. He argued:

> So if you, for example, will spill the kind of oil somewhere in your garden. Who will see? Nobody will see. On a gasoline station if there is some drop of gasoil which is falling down, nobody taking account right? Who will complain on a gasoline station? Nobody will complain because nobody interested. You can imagine the pressure on the pipe while we're bunkering. Just one second [burst] and everybody will pay attention. Maybe it's because other people are taking care more about the sea or the environment at sea and less about the environment ashore.

Because seafarers are up-to-date with the smaller contribution of the shipping industry to global pollution when measured against that of other sectors, they might easily perceive green practices as excessive and out of proportion with environmental goals. This was the view held by a second engineer from Ukraine:

> I know from news [reports] especially from Greenpeace; of 6 per cent of the whole world industries which [emit into the atmosphere], fleet [ships] represent only 5 per cent. So the world fleet work without damage to the environment. It's only high for the [other] industries - I see in world news.

Perhaps it is fair to say that seafarers generally agree about the necessity of protecting the environment but they do have mixed views about the legitimacy of some regulatory requirements and reservations about a number of green practices. Seafarers believe that environmental rules have become stricter for shipping in spite of the industry's lower environmental impact. The stringency of environmental regulations was reflected in the interpretation by one trainee deck officer of how things were expected to be done:

> Garbage [is] number one; do not dispose plastics in any areas. That's very strict. When it comes to bilge water - oily water - that water should pass through the oily water separator with a maximum of 15 parts per million of oil in it before it will be pumped out of the ship.

According to a ship's captain who worried about the growing stringency of environmental rules and the effect it had on his crew, working conditions on board the ship had become more difficult with the growing demands for the industry to take action on the environment:

> Since last year, especially since last year international rules have become too strict. Our life; the seafarers' life has not become too easy with these strict rules.

Many seafarers regard the penalties imposed by some countries as disproportionate and unfair. For example, a third engineer told me about his anxiety levels when refuelling the ship. He said:

> During bunkering; suppose you make this pollution you must report immediately to the [authorities] or the Coastguard that we have pollution here. So that emergency action must be done not to spread this oil from how many miles. So you cannot hide this one. And then after that, big problem for the ship; big problem for the crew [laughs]; and for whom is in charge, especially for me. That's why I am very strict during connection [coupling of hoses]. I don't like it. I do not want to go in jail [laughs]. Yeah that's it. Five thousand US dollars fine! No, this is not a joke.

This belief among ship crews that reporting oil pollution incidents ultimately causes them to incur fines and other penalties was also articulated in the following description of a related incident by one ship's captain. According to him no matter how minor the pollution incident and how effective the ship's response oil spills always result in punitive action from the shore. He explained how:

> It happened on a rainy day during cargo operations, [the ship was] rolling and the water coming down the side. Some small film of the lube oil went into the water and maybe one glass of oil. It was Antwerp port, so the stevedores are just crazy really. They immediately contacted the authorities. I was summoned to the Harbour Master but I had plenty of evidence. We sounded of course immediately the general [emergency] alarm and the crew proceeded correctly and quickly. So we did everything - just in five minutes and everything was secured. When I was summoned to harbour master I spoke to him and so he said many things to us; to the captain to the crew because we resolved the situation very fast - secured everything. But in accordance with the local regulations, the minimum we should pay some fine. It was the minimum.

It is not surprising therefore that seafarers sometimes feel penalised even when they believe that they are doing their best in challenging circumstances. The fear of being held liable or punished for incidents for which other stakeholders, including bunker suppliers and stevedores, are often partly to blame, also affects the perceptions of ship crews about the legitimacy of environmental protection requirements.

This highly punitive enforcement regime can serve to distract seafarers from their commitment to the greater good (in this case environmental protection) which can be potentially negative. One seafarer explained how:

> I tell you very frankly, sometimes even if we discharge some prohibited garbage into the sea, it may be small amounts but it cannot cause big damage. But first thing I am afraid of is the authorities or some disciplinary regulations. Yes, this is my first worry I tell you very frankly. This is our first worry. Second, we worry about some damage to the marine environment but our first worry is we want to avoid any fine, any disciplinary actions against [us from] the shore or Coastguard or something like that.

Interviewees reported participating in the management of a variety of waste streams to comply not only with the standards enforced by legal requirements but also with voluntary initiatives pursued by their company. In relation to recycling, the company had in place a garbage management plan that was being followed by all vessels, as required by MARPOL regulations. According to this plan, solid waste generated on board the ships was segregated into various categories. The quantities were then recorded and discharged to a shore reception facility. As one deck officer described the plan, where possible some of these wastes could be incinerated at sea:

> Well we have to comply with garbage disposal. For instance, we keep a garbage disposal log on board. We have to segregate all garbage; from plastics, recyclables, oily waste. We have separate containers for all these and these are discharged mainly ashore. We do have incinerators on board where we can burn a lot of these stuff. So we can incinerate it.

While their company took steps to reduce ship emissions within its fleet by purchasing compliant fuels from approved bunker suppliers, on board the ships seafarers were cautious about consuming bunkers which would damage the ship's engine or reduce its performance, causing it to burn more fuel and adding to emissions. One engineer explained:

> We would only go to approved bunker suppliers you know. Obviously the Sulphur content has to be, I think it's one percent now. And then we get the bunkers analysed for chemical contamination as well. Once the samples leave the ship, they go to the agent. The agent then couriers them off to the laboratory. It could take up to three weeks. It's not used until we get the analysis through. Because we've just had a case actually where we had an engine problem and that was because of contaminated fuel. It was very abrasive and the piston rings fractured, went into the bottom and we had big problems with the engine.

One junior engineer who confirmed that this practice was being adhered to on board the ships stated further that fuel oils were taken through a purification process to remove any impurities prior to consumption as an added precaution:

> You know bunker is the lowest grade so plenty impurities from this. Especially Vanadium which can destroy the engine. That's why we have this sample before bunkering. After we finish bunkering we bring to the laboratory to make sure that the oil is good. If it passes the laboratory [test] then we can use. But we have the purifiers that all the fuel goes through to

remove as much of the damage in power so that by the time that fuel gets to the fuel injector where it's going into the engine all the nasty bits have gone.

In taking these precautions, seafarers were in effect ensuring that essential engine components (including fuel pumps and injection systems) which can affect the International Air Pollution Prevention (IAPP) certification for their ships' compliance with Nitrogen Oxide emissions limits were adequately maintained.

Sewage generated on board the company's ships was drained into separate holding tanks for grey and black water, before being taken through a treatment plant. Then treated sewage was pumped over the side as clear water within the guidelines. Similarly, oily wastes in liquid form occurring in the ship's machinery spaces were retained in the sludge holding tanks and the oily bilge tank on board the ship in accordance with MARPOL regulations. A second engineer described the separation process:

So it's a question of putting the raw mixture into a holding tank, allowing it settle out and then you usually pump that water up to a further tank which is the immediate tank for the oily water separator, allowing you a little bit further separation. So in effect there should be hardly any oil going into the oily water separator; it should be just water.

Seafarers also reported that there was an alarm system to monitor the content of oil in wastewater being recycled so that the effluent discharged did not exceed the maximum legal limit of 15 parts per million. According to a crew member who confirmed this, every step of the process was carefully documented in the ship's oil record book which had to be 'kept religiously' by the chief engineer. During a tour of the engine room on one of the ships, I learnt that sludge was not incinerated on this particular ship. The duty engineer had commented that the crew were 'very busy' and the process required a lot of preparation, including heating the sludge for evaporation before igniting it and so they simply discharged it in port.

Some of the tasks associated with preserving the environment on board ships described above require time and effort on the part of ship crews. In complying with the requirements, many seafarers are aware of the trade-offs involved. One second officer described how he believed there was a very good return for seafarers on their additional efforts as they meant that seafarers could guarantee a better future for their families:

Actually, it's a little bit more work for us unlike before you just take everything easy. But now it's additional work for us but it's not really hard work. But only additional work but this additional work in exchange for that it's good for our world - for everybody; for the environment because it's not only for us but for the children of the future.

But seafarers also questioned the feasibility of these requirements, especially when they were perceived as allowing for inflexible implementation as in the case of the prevention of oil pollution from ships. According to one chief engineer who had reservations about the practicability of recycling oily wastes using the ship's oily water separator, the mandatory equipment made the process difficult by restricting the discharge of effluent which did not contain oil:

> In general, if we carry out all requirements I think it will be ok. But sometimes it's very difficult to carry out. For example, about bilge water I tell you it's a problem. It's not oily water [being discharged]; just mud. It means it's not so good this design of the oily water separator. It should only restrict oily discharges not everything.

The view that some of the requirements were difficult to fulfil was echoed by their shore-based managers who argued that rules about changing ballast were 'ridiculous' for ships trading on shorter seas routes because of the limited time between port calls.

Seafarers in this study worried less about the workload implications of being green at sea than they did about the unpleasant prospect of penalties and criminal sanctions for infringing environmental protection requirements and it was only reluctantly that they acknowledged any negative impacts on their well-being. A third officer explained:

> Since I commenced my seaman life [green practices] already existed. So it's nothing special for me. But about ten years ago maybe, no such action; no such strict regulations. So nowadays the seamen they have to do more work. But I think this is nothing special; just a normal way of working.

Ship crews have become accustomed to the practice of adjusting to new work environments and the changes that come at the start of a fresh tour of duty. Therefore it seems plausible to assume that because of the nature of seafaring as a career the regulatory changes and practices which affect their work and well-being might easily go unnoticed. Conversely, while some of the consequences of being green at sea may be obvious to seafarers, the precarious nature of their employment and their inability to voice their views at work may make it difficult for them to comprehend whether their lives aboard have been adversely affected.

Fatigue at sea is not new to the shipping industry. Nevertheless, the accounts of ship crews in this study suggest that some green practices at sea might be exacerbating their experience of fatigue. A typical example is air quality emissions regulations in some regions of the world, including North Europe and California.[3] Ship crews are expected to be familiar with the procedures required when they enter these regions and to change over to cleaner fuels when entering the restricted areas. Ships normally run on heavy fuel oil which emits air toxins and other particulate matter into the atmosphere during combustion. Of particular interest to regulators is

---

[3] At the time of conducting this study, the EU regulations required ships berthing in member states' ports to use fuel oil on board with a sulphur content of no more than 0.10%, much lower than the 1% limit enforced under MARPOL Annex VI (Regulation 14 which addresses the Prevention of Air Pollution from Ships). Much of the EU region included emission control areas established under MARPOL Annex VI for SOx: that is the Baltic Sea and North Sea areas. In California which is also a designated emission control area for North America, ocean-going passenger, container and refrigerated cargo ships subject to the At-Berth Regulation must reduce emissions from their diesel auxiliary engines while berthing at a California Port. The regulation currently requires that these ships turn off auxiliary engines and connect to some other source of power; or use alternative control technique(s) that achieve equivalent emission reductions. More information on the At-Berth Regulation is available from the California Air Resources Board (ARB) online at https://ww3.arb.ca.gov/ports/shorepower/shorepower.htm.

Sulphur Oxide emission. The legal limit for Sulphur content in fuel oil varies according to where a ship is trading, consequently when a restricted areas is entered seafarers must follow a changeover procedure in which the ship must switch to burning marine gas oil which is lower in sulphur content but more expensive (currently about US$ 260 more per metric tonne).

A chief engineer explained that on the normal trading routes their ship will run on heavy fuel oil which is cost-effective for ship operators. When going into a designated sulphur emission control area (SECA), including ports and anchorages in countries where additional limits apply, seafarers begin the changeover period 24 hours before entering the SECA. This ensures that their ship is running on compliant fuel before entering the area. However, the process is not straightforward and cannot be achieved by simply flicking a switch. On board the ship, the crew have to carry out a fuel consumption calculation to determine exactly when to start changing over, and to address the associated logistical demands. Engineers on board the ships in this study complained about having to perform the fuel switch-over during their hours of rest to ensure that the ship was burning the correct fuel at the required nautical mile mark. One senior ship's officer reported that such complaints, together with a related concern about accumulating unpaid overtime, were simply dismissed by their shore-based managers who argued that the crew were not managing their time efficiently. Additional technical difficulties are experienced by ship crews when they are required to use low-sulphur fuels. Previous studies[4] have highlighted problems with the supply and storage of low-sulphur fuel particularly for ships with single service tanks. Ship crews also have to grapple with incompatibility between fuel types and delays when changing over from one to another

A third engineer described the extent of the problem:

> It's planning. Also you cannot mix this fuel; suppose the density is 0.988 and another one is 0.999 so you must consume first: make to the lowest from the tank before you use the other one. Otherwise you will [have] too much problems for the purifier. You will become crazy about the density [laughs].

In relation to health impacts, seafarers did not generally believe green practices on board ships exposed them to any health hazards. Those who did were concerned, in part, about coming into contact with bacteria from decaying waste in the ship's general garbage. But there are other potentially hazardous green practices of which ship crews might simply be unaware. When asked how medical waste was handled at sea, seafarers quickly dismissed the possibility of contamination arguing that such wastes only occurred in limited quantities because serious incidents were evacuated ashore. However the management of first aid cases at sea[5] and the self-medicating

[4]For more on technical issues relating to fuel switching on ships refer to US Environmental Protection Agency 2010, Clean Fuels in the Marine Sector, New York: Nova Science. See also AGCS (2012). Issues relating to the practicality of fuel change over on board ships are discussed in Bloor et al. (2011)).

[5]For the occurrence of hygiene or non-infectious medical waste in ships' garbage see National Research Council (1995).

practices (Acejo et al. 2011) of ship crews can in fact contribute to medical and hygiene wastes occurring infrequently in the ship's garbage. This places ship crews responsible for sorting the ships general waste at risk of infection, especially if they are not using adequate protection when performing the task.

Seafarers also appeared to be underestimating the potential for harm to their health if they came into contact with oil and chemicals when dealing with spills on deck. While personal protection is recommended in written procedures for responding to pollution incidents at sea, it is not clear whether ship crews are taking the guidance seriously when cleaning up spills of a smaller nature, especially when they believe that the products are 'safe' and 'environmentally-friendly'.

So what really matters to seafarers when it comes to being green at sea? Contrary to what one would expect, the issues relate more to welfare concerns than to those of health and safety. The fear of being punished for inadvertently infringing environmental rules and the general psychosocial anxiety associated with green practices on board, are among seafarers' major preoccupations. Many ship crews, including some whose views are expressed in this chapter, do not come from communities where environmentally green practices are of concern. Even those who do, and this includes seafarers who have received the appropriate training and support from their employers, cannot go about their duties confidently because of the uncertainty of regulatory inspections in different parts of the world. This is particularly so where additional requirements apply in some jurisdictions, and the enforcement of criminal sanctions for even the smallest infringements, has the potential to contribute to seafarers' experience of psychosocial stress. These experiences of workplace stress can also trigger events of a more serious nature. Extrinsic environmental performance pressures are often matched by the need for strict observation of company programmes and control measures. When preventing or responding to environmental incidents and hazardous occurrences crews might easily overlook safe working procedures. For example, failure to use the recommended personal protection when carrying out pollution prevention activities on board could expose ship crews to dangerous levels of toxic chemicals or other substances hazardous to their health. However, we are still a long way from knowing the extent of occupational health problems among sea-going workers from such exposure.

Conclusions

In exploring the methods used by ship crews to protect the environment this chapter has considered seafarers' commitment to activities related to environmental sustainability and the practices that support this engagement. It is clear from the findings that the environment does matter a great deal to seafarers. All of those interviewed in this study acknowledged the need to protect the environment, frequently citing posterity among the arguments advanced. The certainty that there was a high level of awareness and understanding of sustainability among sea-going personnel is further reflected in seafarers' accounts connecting the impact of everyday actions at work with sustainability using negative socio-economic and ecological impacts as illustrations of how a dystopian future may unfold under practices which encouraged pollution.

In spite of these drivers and the perceived benefits of adhering to green practices at sea, ship crews did not hesitate in expressing disapproval of the strict environmental regulations imposed on the industry. The majority of seafarers said they believed that the shipping industry has become more strictly regulated as a result of the threats to biodiversity and climate change despite what they describe as the industry's 'lower' environmental impact. They argued that the rules were stricter for shipping than for land-based industries where 'green' regulations were not being equally enforced.

Seafarers' mixed views about the legitimacy of environmental requirements described in this chapter mirror concerns by their shore-based managers about the 'unreasonableness' of pollution prevention requirements reported in a wider study (Akamangwa 2013). Elsewhere, such concerns have been found to undermine regulatory objectives (Bardach and Kagan 1982). Such judgments about the compliance practices of other regulatees, arising from the unfair and unequal imposition of regulatory burdens across different sectors, need to be taken seriously in the interest of ensuring a level-playing field in the industry but more importantly, in order to encourage behaviour change among sea-going employees (Tudor et al. 2008) and to promote long-term compliance.

While differences in national and legal regulatory systems mean that some countries legitimately adopt more stringent pollution control standards,[6] it is the scaling of enforcement practices that seafarers are concerned about. The detailed, complex and uncertain nature of some local requirements mean that ship crews could almost always be in breach of the provisions. In regards to the sanctions for violations, the general feeling among seafarers is that such penalties are unfair especially because they target violations which are often unintentional. Additionally, the very prospect of sanctions causes ship crews to experience recurrent moments of fear and anxiety. Not only does this impact adversely on crew morale on board but there are possible health and safety implications to consider in seafarers fulfilling the requirements.

In the current context of environmental sustainability, basic seamanship requires today's sea-going personnel to learn to become part of a green shipboard community. The obligation to cope with regulatory enforcement issues and the environmental responsibilities bestowed upon them is rarely considered. The experiences of seafarers as described in this chapter suggests a difficult situation faced by a community actively seeking to contribute their quota to contemporary global goals of environmental sustainability but who are often constrained by conflicting requirements and resource limitations both within their organisations and also the countries where they trade.

[6]For a discussion of the substantive scope of port state jurisdiction, refer to Molenaar (2007).

So what can we learn about green practices at sea? Are green regulations and company practices putting the environment before workers? Clearly seafarers are employed in a range of environmentally-friendly processes, but what remains a matter for debate is whether the consequences for seafarers are sufficiently considered. If shipping companies and society as a whole continue to benefit from seafarers' commitment to green practices at sea, without turning attention to the implications for work and wellbeing for front-line personnel, ship crews will continue to face unfavourable working conditions.

References

Acejo, I., H. Sampson, N. Turgo, and E. Wadsworth 2011. The Health and Self-medication Practices of Seafarers. *SIRC Symposium*, Cardiff University 6–7 July, 89–107. Cardiff: Seafarers International Research Centre.

AGCS. 2012. Safety and Shipping 1912-2012: From Titanic to Costa Concordia [Internet]. Accessed January 12, 2020. Available from: < https://www.agcs.allianz.com/content/dam/onemarketing/agcs/agcs/reports/AGCS-Safety-Shipping-Review-2012.pdf >.

Akamangwa, N. 2013. *Global Environmental Regulation and Workers in the Shipping Industry*. PhD Thesis, Cardiff University.

———. 2014. *Researching Environmental Compliance Through Semi-Structured Interviews: Perceptions About the Impact on Work and Wellbeing for Ship Crews, SAGE Research Methods Cases*. London: SAGE Publications.

Bardach, E., and R.A. Kagan. 1982. *Going by the Book: The Problem of Regulatory Unreasonableness*. Philadelphia: Temple University Press.

Bloor, M., S. Baker, H. Sampson, and K. Dahlgren. 2011. *Effectiveness of International Regulation of Pollution Controls: The Case of the Governance of Ship Emissions, Interim Report*. Cardiff: Seafarers International Research Centre.

IMO. 2012. *International Shipping Facts and Figures – Information Resources on Trade, Safety, Security, Environment, Maritime Knowledge Centre*. London: International Maritime Organization.

Mitropoulos, E. 2004. Criminalization in Shipping: Human Pawns in Political and Legal Games. Keynote Speech of the *Seventh Cadwallader Annual Memorial Lecture*, 6 October 2004, London, UK [Internet], Accessed January 12, 2020. Available from: < http://www.imo.org/en/OurWork/Legal/JointIMOILOWorkingGroupsOnSeafarerIssues/Documents/1004.pdf >. See also Jefferies, K. 2006. A Marine Insurance Perspective. In: Comité Maritime International Yearbook 2005–2006, pp. 277–282, Antwerp: CMI Headquarter.

Molenaar, E.J. 2007. Port State Jurisdiction: Toward Comprehensive, Mandatory and Global Coverage. *Ocean Development & International Law* 38 (1–2): 225–257.

Mukherjee, P. 2006. Criminalisation and Unfair Treatment: The Seafarer's Perspective. *Journal of International Maritime Law* 12: 325–336.

National Research Council. 1995. *Clean Ships, Clean Ports, Clean Oceans: Controlling Garbage and Plastic Wastes at Sea*. Washington, D.C.: The National Academies Press.

Sampson, H. 2016. Seabirds Matter More Than Us!: Understanding the Complex Exercise of CSR in the Global Shipping Industry. *The Journal of Sustainable Mobility* 3 (2): 101–119.

Tudor, T.L., S.W. Barr, and A.W. Gilg. 2008. A Novel Conceptual Framework for Examining Environmental Behavior in Large Organizations – A Case Study of the Cornwall National Health Service (NHS) in the United Kingdom. *Environment and Behavior* 40 (3): 426–450.

Walters, D., and P. James. 2009. *Understanding the Role of Supply Chains in Influencing Health and Safety at Work*. Leicester: IOSH.

Chapter 11
Safety Aboard Chinese Vessels

Conghua Xue

Introduction

The aim of this chapter is to explore the factors that affect ship to shore safety reporting in the Chinese shipping industry. The study was motivated by of the paucity of research in this specific area. Previous research in shore-based industries suggests that there may be cause for concern in shipping as ashore there is evidence of significant underreporting across a wide range of industries. This study, though it is small in scale, was conducted to partially fill the existing gap. The data used was collected from two major chemical shipping companies in China. Both employer and employees' perspectives were considered in the process of data analysis. Furthermore, the 'social factors' behind the scene of reporting—underreporting, or biased reporting—were explored.

It has been widely acknowledged in the maritime literature that the shipping industry is highly risky (Anderson 2003; Havold 2005; Oltedal and Wadsworth 2010). Seafarer fatalities and injury rates are much higher in seafaring (Lindoe 2007) than the average found in land based industries. The industry also has a higher reported frequency of incidents than some others (Walters 2005). Against this background, Occupational Health and Safety Management (OHSM) is a critical issue.

By tradition, ships are subject to the laws, rules and regulations of their own flag states and in the countries where they sail. For many years there was a lack of multilateral harmonization and uniform standards. However, the introduction of the International Safety Management Code (ISM) in 1998 marked a 'turning point' for the industry. It brought about a fundamental change to the way in which OHSM was previously conducted (Anderson 2003). The International Maritime Organization (IMO), a specialised agency of the United Nations (UN), required every member to

C. Xue (✉)
Jiangsu Shipping College, Department of Arts and Humanities, Nantong, Jiangsu Province, China

V. O. Gekara, H. Sampson (eds.), *The World of the Seafarer*, WMU Studies in Maritime Affairs 9, https://doi.org/10.1007/978-3-030-49825-2_11

implement the Code by enacting corresponding mandatory standards to regulate OHSM in its shipping industry (IMO 2007). The philosophy underpinning the Code is to require shipping managers and seafarers to transform their traditional operational practice into a regulated system-based approach in order to better manage Occupational Health and Safety (OHS) issues and reduce harm to persons, ships and the environment (Anderson 2003; Bailey 2006).

According to the ISM Code, all shipping companies (subject to the Code) are required to establish mandated forms of safety management systems (SMSs). An Occupational Health and Safety Management System (OHSMS) should consist of some essential elements contained in the Code with safety reporting an integral part of a safety management system. The reporting of events is of great value for 'proactive remedies', 'organizational learning', and 'continuous improvement' as well as 'increased safety' (Ogbonnaya and Valizade 2015; Oltedal and Wadsworth 2010; Oltedal and McArthur 2011; Psarros et al. 2010). The smooth functioning of the reporting system is a precondition for successful organizational management and this requires an effective reporting culture (Graham et al. 2002; Havold 2000), one of the key features of a high reliability organization (HSE 2000; Kuhn and Youngberg 2002; Reason 1997).

A major finding from studies of land-based industries showed that the 'underreporting' of safety-related events was omnipresent (Oltedal and McArthur 2011). To a great extent, this is echoed by the limited amount of pre-existing research related to the shipping industry. For example, the ten-year study of maritime casualty/accident databases (1997–2007) from Lloyd's Register Fairplay and Norwegian Maritime Directorate showed that more than 60% of accidents were underreported (Psarros et al. 2010). In general, the literature suggests that underreporting is a 'considerable problem' in this industry, and 'a culture of underreporting' of safety related occurrences is prevalent (Bhattacharya and Tang 2012; Bhattacharya and Tang 2013; Ellis et al. 2010; IMO 2008; Oltedal and McArthur 2011). Such underreporting undermines the normal and effective operationalization of established safety management systems, as stated by Oltedal and McArthur (2011, p. 331):

> A fundamental pillar of safety management is that information reported into the system is reliable and reflects the actual situation in working operations. Thus, under-reporting of safety related events constitutes a major threat to the efficiency and utility of a safety management system.

This chapter is going to explore the reporting practices in the Chinese shipping industry. It is informed by some of the findings of a qualitative study which I undertook in recent years. As part of this I carried out interviews with 47 seafarers while sailing on board their ships and making observations. The fieldwork was mainly conducted in two major Chinese chemical shipping companies (C1 and C2 hereafter) where I also conducted 13 interviews with managers and superintendents. The findings of this study are presented from both the management and the crew's perspectives. Furthermore, the influential factors that affect safety reporting will be explored.

Contradictory Messages from Managers

Managers in both companies strongly stated their commitment to encouraging accident reporting. Their stated objective was to ensure that remedial actions were taken after all reported incidents for the purpose of the continuous improvement in safe operations and management.

The Publicly Stated Commitment by Managers to Reporting: 'We Encourage Reporting'

The reporting of accidents was seen to provide a 'window' which allowed managers to consider shipboard work practices and provided a way of directing safety improvements for 'the ship, the company and its fleet'. As such it had considerable implications for promoting shipboard safe working practices. Data showed that the managers of both companies shared a similar safety attitude towards crew reporting—phrases like the 'non-blame attitude' or 'non-blame culture' were frequently mentioned in discussing the principles of their safety management policy. For example, one superintendent said:

> The company is always advocating a no-blame policy. You (crew) may report whatever you want. We hope you report ten near-misses, but we don't want to see one accident.

Furthermore, in order to eliminate the misgivings of crew members in making safety reports, 'fair treatment' was also guaranteed in text form. For example, a paragraph in the SMS of C1, stated:

> Company guarantees that the person who makes the report will not be treated unfairly; instead, the company will give awards to those who are helpful in improving company's safety management and environment protection.

In terms of the role of reporting in the improvement of safety management, it was regarded as 'good practice' that could contribute to ship's safety. For example, one superintendent said:

> For a major case, there is a need for the company to make countermeasures. For a minor case, it could remind others to care more about it. It's a good practice. It's for the good of safety management.

In consideration of the fact that there might be certain factors that affected a crew member's motive for reporting, both companies insisted that there was 'no ground' for the crew to have any hesitation. For example, a manager explained:

> (If) you (crew) hide problems, you do not fully understand the essence of the ISM and SMS. If you found problems and made reporting, it was the company to hold accountability. If you hide and they are disclosed by the company, you will take full responsibility.

Therefore, both companies' publicly stated attitudes were clear: that reporting helped to promote shipboard safe working operations and practices. If a problem was not reported, it would be very likely to 'develop into an accident sooner or later', which would lead to 'damaging consequences' (superintendent)—which was believed to be undesirable to both the management and crew.

The Received Message from Management: 'Fewer Reports are Better'

As stated earlier, in both companies, there was what appeared to be overwhelming agreement relating to the desire to encourage crew to engage in safety reporting. However, the data also suggested another seemingly contradictory view that: 'the less reporting (there was) the better'. Notwithstanding the management's publically stated commitment to 'near miss' reporting, and accident reporting more generally, they were not happy to see problems reported from ships. For example, a manager said:

> If there is no such a (problem) report, it's good news. It signifies that that ship's management is good. Every aspect on board is good.

In a similar way, one superintendent also stated:

> If the captain doesn't report any problem, and neither does the chief engineer, this ship is perfect. It shows that everybody is very good.

From such comments, it becomes clear that there was a common understanding among the managers, which was at odds with their stated objectives of encouraging near-miss reporting. The 'number of reported events' was considered to be an important indicator of the quality of shipboard safety management. In this sense, less reporting was equated with 'better' ship management. It is self-evident that if such an attitude is conveyed to seafarers then near miss reporting is likely to be constrained.

One of the major duties of shore management is to monitor the completion of a ship's voyage plan. From the management perspective, the number of reported cases becomes one of the important indicators for measuring the successfulness of a voyage. For example, a manager commented:

> If you (ship) completed the voyage, and didn't report any incidents/accidents, this meant that the ship didn't cause a major economic loss to the company and successfully completed the voyage tasks.

Consequently, it seems that in contrast to the apparent commitment to near-miss and accident reporting, such reports were not actually desired by the companies' management. Reason (1997) had similar findings from research at organizational level—low reporting frequency may suggest an 'image of safety' but he warned that it may not reflect reality and as a consequence the improvement of workplace safety could be seriously compromised. It seems that whilst company managers understood this message to the extent that they could and would emphasize the importance of incident reporting they had not understood it (or internalized it) well enough to be free of the overwhelming view that a ship reporting few incidents (or none) must be a very safe ship.

So far, the discussion has drawn upon the perspective of the company management. The picture is now presented from the crew's perspective in terms of their understanding of the requirement to report safety-related issues.

The Message Conveyed to the Crew: If Accidents Occur Then There Must Be Something 'Wrong' with the on Board Supervision

According to the reporting requirements of the SMS in each company, each crew member had a responsibility to report accidents if they have safety implications, no matter how minor they were. Most crew members seemed well aware of this stated requirement. However, in reality there was a wide gap between what the management expected and what the crew did in terms of reporting practices. The research revealed that a significant number of safety-related issues were underreported. It also identified biased reporting.

Given the formal obligation of the crew to make reports, it was noticeable how many seafarers were reserved in their comments when asked about accident reporting. Surprisingly few agreed that 'all safety related problems were fully reported according to the facts'.

Ratings, were particularly uninterested in reporting safety-related issues. In particular they demonstrated indifference towards making near-miss reports. One rating explained:

> Generally it would not. The near miss. . .there are no real consequences. . .we feel it has passed and there is no need to report it. What is it for?

It could be said that their lack of interest appeared to be because they thought reporting was done by senior officers and it was therefore unnecessary for them to make reports. For example, one rating said:

> The reporting is done by the captain. Whether he reports to the company, it's up to him. The low rank crew would not report. The low rank crew. . .it's unnecessary to talk about this. There is nothing to do with my job.

Consequently the officers might be expected to be more active in making reports. However, even amongst officers voluntary reporting was rare in both companies. A second officer expressed his unwillingness to report near-miss cases in the following way:

> It's rare. I didn't meet such a case. Who voluntarily made such reporting? It's only me who knew it, and nobody else knew it. I kept it in my mind then that's ok. I would not talk to captain if he didn't see.

This is consistent with the finding by Oltedal and Wadsworth (2010), that crew working on an individual basis (alone) are less likely to report any accidents which occur. As an 'alternative' way, 'self-reflection' was commonly referred to by some crew as the 'substitute' for reporting. For example, a chief officer said:

> It was rare (to report). If you reported to the company, it would cause trouble. But in reality, we would not report. It would be digested on board unless it had serious consequences.

Fear of 'trouble' (for the whole crew and not simply the individual reporting an incident) was suggested as a reason for underreporting and this will be returned to in due course. In C1, in order to encourage more reporting of near misses, a box was placed in public places on the two ships. During my time on board, questions were raised about how individual crew contributed to the near-miss box. The interviewees' reaction seemed to vary, some gave awkward smiles and some were unwilling to talk about their own experiences, just giving a superficial answer saying that it was the company's requirement. However a second officer gave a clear and firm response, 'it was empty…nobody care about it'. This general impression showed that commitment to submitting reports to the near miss box remained weak (notwithstanding the superficial anonymity it provided[1]).

The discussion in this section shows that underreporting of shipboard accidents and near-misses was common. Few safety-related problems were reported unless there was a significant consequence with which the crew could not cope without shore support.

Biased Reporting and Underlying Social Factors

Not only did this study find considerable under-reporting of accidents and near-misses, it also found that the reporting in both companies could be biased in one way or another. It seemed that the crew, particularly the senior officers, would carefully deliberate as to what to state prior to giving any account to their companies. Their 'general principles' appeared to be to focus on trivial matters so that some matters could be reported as required by the company without reflecting badly on the crew. One suggested that:

> Basically for us, the principle of reporting is to report only the good not the bad, to avoid the critical points and dwell on the trivial (Captain).

> We had certain consideration…The ship could not report all the issues [to the company]. Also, [the ship] could not report nothing. [So] some innocuous cases might be reported (Chief Officer).

Reported incidents demonstrated that the crew tended to report 'innocuous' cases or 'something unimportant' to their companies. For example, a chief officer said:

[1]Crews are so small and subdivided in terms of role and department that it is unlikely that anonymity could in fact prevail.

> The crew make reporting to the captain. . .it is rare. Most reports made were minor issues. Like in the kitchen, the flour was put on the fire prevention station, where it was not allowed.

Given the necessity of reporting serious cases such as incidents/accidents which were impossible to hide, the data showed further bias. During my time on board, I came across a chief engineer who had worked for C1 for thirty years before coming to C2, and he talked about his strategy in dealing with such reporting:

> First, the reporting should not link to my own responsibility; second, (it) should not link to my colleagues; third, (it) should not link to company leaders. If you discharge all the responsibility to your company, do you mean that the company's management is not effective? No. This is not good. Then how to deal with this? Try to find some causes from our own, to find some from external objective environment. The rationale is not to [negatively] affect, or criticize, anybody.

Therefore, it could be seen that the reporting would be 'manipulated' by the crew, while the real situation would not be truly reflected. Thus it is apparent that the four major factors that influenced safety reporting were managerial, cultural, personal and occupational. These are detailed as follows.

The managerial factor arose as a result of fear of condemnation for bad management practice, with the crew holding a strong collective view that if a problem was reported it would imply that the ship's on board safety management was bad. A third officer explained:

> If you report, it is certainly not good for the ship. It implies that this ship's work was not done well. The company would think your ship has safety problems [that] this ship's leader was not good.

Not only would the company's leaders think the ship management was not good, but they would also doubt the ship leader's competence. One second engineer stated:

> If you could not solve problems on board and they were reported and you need support from the shore base the (company) leaders would have second thoughts. It might mean that your individual competence is bad.

The seafarers on board held the same understanding that is created in the literature on employee performance. This suggests that problem solving is central to success in modern organisations (Tews et al. 2010). While seafarers felt obliged to show problem solving skills on board they were reluctant to demonstrate these in relation to the follow-up of minor incidents associated with safety. According to the SMS, even where an incident did not lead to a major problem on board (perhaps following seafarer intervention) it should still be entered into the System to be reported to shore-side management. In these cases, however, seafarers were afraid that negative judgements associated with the original event would outweigh any positive conclusions that might be arrived at in relation to the way they had 'problem solved' after an event had taken place. Therefore on board reports were rarely made. Furthermore, in the chemical shipping industry, it is common for chemical tankers to have industrial external inspection, typically inspection from major petro-chemical companies. Reporting was also affected by fears relating to such inspection. For instance, a second engineer said:

> Also, it (the reporting) is not good for external inspection. If the inspectors found that you had more problems reported, they would doubt your ship's management and check in more detail.

Therefore, it is clear that, for fear of the condemnation of bad management, crew showed a selective attitude in any safety-related problem reporting.

If a safety problem was reported to the company, it would be investigated by the management of the company. The research showed that the 'perceived investigation result' didn't encourage crew reporting. Field notes record a few personal injuries on the four ships, and none of them were reported. Among these, one injury case was described as follows:

> The rating showed his finger pervasive with the blood. The finger was hit by a roller in the engine room. His right fingers pressed the root of the finger that was hurt, he gnashed his teeth, and showed pain on his face.

The cut was further treated and shore medical assistance was called on arrival at a foreign port. A second engineer commented about this injury:

> It would not be reported. If it is reported, the company would think it is mainly because of violation of procedures. Safety bonus would be deducted from top (leader) to the bottom (ratings). But the real cause is fatigue.

On board the ship, almost all the crew I met thought the injury was caused by fatigue. Meanwhile, they strongly believed that any investigation would conclude that it was more simply caused by 'the violation of procedures' by individuals on board. A third engineer talked about his experience:

> More than 90 percent of the company's investigation conclusions were violation of operational procedure. They thought if it was not (because of it), it (injury) would not happen. If you saw many safety circulars (sent on board), they were all about violation of operations.

Research by Ellis et al. (2010) show that the pattern of *reporting* of seafarers injuries is socially constructed. In this research, data showed the crew's past experience in reporting offended their sense of justice—as a result they felt that reporting injuries was not in their interest but would be like 'lifting a stone to drop it onto one's own feet' (Chinese proverb). Under such circumstance, the crew would rather choose not to report. The literature indicates that 'human error' investigation approaches (Oltedal and McArthur 2011; Pantouvakis and Karakasnaki 2016, 2018; Psarros et al. 2010) and a 'person oriented' focus (Oltedal and Wadsworth 2010) can lead to a failure to identify 'real causal factors'. The example described above shows some correspondence with the existing literature, inasmuch as in this incident the underlying ('real') cause of the accident—fatigue—was regarded as something that any investigation would leave unmentioned. It could be seen that the 'perceived' response from the company affected the crew's willingness to report.

Research has found that safety reporting is affected by national culture (Havold 2000; Hofstede 1991)—in this context—the Chinese culture. Previous research has indicated that the Chinese traditional culture—Confucianism—persists in modern enterprises (Yang and Zheng 1989) and this research found that some Chinese cultural elements also affected the reporting.

In reporting, crew members tended to avoid the potential negative impact of the reported issues on the shore management, particularly the superintendent in charge of the ship. A chief officer elaborated:

> About what to report, there is much knowledge inside. We could not directly report if the reporting related to the superintendent's duty (fault). The superintendent in charge (of this ship) would be questioned or even reprimanded by the senior manager.

According to the safety management system, all the written reports were by senior managers as well as relevant departmental managers. Most of the crew, did not want their superintendent to be blamed because certain problems on board were reported. Such a consideration was augmented by the fact that he had the power to arrange crew appointments.[2] Furthermore, data indicated that reporting a problem could potentially offend one particular department. For example, a chief officer said:

> The Marine Department, they wanted ships to report less problems, right? You [ship] reported more [problems], and it would be no good for the company senior managers to see that. Try to report less.

It became obvious that the nature of problems was considered by the crew before a report was made. In order to avoid offending shore management, some crew voiced the fact that pre-communication with a company's superintendent would be done prior to a formal written report. In general, the reporting would be 'guided' by the superintendent in terms of what to say and how to report. One of the core values of Confucianism is the 'respect for hierarchy' (Fang 1999). The fear of offending seniors was deeply embedded in the thoughts of the Chinese crew and had a marked impact on reporting practices.

In addition the research found that reporting could affect the interpersonal relationships between seafarers both on board and when they returned home. A chief officer explained:

> When reporting to the company, the captain would consider the crew's interest. When we are [back] ashore, the superior-subordinate relationship doesn't exist anymore. We were colleagues. . .brothers.

It could be seen from the quote that the negative impact of reporting on personal relationships was considered by the senior officers on board. There is an ancient Chinese saying which addresses interpersonal relations and suggests that 'harmony matters'. In general, harmonious relationships are prized by the Chinese as one of the core values of Confucianism (Fang 1999; Porter 1996). This also applies in organisational contexts. Personal relationships could be disharmonized if a report was submitted against crew members' wishes. An example is given below:

> You made such a report, then you offended that person. . .we all knew each other and were not willing to offend others (Rating).

---

[2]Part of the role of a superintendent is to evaluate crew's performance, and make suggestions for crew arrangements on a ship he supervises.

A chief officer described a serious near miss—the captain saw an appalling scene when he went to the bridge:

> It's the third officer's duty. . .The Captain saw a very big ship ahead, and he could not see the sky. . .you could imagine how close it was (with that ship). . .The captain immediately took control. . .Luckily, it (accident) was avoided.

Principally, it was a typical near miss that had far reaching safety implications in terms of shipboard risk management. But it was not reported to the company because of its potential impact on a third officer:

> You say, would he [captain] report this case to the company? For sure, he would not. If he reported [to the company], he would damage the third officer. The third officer would hate him forever. . .definitely finish [his career].

This example demonstrates how reporting could damage relationships. A chief engineer expressed this in a similar way when he told me that:

> The young crew. . .they are very kind in usual time. But he had a dangerous behaviour because of his carelessness. Would I kick him out? Try our best to remedy on board, rather than something else [such as reporting].

Given the fact that ultimately decision-making lay in the captain's hands, some of the crew considered that the quality of the relationship between crew members and the captain could determine whether an incident was reported or not. For instance, a second officer said:

> If the captain has a good relationship with me, he might cover this for me. If the captain doesn't have a good relationship with me, or he dislikes me, he would report this.

These examples illustrate the ways in which personal relationships influence decisions in relation to the reporting of safety-related incidents.

Crew members also took into account their personal interests when they decided whether a safety related problem would be reported or not. For example, a rating said:

> It [reporting] directly affects individual interest. . .bonus, salary, and company's appraisal.

Consideration of these kinds of issues was expressed by a significant number of crew members in both companies. In C1, recent salary reforms aligned salaries more closely with performance appraisal. A captain explained the situation:

> Personally my salary is often deducted by the company. Now it is tricky. If there is a problem to be reported, my money would also be deducted.

The interviews revealed that such reporting was also regarded as having the potential to impact on future appointments. For example, a second officer said:

> Although it is said there is not any unfair treatment, in reality it would still have potential affect. Apart from safety bonus, the company would have other considerations on the next (job) appointment.

In both companies, anonymisation was required for the reporting of near misses. However, it was considered to be easy to identify who had made the report and also who was involved in the reported incident. The reason was that shipboard work allocation was 'one radish; one whole', as the crew termed it, which meant there was very little overlap in terms of each crew member's duties. Therefore, in practice anonymisation seemed to have little effect. In C1, if someone was found to have caused an 'unusual' safety problem on board a ship, then in the future seafarers believed that they might be dispatched to another company working as an 'exported' seafarer. This was regarded as very negative because it was seen as 'punishment' for bad performance and was also generally regarded as involving joining ships where conditions were worse than they were on the company's own vessels.

Therefore, it became clear that crew members' fear of reporting was related to the perception that individual interests were likely to be damaged as a result of making a report. Consequently, the reporting tended to coalesce around non-human related problems. As one superintendent in C1 said: 'mostly the reporting was about the equipment' and 'it was rarely about crew themselves'.

Finally, it seemed that the fluidity of employment further weakened crew members' willingness to report incidents. In C2, the majority of the crew were employed on short term contracts. They were particularly reluctant to report incidents. For example, one senior bosun reflected on his thirty years of experience as a seafarer and said:

> I met many occasions of near misses. In general I would not report. We are the freelance seafarers. I worked in this company today, it's uncertain that I would leave some day. Why should I care about it? It would not be reported until there is an accident.

The unwillingness to report incidents also related to a desire among long-serving seafarers to be returned to familiar vessels. For example, a third officer said:

> If you were only on board for a few months, you reported this and that, wanting to change everything, and then you were going to leave. . .many people don't want to do like that. Next time, I might change to another ship. I would not go to this ship again.

Although crew in both companies had differing contractual terms and conditions the data did not significantly differ between them.

Conclusion

Effective communication within an organisation is considered a prerequisite for successful safety management (Leiss 2004), and one of the valuable characteristics of an organisation with strong safety culture (Michael et al. 2006). The examination of both management's and crews' perspectives showed that there was a significant gap between what the management expected (although this in itself was contradictory) and what happened in reality. Shipboard safety reporting was affected by a complex combination of managerial, cultural, personal as well as occupational factors, which were made manifest in both underreporting and biased reporting.

To sum up, the study revealed that although the importance of safety reporting is widely acknowledged, the crew did not seem to understand its importance and therefore prioritized other issues such as concern for their personal interests and relationships. Despite the strong impression given by the management of a desire to pursue a no-blame attitude in safety reporting, they tended to say one thing but actually mean another. A particularly clear example of this was provided by their contradictory stance relating to reports. Whilst they recognized that reporting was part of good safety management they concurrently took reports to indicate that different practice was being followed on board. In general, the data suggests that safety reporting practices fail to function properly if managers do not adjust their attitudes and behaviour.

Based on the results of this study, it seems that there is a need for considerable training for both managers and crew in terms of the attitudes and behaviour that underpin the proper functioning of a safety management system. The research depicts a complex picture which should be considered by those maritime practitioners or policy-makers concerned with improvements to the globalized shipping industry.

Acknowledgement The simplified version of this manuscript has been presented at the 5th International Conference on Management and Service Science. It is part of the research outcome of the Qing Lan Project and "226" Talent Project.

References

Anderson, P. 2003. *Cracking the Code: The Relevance of the ISM Code and Its Impact on Shipping Practices*. London: Nautical Institute.

Bailey, N. 2006. Risk Perception and Safety Management Systems in the Global Maritime Industry. *Policy and Practice in Health and Safety* 4 (2): 59–76.

Bhattacharya, S., and L. Tang. 2012. Fatigued for Safety? Supply Chain Occupational Health and Safety Initiatives in Shipping. *Economic and Industrial Democracy* 34 (3): 383–399.

———. 2013. Middle Managers' Role in Safeguarding OHS: The Case of the Shipping Industry. *Safety Science* 51 (1): 63–68.

Ellis, N., M. Bloor, and H. Sampson. 2010. Patterns of Seafarer Injuries. *Maritime Policy and Management* 37 (2): 121–128.

Fang, T. 1999. *Chinese Business Negotiating Style*. London: Sage Publications.

Graham, G.M., et al. 2002. Safety Reporting and Aviation Target Levels of Safety. In *Investigation and Reporting of Accidents*, ed. C.W. Johnson, 68–77. Scotland: University of Glasgow.

Havold, J.I. 2000. Culture in Maritime Safety. *Maritime Policy and Management* 27 (1): 79–88.

———. 2005. Safety Culture in a Norwegian Shipping Company. *Journal of Safety Research* 36 (5): 448–458.

Hofstede, G. 1991. *Cultures and Organisations: Software of the Mind*. Berkshire: McGraw-Hill Book Company.

HSE. 2000. *Leading Health and Safety at Work*. London: HMSO.

IMO. 2007. *Guidelines for the Operational Implementation of the International Safety Management (ISM) Code by Companies*. London: International Maritime Organization.

———. 2008. *Guidance on Near-Miss Reporting*. London: International Maritime Organization.

Kuhn, A.M., and B.J. Youngberg. 2002. The Need for Risk Management to Evolve to Assure a Culture of Safety. *Quality and Safety in Health Care* 11 (2): 158–169.

Leiss, W. 2004. Effective Risk Communication Practice. *Toxicology Letters* 149 (2004): 399–404.

Lindoe, P.H. 2007. Safe Offshore Workers and Unsafe Fishermen – A System Failure? *Policy and Practice in Health and Safety* 5 (2): 25–39.
Michael, J.H., et al. 2006. Production Supervisor Impacts on Subordinates' Safety Outcomes: An Investigation of Leader-member Exchange and Safety Communication. *Journal of Safety Research* 37: 469–477.
Ogbonnaya, C.N., and D. Valizade. 2015. Participatory Workplace Activities, Employee-level Outcomes and the Mediating Role of Work Intensification. *Management Research Review* 38 (5): 540–558.
Oltedal, H., and E. Wadsworth. 2010. Risk Perception in the Norwegian Shipping Industry and Identification of Influencing Factors. *Maritime Policy & Management* 37 (6): 601–623.
Oltedal, H.A., and D.P. McArthur. 2011. Reporting Practices in Merchant Shipping, and the Identification of Influencing Factors. *Safety Science* 49: 331–338.
Pantouvakis, A., and M. Karakasnaki. 2016. An Empirical Assessment of ISM Code Effectiveness on Performance: The Role of ISO Certification. *Maritime Policy & Management* 43 (7): 874–886.
———. 2018. The Human Talent and Its Role in ISM Code Effectiveness and Competitiveness in the Shipping Industry. *Maritime Policy & Management* 2018 (2): 1–16.
Porter, R. 1996. Politics, Culture and Decision Making in China. In *Management Issues in China: Volume I – Domestic Enterprises*, ed. D.H. Brown and R. Porter. London: Routledge.
Psarros, G., R. Skjong, and M.S. Eide. 2010. Under-Reporting of Maritime Accident. *Accident Analysis and Prevention* 42: 619–625.
Reason, J.T. 1997. *Managing the Risks of Organisational Accidents*. Aldershot: Ashgate.
Tews, M.J., et al. 2010. Beyond Objectivity: The Performance Impact of the Perceived Ability to Learn and Solve Problems. *Journal of Vocational Behaviour*: 1–12.
Walters, D. 2005. International Developments and Their Influence on Occupational Health and Safety in Advanced Market Economies. In *Occupational Health and Safety*, ed. C.L. Peterson and C. Mayhew, 13–30. New York: Baywood Publishing Company.
Yang, G., and B. Zheng. 1989. Empirical Test of a Neo-Confucians Hypothesis. In *Ancient Management Thoughts and Chinese Management*, ed. Y. Jiang and J. Min, 34–52. Beijing: Economic Management Press.

Chapter 12
Multiple Roles and Role Conflict: Seafarers As Economic, Humanitarian and Security Actors

Amaha Senu

Introduction

Undocumented migrants at sea and maritime stowaways in ports impinge upon the world of the seafarer in ways that are often challenging.[1] According to the International Chamber of Shipping (ICS 2018), merchant ships rescued around 100,000 migrants in the Mediterranean in the period between 2015 and 2018 (ICS 2018). The operations, involving migrants at sea, pose significant challenges to seafarers in terms of scale, safety and security and differ from conventional rescue operations such as the rescue of crew members from an abandoned ship (ICS 2015, p. 2). While seafarers are, as far as practicable, bound by law to render assistance and come to the rescue of anyone at sea under the UNCLOS, SOLAS, SAR and SALVAGE Conventions,[2] the provisions in these legal instruments do not take account of the challenges which such large scale rescue operations entail. Seafarers are neither adequately trained nor resourced to undertake such activities although they are legally obligated to do so (ICS 2015; Kilpatrick and Smith 2015; Kilpatrick 2017).

This chapter is partly based on an earlier version presented at the Department for Politics and International Relations Postgraduate Research Conference at Cardiff University, UK, on the 7th of May 2014. I am grateful to Professor Christian Bueger, Jan Stockbruegger and the editors of this volume for their constructive comments.

[1]Seafarers are construed broadly in this chapter to encompass those working on fishing vessels although the discussion largely revolves around those working on merchant cargo ships.

[2]United Nations Convention on the Law of the Sea (UNCLOS) 1982; International Convention for the Safety of Life at Sea (SOLAS) 1974; International Convention on Maritime Search and Rescue (SAR) 1979; International Convention on Salvage (SALVAGE) 1989.

A. Senu (✉)
Johannesburg Institute for Advanced Study, University of Johannesburg, Johannesburg, South Africa

V. O. Gekara, H. Sampson (eds.), *The World of the Seafarer*, WMU Studies in Maritime Affairs 9, https://doi.org/10.1007/978-3-030-49825-2_12

The shipping industry as a whole, in conjunction with relevant institutions such as the International Maritime Organization (IMO) and the United Nations High Commissioner for Refugees (UNHCR), has been proactive in attempting to provide guidance for seafarers to help them cope with the challenges they face when encountering migrants at sea (ICS 2015; IMO et al. 2015; Kellett et al. 2015). While various industry publications, and to a lesser extent reports in the media, have emphasised the challenges and problems seafarers contend with when encountering undocumented migrants, the academic literature has largely avoided substantive engagement with the implications of undocumented migration for seafarers. Although there are notable exceptions that specifically focus on shipping and, to a limited extent, on seafarers (Maccanico 2012; Maquet and Zortea 2013; Basaran 2014, 2015; Aarstad 2015; Goddard 2015; Kilpatrick and Smith 2015; Kilpatrick 2017), the lived experiences of seafarers are not given a central place in the academic literature on migration governance, border control, and humanitarianism at sea. Instead the emphasis tends to be on analyses of the provisions in various legal instruments as opposed to a focus on and an analysis of the experiences of seafarers in their interactions with migrants at sea (Ort 1991; Tauman 2002; Bailliet 2003; Davies 2003; Coppens and Somers 2010; Coppens 2013b). The literature relating to the encounters of seafarers with stowaways, a group which also carry significant implications for shipping, similarly demonstrates a scarcity of data relating to their experiences (Mason 1987; Jarvis 1988; Ort 1991; Nourse 1993; McConnell 1997; Steglich 1999).

This chapter aims to situate seafarers at the centre of the discussion of undocumented migration. As such, it explores the tensions, contradictions and outcomes that arise from the often-diverging expectations placed upon them. I attempt to demonstrate how seafarers are forced to assume multiple and conflicting roles, i.e. economic, humanitarian and security roles, in their interactions with migrants in the maritime sphere. The academic literature, documents from relevant institutions and publicly available sources on migration across the Mediterranean, as well as data from my own research on maritime stowaways, are drawn upon here to make the argument that serious implications for both seafarers and migrants emerge when seafarers find themselves compelled to navigate these conflicting roles.

Rescuing Migrants in the Mediterranean Sea

Rescuing migrants at sea is a significantly more challenging task for seafarers than the rescue operations merchant ships routinely engage in. Cases such as that of *MV King Jacob* where close to 800 migrants perished when a migrant boat collided into the ship attempting to render assistance (Miglierini 2016; https://deathbyrescue.org/report/narrative/), highlight the hazardous nature of large-scale rescue operations. Nevertheless, as previously stated, the provisions in the legal texts establishing the foundations of humanitarianism at sea oblige seafarers to engage in such large-scale rescue operations involving migrants.

Captain Jamie Wilson, who was involved in the rescue of 907 migrants off the coast of Libya in January 2017, indicated that although his crew were prepared for the possibility of encountering migrants, albeit without any previous rescue experience, they were overwhelmed by the sheer numbers (BBC 2017). His account affirms that humanitarianism at sea usually takes precedence over any other considerations for many seafarers.

> As captain, you're bound by law to proceed to help anyone in danger, [...] There's no grey area for me as captain - you have to go and assist. My duty is to save lives at sea. (BBC 2017)

However, there is also a level of anxiousness on the part of seafarers when they encounter migrants at sea. Migrants are often found in large numbers, and there are concerns that they may pose health and safety risks to seafarers. On 22 October 2014, the dry bulk carrier *MV CS Caprice* was alerted by Malta's Rescue Coordination Centre to proceed to the assistance of a boat in distress carrying migrants. Whereas the ship had only 20 crew members on board, the migrants they eventually rescued numbered 510 individuals. Captain Rajesh Dhadwal, who was the designated person ashore (DPA) providing guidance to the crew at the time, indicated that the crew had reservations and concerns. His account highlights the health, safety and security concerns that are often felt by seafarers in such situations together with the desire to uphold their humanitarian obligations.

> The human spirit has to lift itself to another level. You cannot attempt this scale of operation if you are thinking about compensation or 'what if the migrants have Ebola?' or 'what if there are terrorists among them and they take over the ship?' You have to put aside the 'what ifs'. [...] Isis has said it might use this as a channel to export terrorism, this is a real threat and it becomes so real when you start talking about gas tankers where, if people took over the ship, you would be facing an environmental disaster. [...] When you are in the middle of the sea, with so many people with no papers, how can you stand off and not help them, thinking of all the various scenarios? If they die and they were not criminal or terrorists, then who is liable for their deaths? (Fairplay 2015).

Considering the rescue operation took place at the time of the Ebola epidemic in West Africa and the political crises in Libya and Syria, his account highlights the profound health and security concerns seafarers could have when engaged in rescuing migrants in the Mediterranean Sea and beyond. Indeed, what Valverde (2014, p. 384) calls 'the affective dimensions of security' are ever present on board in these situations whereby seafarers' concerns can be influenced by the discursive climate where criminality and terrorism are often invoked alongside issues of migration (Huysmans 2000, 2006). Furthermore, there have been cases in which migrants became uncooperative, demanding to be taken to specific destinations, and leaving seafarers with no alternative but to acquiesce to their demands. The case of *MV Tampa* is one example in which 440 rescued migrants threatened to commit suicide and undertake hunger strikes unless they were taken to Australia, which prevented the captain from proceeding to his intended next port of call, Singapore (Tauman 2002; Bailliet 2003; Kenney Jr and Tasikas 2003). A more recent example is the case of the cruise liner *Salamis Filoxenia* which rescued about 300 migrants who subsequently refused to disembark in Cyprus, demanding to be taken to Italy instead. The standoff was reported to have cost the company 'hundreds of thousands of euros' (BBC 2014). This should also be considered in the context of the longer period of time that migrants can sometimes remain on board.

In the case of the *MV CS Caprice*, the crew cared for the migrants on board for 4 days because weather conditions necessitated their disembarking at a different port from that initially planned. Interestingly, the DPA pointed out that the charterers had refused to pay for the 4 days that they considered the ship was 'off-hire', highlighting the charter-party issues which ship owners may be faced with (Fairplay 2015). The cost to owners is further exacerbated when there is lack of clarity as to where the migrants should be taken. For instance, there has been a long dispute between Italy and Malta concerning the responsibility for allowing disembarkation onto their respective territories (see Coppens 2013a, b for a detailed discussion on this). The lack of clarity on the disembarkation of migrants was also highlighted by the DPA in the case of *MV CS Caprice.*

> When we picked up that group of 510 people, we did not know where we would be able to take them; we did not know how long they would be with us. [. . .]We need clear guidelines explaining: in the Mediterranean Sea, within these boundaries, migrants should be taken to so and so place, or reported to so and so. (Fairplay 2015)

A case involving a Maltese fishing boat *Budafel* in 2007 with a crew of four, brings forth the tension that arises from the diverging humanitarian, security and economic considerations more clearly. Twenty-seven migrants were forced to hold on to the tuna pen for what was initially reported as 24 h when the crew refused to allow the migrants to board their vessel while the Maltese and Libyan authorities argued about which country should assume the responsibility of taking them. The owner explicitly indicated security concerns as the rationale behind the fisher's decision in prohibiting the migrants from boarding. His account highlights the tension between the commitment to humanitarian assistance and the security concerns of the sailors on board.

> "As a Maltese, I'm prepared to assist people, but there's a limit to everything. What if these 24 strong men rebelled and tried to assume control of the boat?" he asked, admitting that the immigrants' lives were at stake. (Grech 2007).

Interviews by the Italian Council for Refugees (CIR) with the survivors after they were rescued by the Italian navy, however, revealed that the migrants actually clung to the buoys around the tuna pen for 3 days. The four crew members of the *Budafel* provided the migrants with some fruit and water while stopping short of allowing the migrants to board the vessel (CIR 2007, p. 3). Basaran (2015, p. 213) refers to such practices as 'humanitarianism light' inasmuch as they involve 'providing directions, water, and possibly food to people in distress, but without taking them on board, hence avoiding complications associated with rescue.' What is interesting here is while Malta and Libya wrangled back and forth arguing which country should assume responsibility, the Maltese Justice and Home Affairs Minister informed reporters that the Maltese authorities had emphasised to the Captain of the *Budafel* that he was obligated to take the migrants on board if they were in any danger (CIR 2007, p. 3).

This clearly underscores the tension between the humanitarian roles expected of seafarers and the contradictory considerations that stem from security considerations in which seafarers are simultaneously concerned about their own safety as well as the difficulty of obtaining the consent of states to disembark the migrants. Furthermore, it was also reported in the above case that the captain had argued ‘he could not take the persons to Malta as he could not risk losing the € 1 million-worth catch of tuna being hauled by the ship, which was heading to Spain’ (CIR 2007, p. 3), drawing our attention to the economic considerations that come into play when seafarers rescue migrants at sea.

In addition to the operational challenges of rescuing migrants, the anxieties and fears felt by seafarers and the associated economic cost of rendering assistance, the margins of humanitarianism at sea have been shrunk by states’ border security regimes. The long-standing legal duty to render assistance at sea has been gradually eroded through increasing laws and practices at the national, regional and supranational levels effectively discouraging rescue at sea that is not sanctioned by states. As Cuttitta (2014, p. 33) and Basaran (2014, p. 367) note, non-state actors are discouraged from independent rescue and assistance through the introduction of legislation that gradually chips away the protection humanitarian acts are afforded from criminalisation. This trend is also noted by Fekete (2009) and Williams (2016) who point out that activists, sympathetic politicians, medical professionals and ordinary citizens have all been prosecuted for acting in accordance with humanitarian ideals in relation to undocumented migrants in different countries.

In the case of Mediterranean migration, this is done through ‘anti-smuggling legislation’ that can criminalise independent rescue efforts (Basaran 2014). The cases of *MV Cap Anamur*, *MV Fakhreddine Morthada* and *MV Mohamed el-Hedi* are some of the well-known examples of seafarers being prosecuted for rescuing migrants at sea and taking them to a place of safety (Statewatch 2007; Basaran 2014).

MV Cap Anamur, eponymously named after the non-governmental organization (NGO) it belonged to, was involved in rescuing migrants in the Mediterranean, and in June 2004 the vessel rescued 37 migrants in the area between Libya and the Italian island of Lampedusa. The president of the German NGO Cap Anamur, the captain and the first *[sic]* officer were arrested and faced charges of helping the migrants to enter Italy illegally. This took place after the ship stayed over 2 weeks at sea awaiting permission to enter, ‘amid a shortage of supplies, threats from the migrants that they would jump into the sea, and worsening physical and psychological conditions experienced by both migrants and crew members’ (Statewatch 2007). While the accused were finally acquitted (BBC 2009), the charging of the personnel in the first place led the NGO to terminate its rescue activities in 2004 (Cusumano 2017, p. 92).

Similarly, the crew of the Tunisian fishing boats *Fakhreddine Morthada* and *Mohamed el-Hedi* rescued 44 migrants in August 2007 and proceeded to Lampedusa disregarding non-disembarkation orders by the Italian authorities. They were promptly arrested and tried on charges of smuggling which were subsequently dropped. However, the captains of each vessel were convicted of ‘charges of resisting public officer and committing violence against a warship', and sentenced to two and half years imprisonment as well as a fine of € 444,000 each, which were subsequently dropped following appeal (Basaran 2014, p. 376). Although all the seafarers were ultimately exonerated, the trials lasted many years, the fishing vessels were confiscated for long periods and rendered unusable, 'effectively amounting to the loss of [the fishers'] economic livelihoods' (Basaran 2014, p. 376). Although all the above cases led to eventual acquittals, Basaran (2014, p. 377) emphasises that the prosecution process and the cost of the criminal procedure were effectively used as a deterrent to humanitarian acts unsanctioned by the state.

It is worth reconsidering the implications of such developments for seafarers and migrants alike. There are certainly precedents in which fishing and cargo vessels have been refused entry into port after having rescued migrants. One case involved a Spanish fishing vessel *Francisco Y Catalina* that rescued 51 migrants on 15th July 2006 and was denied permission to land in Malta. The ship was forced to anchor six miles from the coast for 6 days under extreme overcrowding, with some of the migrants falling ill (Maccanico 2006). Similarly, on 30th January 2007 *MV Marina I* sent a distress call to the Spanish Coastguard after rescuing over 300 undocumented migrants. Nevertheless, it took 2 weeks for the various nations involved (Spain, Senegal and Mauritania) to come to an agreement and disembarkation to take place (Coppens and Somers 2010; Coppens 2013b). A third example is that of the Turkish vessel *Pinar E* that rescued 140 migrants in April 2009 and the high-profile dispute that ensued for 4 days between Malta and Italy regarding who would be responsible for the migrants (HRW 2009; The Telegraph 2009). There is also the case of the oil tanker *MT Salamis* which rescued 102 migrants on 5th August 2013 and the 2 days standoff that followed between the vessel and Maltese authorities due to disagreement over disembarkation (MaltaToday 2013; WatchTheMed 2013).

When such disembarkation refusals and delays combine with the threat of sanction and prosecution, the economic cost of rescue, seafarers' fears and anxieties and the significant challenge of providing humanitarian assistance to large numbers of migrants while having only a handful of crew on board, some seafarers might deem 'looking the other way' to be an easier option. There are a number of testimonies from migrants that suggest that some ships simply pass by without rendering assistance at sea (CIR 2007; HRW 2009; Strik 2012; Heller and Pezzani 2016). Such actions self-evidently put the migrants' lives at risk. Furthermore, seafarers who are guilty of such actions may, nevertheless, suffer from the psychological consequences of their failure to stop and assist fellow humans in distress.

Stowaways

Maritime stowaways have a pedigree as old as shipping itself, and some of the challenges they pose to shipping are not new. However, contemporary stowaways produce significant tensions for seafarers in terms of their economic, security and humanitarian obligations. When the vessel is in port, seafarers are preoccupied with associated security and economic roles whereas humanitarian roles are introduced when stowaways are detected on board while the vessel is at sea.

Stowaways have always entailed an economic cost to ship owners and, hence, a number of procedures have long been prescribed to seafarers to prevent stowaways from boarding and to detect them before a ship departs from port. Some of the recommended practices include: controlling access to the ship from both shore and sea while the ship is berthed and at anchor; implementing an identification pass system at the ship's gangway; roving patrols and the maintenance of a security watch; sealing off restricted areas on board; adequate lighting at night; a systematic stowaway search assisted by a checklist prior to departure; making use of technologies such as CCTV cameras, CO_2 and heat detectors, automatic intrusion detection devices (AID) and alarm systems to detect stowaways (Parrit and Parker 1992; Holder 1997; Robertson 1997; NEPIA 2001; Miller 2009; BIMCO 2013; Jones 2014; GARD n.d.). While these procedures were recommended as early as the 1990s, the introduction of the International Ship and Port Facility Security Code (ISPS) following the 9–11 terrorist attacks formalised these procedures and rendered them mandatory, making the presence of stowaways on board a breach in a ship's security plan implementation. Thus, prevention of boarding by unauthorised personnel, including stowaways, is now part of the explicit security roles seafarers are obliged to assume in ports. However, seafarers also have primary economic and operational obligations to their employers, such as cargo work, liaising with various parties, bunkering, maintenance and so on. Reconciling the above security and commercial expectations can often be challenging for seafarers, particularly when their security measures are not complemented by an effective port security infrastructure, as the following account from one captain highlights.

> From the ship's side, we were left to do all the work with no extra help for the crew. My company said right from the start when we first started setting up ISPS code, a lot of the captains wrote to say, 'okay, we need one extra seaman on deck.' 'No way. No, you're not getting any extra man.' So, we had to do it all ourselves. But what we saw from our side, we're going through all this huge, massive procedures, setting up procedures on board, and audits and inspections and security measures, and the ports are doing nothing. We go to some ports and there's thousands of people just wandering around the jetty. And we're the ones who have to try and stop them getting on board. But nobody was taking the trouble to try and stop them getting into the ports. [...]So, a lot of things didn't get done in port that we'd like to have done. All the maintenance, painting and cleaning. There's the whole crew that's just occupied in manning the gangway and walking up and down the ship's side, you know, looking over the side, canoes, boats. It was a huge burden on the ships. (Capt. Smith, British)

Nonetheless, the security measures taken by seafarers do not always prevent stowaways from boarding ships. My research on stowaways indicates their creative adaptability to measures put in place to deter their movement. This strongly resonates with observations made about the creative agencies of other groups of undocumented migrants on the move (Papadopoulos and Tsianos 2013; Andersson 2014). Furthermore, interviews with stowaways and security experts also revealed that stowaways are, at times, able to avoid detection even when thorough searches are conducted with professional experts assisted by sniffer dogs.

The reaction of seafarers can be quite strong when they discover stowaways at sea. This is due to a number factors that include: frustration over breaches in both ship and port security arrangements; awareness of the significant cost stowaways entail to ship owners and their protection and indemnity (P & I) club insurers; the added workload that comes with caring for and monitoring stowaways on board as well as the pervasive concerns about implications for seafarers' jobs and careers. In addition, the affective dimensions of security alluded to earlier are prominent, particularly in the initial interactions between seafarers and stowaways during which time both groups are fearful and apprehensive. For seafarers, this is due to the link made, in the industry discourse, between piracy, terrorism, criminality and stowaways. In addition, there have been incidents in which a small number of stowaways became violent and effectively hijacked the ship, reinforcing the security concerns of having stowaways on board (BBC 2000; Cooper 2014; Scully 2017). For the stowaways, their concerns are about the potentially violent reactions by seafarers, perceptions that are based on shared past experiences. Such apprehension during the initial encounter at times manifests itself in seafarers carrying 'protective tools'.

> Third officer and duty AB were scared because the incident happened at night time. [. . .] We carried some steel pipe, and ropes and some wood. So, Bosun, AB, and fitter and some of the young guys, I think at least five or six people carry some of the protective tool to, yes, to protect ourselves against these two guys, yes. Because when we heard this news actually, we didn't know how many stowaways we had on board. How many African guys, what kind of weapon they had, maybe some knife or maybe some of the more dangerous weapon. So, we use some protection too, yes. (Capt. Yang, Chinese)

When stowaways are found on board, seafarers are legally obligated to treat them in a humane manner which includes monitoring their health, providing adequate food and suitable accommodation, abstaining from any form of maltreatment, avoiding putting them to work as well as allowing them to exercise daily (IMO 2011; Jones 2014; NEPIA 2015; GARD n.d.). However, seafarers are also instructed to maintain security procedures throughout the period stowaways are on board including locking-up the stowaways, supervising their exercise, posting a crew member as a continuous security watch and segregating stowaways into smaller numbers if they are present in large numbers. These security roles, both in ports and at sea, are embraced reluctantly by seafarers who were keen to point out during interviews that they are not security professionals.

Ship masters are also advised to ensure interactions between crew members and stowaways are kept to the absolute minimum so as to inhibit the development of a sympathetic relationship which might prompt seafarers to provide unauthorised assistance to the stowaways. This could take the form of disembarking them without notifying the appropriate authorities or assisting them to escape from the ship while in port. My interviews with both seafarers and stowaways reveal instances in which seafarers, becoming sympathetic to the life stories of stowaways, helped them with covert disembarkation. The situation should be understood in the context of many jurisdictions refusing permission for stowaways to disembark, forcing ships to sail with stowaways still on board. However, while authorities are often reluctant to allow their disembarkation even for the purpose of repatriation at the ship owners' expense, most are quite adamant that seafarers should treat stowaways in accordance with the relevant regulations and recommended practices. For instance, one seafarer, who had very young stowaways on board for months, highlighted the contradiction in state policies and practices of checking the onboard treatment of stowaways while simultaneously refusing their disembarkation.

> These people were coming to us to interview us about, and it seems like all of them have the same checklist, about how we are treating them, what are we feeding them, and all of that. [...] And then they keep asking us the same questions which we after that realised that it was just a checklist. 'What are you doing with them? What are you feeding them?' Of course, we are feeding them the same food that we eat. 'Are you beating them or torturing them?' C'mon, why should we torture them? 'Are you locking them up?' No, we are not locking them up. [...] We roamed the world with them for four months, but no one really wanted to take them. And the same thing every port, delays, quarantine, checklists, same stupid questions, nobody's taking them until the captain was sacked from the company because of that at a later stage as we know. (Capt. Karim, Egyptian)

As the above account suggests, there are instances where stowaways can have serious implications for the jobs and careers of seafarers because ship owners can incur significant costs when stowaways are found on board. P & I Clubs cover the direct costs associated with stowaways such as the cost of their maintenance on board, disembarkation and repatriation costs including fines by states, the cost of fuel for any diversion for the purpose of repatriation and so on. However, the costs of delays or being rendered 'off-hire' in the case of charter-parties are not covered. Hence, some ship owners can penalise seafarers as they deem them to have failed to meet their obligations. The fear produced by such actions is exacerbated due to the prevalence of temporary employment in shipping and a sense of being easily replaceable (Kahveci and Nichols 2006; Bhattacharya 2011; Xue et al. 2016).

The combined effect of the aforementioned factors can be so severe that 'solutions' resorted to by seafarers can include stowaways being forced off the ship onto makeshift rafts in the middle of the sea. Based on interviews with stowaways and seafarers as well as analysis of various documentary data, I have compiled a number of such incidents. My data indicates interesting patterns such as the provision of floating aids along with water and, at times, food in most cases (see Senu 2018, pp. 258–259). Although these actions by seafarers are certainly criminal and inhumane, it is clear that many of them make attempts to mitigate the consequences of their actions through the 'humane' supply of provisions to aid survival. This conjures up the 'humanitarianism light' (Basaran 2015, p. 213) approach alluded to earlier in the chapter that arises, in part, from the conflicting roles associated with economic, humanitarian and security obligations.

Conclusion

Heller and Pezzani (2016, p. 14) point out that when the Italian military-humanitarian rescue mission *Mare Nostrum* was in place, 42,061 migrants were rescued by commercial shipping accounting for 25% of the total number. However, with the termination of *Mare Nostrum* this increased to 30%. This surge subsequently reduced following the expansion of rescue missions by Italian authorities, the involvement of FRONTEX, EUMEDNAVFOR, an Irish governmental humanitarian mission as well as various NGOs (Cuttitta 2018, pp. 638–639). This emphasises the importance of commercial shipping in rescues, particularly when the presence of other more suited actors to undertake large-scale rescues at sea is reduced. Considering the significant numbers of migrants who perish on the Mediterranean Sea (https://missingmigrants.iom.int/region/mediterranean), the involvement of shipping in saving lives at sea is crucial.

Nonetheless, as various stakeholders in the shipping community have emphasised to governments in the EU, commercial ships and their crews are not equipped to undertake large-scale rescues (ECSA 2015). Furthermore, rescuing and dealing with migrants entails significant challenges and imposes conflicting expectations on seafarers' performance. While this is widely acknowledged by those in the shipping industry, the academic literature has lacked substantive engagement with the roles of seafarers in migration governance, save for a few exceptions. This chapter has sought to centre seafarers at the heart of the debate by attempting to flesh out the tensions that emerge from diverging economic, humanitarian and security expectations in relation to two groups of migrants. As highlighted in the chapter, such diverging expectations have serious implications for both seafarers and migrants. Acknowledging and addressing these tensions is crucial to the alleviation of the burden on seafarers, while at the same time is very likely to prevent deaths and save lives at sea.

References

Aarstad, Å.K. 2015. The Duty to Assist and Its Disincentives: The Shipping Industry and the Mediterranean Migration Crisis. *Mediterranean Politics* 20 (3): 413–419.

Andersson, R. 2014. *Illegality, Inc.: Clandestine Migration and the Business of Bordering Europe*. Oakland: University of California Press.

Bailliet, C. 2003. The "Tampa" Case and Its Impact on Burden Sharing at Sea. *Human Rights Quarterly* 25 (3): 741–774.

Basaran, T. 2014. Saving Lives at Sea: Security, Law and Adverse Effects. *European Journal of Migration and Law* 16 (3): 365–387.

———. 2015. The Saved and the Drowned: Governing Indifference in the Name of Security. *Security Dialogue* 46 (3): 205–220.

BBC. 2000. Stowaways Hijack Ship. [Online]. Available at: http://news.bbc.co.uk/1/hi/world/south_asia/786664.stm. Accessed 3 July 2016.

———. 2009. Italy acquits migrant rescue crew. [Online]. Available at: http://news.bbc.co.uk/1/hi/8295727.stm. Accessed 19 Jan 2014.

———. 2014. Cyprus police end migrant stand-off abroad cruise ship. [Online]. Available at: http://www.bbc.co.uk/news/world-europe-29358265. Accessed 04 Dec 2017.

———. 2017. Award for Scottish ship's captain who rescued 907 migrants. [Online]. Available at: http://www.bbc.co.uk/news/uk-scotland-tayside-central-41472873. Accessed 04 Dec 2017.

Bhattacharya, S. 2011. Sociological Factors Influencing the Practice of Incident Reporting: The Case of the Shipping Industry. *Employee Relations* 34 (1): 4–21.

BIMCO. 2013. *The Ship Master's Security Manual: Guidance and Advice on Stowaways*. Bagsværd: BIMCO Informatique A/S.

CIR. 2007. CIR Report Regarding Recent Search and Rescue Operations in the Mediterranean. [Online]. Available at: http://www.europarl.europa.eu/hearings/20070703/libe/cir_report_en.pdf. Accessed 28 June 2015.

Cooper, N. 2014. Hostage to Stowaways. *Seaways* (April issue): 4–5.

Coppens, J. 2013a. The Essential Role of Malta in Drafting the New Regional Agreement on Migrants at Sea in the Mediterranean Basin. *Journal of Maritime Law & Commerce* 44 (1): 89–115.

———. 2013b. The Lampedusa Disaster: How to Prevent Further Loss of Life at Sea? *The International Journal of Marine Navigation and Safety of Sea Transportation* 7 (4): 589–598.

Coppens, J., and E. Somers. 2010. Towards New Rules on Disembarkation of Persons Rescued at Sea? *The International Journal of Marine and Coastal Law* 25 (3): 377–403.

Cusumano, E. 2017. Emptying the Sea with a Spoon? Non-governmental Providers of Migrants Search and Rescue in the Mediterranean. *Marine Policy* 75 (1): 91–98.

Cuttitta, P. 2014. From the *Cap Anamur* to *Mare Nostrum*: Humanitarianism and Migration Controls at the EU's Maritime Borders. In *The Common European Asylum System and Human Rights: Enhancing Protection in Times of Emergencies. CLEER Working Papers 2014/7 ed*, ed. C. Matera and A. Taylor, 21–37. The Hague: T.M.C Asser Institute.

———. 2018. Repoliticization Through Search and Rescue? Humanitarian NGOs and Migration Management in the Central Mediterranean. *Geopolitics* 23 (3): 632–660.

Davies, M. 2003. Obligations and Implications for Ships Encountering Persons in Need of Assistance at Sea. *Pacific Rim Law & Policy Journal* 12 (1): 109–141.

ECSA. 2015. *Humanitarian Crisis in the Mediterranean Sea*. Brussels/London.

Fairplay. 2015. Captain calls for 'diplomatic' leadership and guidelines in Med rescues. [Online]. Available at: https://fairplay.ihs.com/article/17652/news-insight-master-recounts-migrant-rescue. Accessed 04 Dec 2017.

Fekete, L. 2009. Europe: Crimes of Solidarity. *Race & Class* 50 (4): 83–97.

GARD. n.d. GARD Guidance on Stowaways. [Online]. Available at: http://www.gard.no/Content/13385148/Guidance%20on%20stowaways.pdf. Accessed 06 Aug 2013.

Goddard, K.S. 2015. Rescuing Refugees and Migrants at Sea: Some Commercial Shipping Implications. *The Journal of International Maritime Law* 21 (5): 352–367.

Grech, H. 2007. Illegal immigrants floating in limbo. *TIMES OF MALTA* [Online]. Available at: http://www.timesofmalta.com/articles/view/20070528/local/illegal-immigrants-floating-in-limbo.16401. Accessed 28 June 2015.

Heller, C., and L. Pezzani. 2016. Ebbing and Flowing: The EU's Shifting Practices of (Non-) Assistance and Bordering in a Time of Crisis. *Near Futures* [Online] 1. Available at: http://nearfuturesonline.org/ebbing-and-flowing-the-eus-shifting-practices-ofnon-assistance-and-bordering-in-a-time-of-crisis/. Accessed 28 Nov 2017.

Holder, A. 1997. Stowaways. In *Shipping at Risk: The Rising Tide of Organised Crime*, ed. E. Ellen, 230–246. Paris: ICC Publishing SA.

HRW. 2009. *Pushed Back, Pushed Around: Italy's Forced Return of Boat Migrants and Asylum Seekers, Libya's Mistreatment of Migrants and Asylum Seekers*. New York: Human Rights Watch.

Huysmans, J. 2000. The European Union and the Securitization of Migration. *Journal of Common Market Studies* 38 (5): 751–777.

———. 2006. *The Politics of Insecurity: Fear, Migration and Asylum in the EU*. Abingdon: Routledge.

ICS. 2015. *Large Scale Rescue Operations at Sea: Guidance on Ensuring Safety and Security of Seafarers and Resued Persons*. 2nd ed. London: International Chamber of Shipping.

———. 2018. Shipping Industry Increasingly Worried About EU Member States' Policy on Migrants Rescued at Sea. [Online]. Available at: http://www.ics-shipping.org/news/press-releases/view-article/2018/06/26/shipping-industry-increasingly-worried-about-eu-member-states-policy-on-migrants-rescued-at-sea. Accessed 29 Dec 2018.

IMO. 2011. Revised Guidelines on the Prevention of Access by Stowaways and the Allocation of Responsibilities to Seek the Successful Resolution of Stowaway Cases. *Resolution FAL.11 (37) adopted on 9 September 2011*.

IMO., et al. 2015. *Rescue at Sea: A Guide to Principles and Practices as Applied to Refugees and Migrants*.

Jarvis, R.M. 1988. Rusting in Drydock: Stowaways, Shipowners and the Administrative Penalty Provision of INA Section 273 (d). *Tulane Maritime Law Journal* 13 (1): 25–49.

Jones, S. 2014. *Stowaways by Sea: Maritime Security Handbook*. London: The Nautical Institute.

Kahveci, E., and T. Nichols. 2006. *The Other Car Workers: Work, Organisation and Technology in the Maritime Car Carrier Industry*. Basingstoke: Palgrave Macmillan.

Kellett, J., et al. 2015. Best Management Practices for Large Scale Rescue Operations at Sea. In *InterManger Large Scale Rescue At Sea Workshop*. Brussels: Allmode Limited.

Kenney, F.J., Jr., and V. Tasikas. 2003. Tampa Incident: IMO Perspectives and Responses on the Treatment of Persons Rescued at Sea. *Pacific Rim Law & Policy Journal* 12 (1): 143–178.

Kilpatrick, R.L. 2017. *The 'Refugee Clause': Why Contractual Allocation of Rescue Costs is Critical During Periods of Mass Migration at Sea. NUS Centre for Maritime Law Working Paper*. Singapore: National University of Singapore.

Kilpatrick, R.L., and A. Smith. 2015. The International Legal Obligation to Rescue During Mass Migration at Sea: Navigating the Sovereign and Commercial Dimensions of a Mediterranean Crisis. *U.S.F Maritime Law Journal* 28 (2): 141–194.

Maccanico, Y. 2006. EU/Africa: Carnage continues as EU border moves south. *Statewatch Immigration Analysis* [Online] (55). Available at: http://www.statewatch.org/news/2006/sep/Immigration-analysis.pdf. Accessed 18 Jan 2014.

———. 2012. Securitising Maritime Transport: Shipping Merchandise and Dealing with Stowaways. *Statewatch Journal* 22 (1): 9–13.

MaltaToday. 2013. Salamis heads to Italy as Malta refuses access to rescued asylum seekers. [Online]. Available at: http://www.maltatoday.com.mt/news/national/28928/slideshow-salamis-adrift-malta-refuses-access-to-rescued-asylum-seekers-20130806#.WiTEJmdLE5v. Accessed 02 Dec 2017.

Maquet, P., and J.B. Zortea. 2013. Sanctions for Stowaways: How Merchant Shipping Joined the Border Police. *Statewatch Journal* 23 (2): 38–42.

Mason, M. 1987. Alien Stowaways, The Immigration and Naturalization Service, and Shipowners. *Tulane Maritime Law Journal* 12 (2): 361–371.

McConnell, M. 1997. "Forward This Cargo to Taiwan": Canadian Extradition Law and Practice Relating to Crime on the High Seas. *Criminal Law Forum* 8 (2): 335–351.

Miglierini, J. 2016. Migrant tragedy: Anatomy of a shipwreck. *BBC News* [Online]. Available at: http://www.bbc.co.uk/news/world-europe-36278529. Accessed 03 Dec 2017.

Miller, M.S. 2009. The Stowaway Problem: Revisiting the 2002 Amendments to the FALL Convention. *Currents* 29: 4–7.

NEPIA. 2001. Stowaways: An Increasing Problem. *Signals* Special Edition (6).

———. 2015. Stowaways. *Loss Prevention Briefing* [Online]. Available at: http://www.nepia.com/media/278327/LP-Briefing-Stowaways-July-2015.PDF. Accessed 18 Feb 2015.

Nourse, D.A. 1993. Detention of Stowaways: Who Should Bear the Cost? *USF Maritime Law Journal* 6 (2): 435–448.
Ort, B.A. 1991. International and US Obligations Toward Stowaway Asylum Seekers. *University of Pennsylvania Law Review* 140 (1): 285–366.
Papadopoulos, D., and V.S. Tsianos. 2013. After Citizenship: Autonomy of Migration, Organisational Ontology and Mobile Commons. *Citizenship Studies* 17 (2): 178–196.
Parrit, B.A.H., and C.J. Parker. 1992. The Answer: A Practical Response to the Stowaway Problem. In *Stowaways by Sea: Illegal Immigrants-Refugees-Asylum Seekers: A Nautical Institute Practical Guide to a Growing International Problem*, ed. B.A.H. Parrit, 115–120. London: The Nautical Institute.
Robertson, B. 1997. Preventative Security. In *The Mariner and the Maritime Law: Seminar 8 Stowaways*, 35–42. North East Branch: The Nautical Institute.
Scully, D. 2017. Chaos shits Technomar bulker as crew threatened by Nigerian stowaways. [Online]. Available at: http://splash247.com/chaos-hits-technomar-bulker-as-crew-threatened-by-nigerian-stowaways/. Accessed 03 Dec 2017.
Senu, A. 2018. *The Global Assemblage of Multi-Centred Stowaway Governance.* Unpublished PhD Thesis, Cardiff University.
Statewatch. 2007. Criminalising solidarity- Cap Anamur trial underway. *Statewatch News Online* [Online]. Available at: http://www.statewatch.org/news/2007/apr/03italy-cape-anamur.htm. Accessed 17 Jan 2014.
Steglich, E. 1999. Hiding in the Hulls: Attacking the Practice of High Seas Murder of Stowaways Through Expanded Criminal Jurisdiction. *Texas Law Review* 78 (6): 1323–1346.
Strik, T. 2012. *Lives Lost in the Mediterranean Sea: Who Is Responsible?* Strasbourg: Committee on Migration, Refugees and Displaced Persons, Council of Europe.
Tauman, J.E. 2002. Rescued at Sea, But Nowhere to Go: The Cloudy Legal Waters of the Tampa Crisis. *Pacific Rim Law & Policy Journal* 11 (2): 461–496.
The Telegraph. 2009. Italy to allow disputed migrant ship to dock. [Online]. Available at: http://www.telegraph.co.uk/news/worldnews/europe/italy/5184979/Italy-to-allow-disputed-migrant-ship-to-dock.html. Accessed 02 Dec 2017.
Valverde, M. 2014. Studying the Governance of Crime and Security: Space, Time and Jurisdiction. *Criminology and Criminal Justice* 14 (4): 379–391.
WatchTheMed. 2013. Tanker 'Salamis' carrying migrants stopped from entering Malta. [Online]. Available at: http://watchthemed.net/reports/view/18. Accessed 03 Dec 2017.
Williams, J.M. 2016. The Safety/Security Nexus and the Humanitarianisation of Border Enforcement. *The Geographic Journal* 182 (1): 27–37.
Xue, C., et al. 2016. Who is Dominant? Occupational Health and Safety management in Chinese Shipping. *Journal of Industrial Relations* 59 (1): 65–84.

Part III
Support for Seafarers and Their Families

Chapter 13
Union Organising in the Context of Regional Labour Market Decline: The Case of Nautilus International

Victor Oyaro Gekara

Introduction

Over the past few decades the impact of globalisation on society and industry at the national level has been immense and has been studied and extensively documented in the literature. Some of the major benefits and losses accruing from economic globalisation, particularly since the late 1970s have been debated by dominant political economy commentators (see e.g. Harvey 2005; Held et al. 1999; Strange 1996; Scholte 2000; Stiglitz 2002; Giddens 2002; Chomsky 2017). An important aspect of the globalising process has been the extensive restructuring of production and distribution patterns in search of cheaper resources, through aggressive outsourcing and offshoring. The result for many national economies, particularly advanced industrial states, has been a drastic decline in traditional industries affecting both labour and capital (Dunning 1993; Beck 2005; Perraton 2019). This chapter examines the decline in the seafaring labour markets of the so-called Traditional Maritime Countries (TMN), and the implications for union organising focusing on the UK and its seafaring labour. It examines the creation of Nautilus International (NI) Union via a merger of unions for maritime professionals across different countries in Europe initially beginning with Great Britain, the Netherlands and later Switzerland. This was a uniquely strategic response to declining membership and weakening organising capacity. Some of the key challenges associated with unions trying to organise and represent their members in the context of industrial and labour market decline are explored.

The particular focus in this chapter is the decline in the national seafaring labour markets of European Traditional Maritime countries such as Britain, Germany,

V. O. Gekara (✉)
School of Accounting, Information Systems and Supply Chains, RMIT University, Melbourne, VIC, Australia
e-mail: victor.gekara@rmit.edu.au

V. O. Gekara, H. Sampson (eds.), *The World of the Seafarer*, WMU Studies in Maritime Affairs 9, https://doi.org/10.1007/978-3-030-49825-2_13

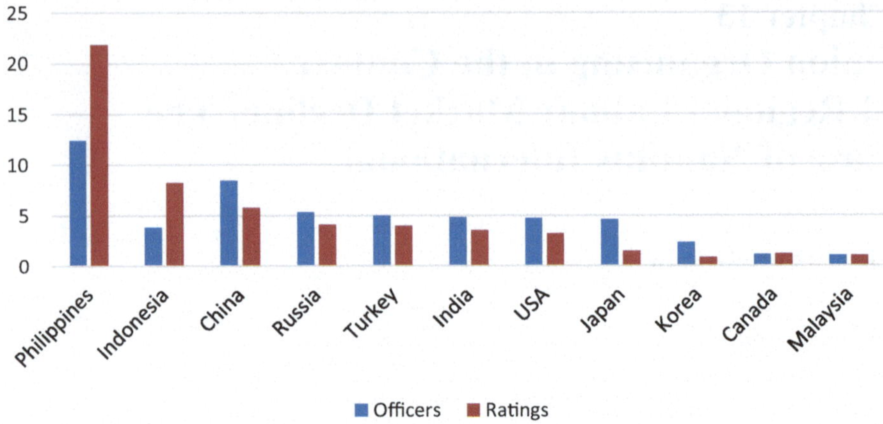

Fig. 13.1 Eleven top seafarer supply countries as of 2003. Source: Adapted and recreated by author from APEC accreditation of seafarer manning agencies project, 2005

Netherlands and Denmark. This resulted, from economic globalisation and deregulation within national economies in response to emerging neoliberal government policies in the 1980s and 1990s. (McConville 1999; Gekara 2010b). The seafaring labour market follows the hierarchical structure of the crew on-board ships and is broadly divided into two segments: officers and ratings. Senior staff responsible for the commercial and technical management of the ship are drawn from the officers' market segment, while ratings, i.e. lower level operational staff, are recruited from the ratings' market segment. The discussion here specifically relates to officers. Thus, use of the term 'seafarers' will in most cases, unless otherwise qualified, be in reference to officers.

As cheaper sources of seafaring labour opened up in low-cost developing regions, many European ship owners opted to recruit their crew from countries such as the Philippines, China, India and Indonesia and, with time, almost entirely abandoned their local labour markets. Figure 13.1 shows that by the end of the twentieth century, the majority of seafarers, both officers and ratings originated from developing countries. Note that no Western European country is represented in the top 10 list of seafarer supply by this time, and the only European country on the list, Russia, is comparatively low-cost. From the OECD, only the US, Korea and Canada appear, albeit, with very small numbers.

In the UK this shift in the supply of seafarers inevitably led to a general weakening of the labour market just as had occurred in many other similar countries. Employment opportunities for national seafarers shrank with shipping companies reducing investment in recruitment and training activities. Eventually there was a general decline of interest in the occupation even in areas that had always been considered as traditional seafaring communities such as Glasgow, Liverpool, Aberdeen and Southampton (see Gekara 2010a). With regard to labour organisation and representation, the unions acting for seafarers experienced a drastic decline in their membership and, by extension, their financial and political influence. It is within this context that this chapter describes the way in which three Unions, representing seafarers in North Western Europe, sought to revitalise their position through a unique form of cross-border amalgamation into a single union known as Nautilus International (NI). The chapter draws on a qualitative social science study, which was designed to examine the limitations of local policy responses to globalisation-induced problems. The research examined the waning of British shipping as a result of processes of economic globalisation and deregulation in the 1980s and 1990s and the impact of locally designed and implemented policy responses, predominantly the tonnage tax initiative. An important aspect of the study was the decline in British seafaring and the implications for, and response from, local maritime unions.

In the following sections I examine this decline as part of the overall global economic and regulatory shifts that led to an unlikely initiative by the union leaders, the process and result of their efforts, the challenges involved in the process, and conclude with an assessment of its success and conjecture as to its future.

The British Seafaring Labour Market in Decline

The globalised nature of the shipping industry has been analysed extensively, with the consistent conclusion that, undeniably, it stands out as exemplar of industrial globalisation and corporate foot-looseness (DeSombre 2006). Often highlighted is the international ownership of shipping capital and the means by which it is operated, the global nature of crew sourcing and employment and the ease with which a ship's nationality can be shifted from state to state (Alderton et al. 2004; Sampson and Schroeder 2006). As Kahveci and Nichols (2006) observe, ownership and nationality of ships are both vague and fictitious because they are increasingly difficult to ascertain and can be switched and shifted with extreme ease. Whereas this arrangement presents enormous benefits for business, in this case ship-owners, the impact for labour has been a significant decrease in resources, political influence and bargaining power (Lillie 2006; DeSombre 2006; Gekara 2010b).

Whilst many seafarers are employed on the international labour market, within Europe there nevertheless remains a relationship between the numbers of domestic seafarers in employment and the size of the national registered fleet. A number of factors are at play here including the nature and structure of the internal labour market, the training opportunities available including funding and access to training institutions, and also perceived career prospects. As highlighted previously from the mid-1970s the British shipping industry was in decline across all major aspects, including the registered fleet.

As illustrated in Fig. 13.2, the UK fleet steadily declined from 1976 through to the end of the century as a result of ship owners flagging out their vessels away from the national registers of advanced industrial maritime countries. This resulted from the fact that they were considered more stringently regulated and costlier to operate from than low-cost flags in developing regions (for an in-depth discussion of the flagging out phenomenon refer to Carlisle 1981; Metaxas 1985).

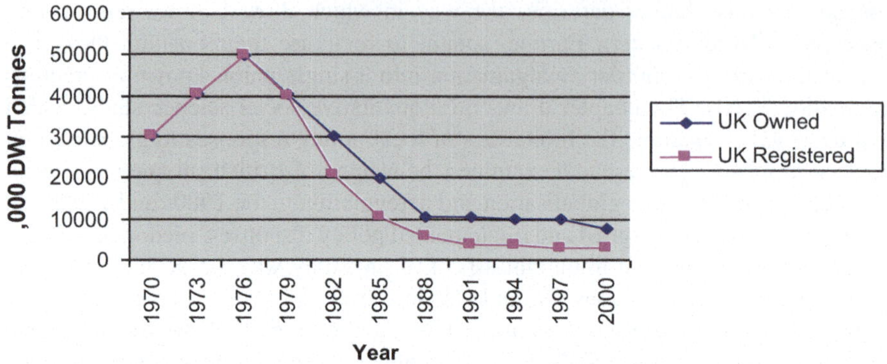

Fig. 13.2 UK owned and registered fleet 1970 to 2000. Source: UK Chamber of Shipping. (Adapted and recreated by author from Brownrigg et al. 2001)

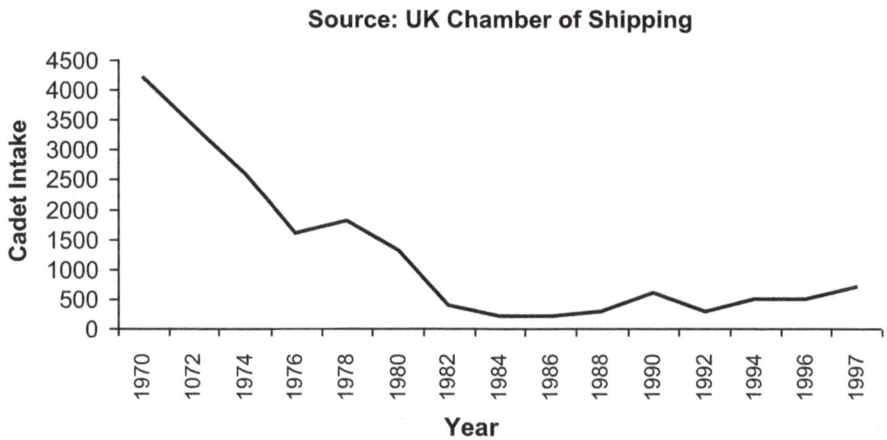

Fig. 13.3 Recruitment of cadets between 1970 and 1997. Adapted and recreated by author from Gardner et al. (2001)

Since ship owners in the UK traditionally bear much responsibility for recruiting and training cadets, as well as providing employment for qualified officers, flagging out has resulted in a corresponding decline in training funding, training opportunities and, even more problematically, employment opportunities for British seafarers. Consequently, as Fig. 13.3 illustrates, the impact of the decline in the national fleet was to cause a considerable reduction in the numbers of cadets recruited annually. This fell from about 4300 in 1970 to about 1000 cadets per year from the mid-1980s onwards.

Similarly, a survey of the number of officers employed on the UK fleet between 1980 and 1998 (Fig. 13.4) confirms the above observations as the number dropped steadily from around 25,800 in 1980 to about 9000 in 1991 then levelled out towards

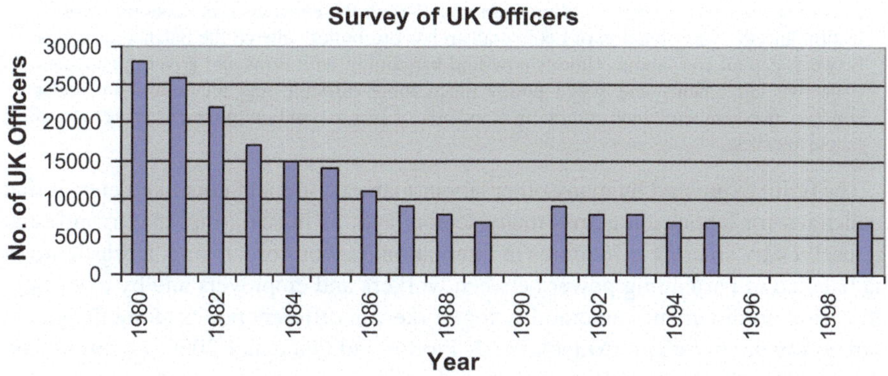

Fig. 13.4 The number of British officers employed in the UK fleet between 1980 and 1998. Source: UK Chamber of Shipping (adapted and recreated by author from Brownrigg et al. 2001)

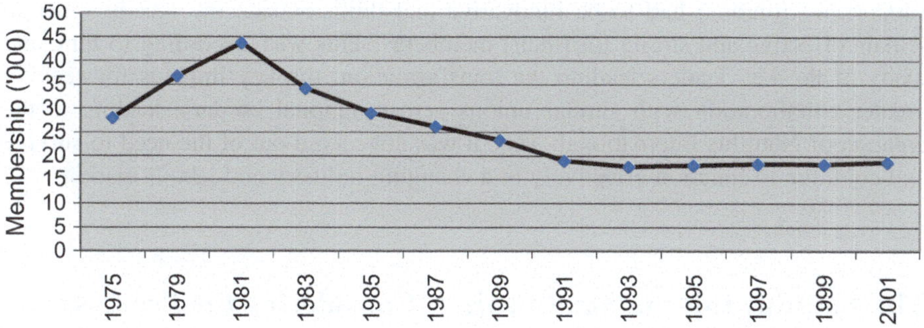

Fig. 13.5 NUMAST membership trend between 1975 and 2001. Source: Created by author from Nautilus International annual reports, 1975–2001, The British Certification Officer, https://tinyurl.com/wgqeakw [24/11/2019]

the end of the century (see also Brownrigg et al. 2001; Leggate and McConville 2005).

The third area of decline, and one which forms the core focus of this chapter, is union membership. Figure 13.5 shows the trend of membership for National Union of Marine, Aviation and Shipping Transport Officers (NUMAST), the key union for seafarer officers in Britain from the early 1980s to 2006. Union membership diminished during this period in tandem with the national shipping fleet, cadet recruitment and the number of officers employed in the British shipping fleet. The consistent decline across all these aspects of the industry is unsurprising since they are intimately intertwined and cross-dependent.

As union membership decreased, so did the union's capacity to effectively represent workers and ensure effective protection of labour standards and working conditions in an increasingly vulnerable labour market. These developments were not unique but broadly representative of the general predicament of labour in most advanced industrial countries. As Peters (2008, p. 85) observes,

> [...] over the past 25 years [starting from mid-1980s], the emergence of economic globalization and the consolidation of neoliberalism has profoundly altered the balance of power between capital and labour. Unions now find bargaining with firms and governments over collective agreements and social policy much more difficult, and all unions are under constant pressure to defend minimum standards of income and employment protection in labour markets.

The point expressed by many other labour market commentators like Peters is that challenges for labour cut across many sectors and, as in seafaring, they manifested themselves by creating difficulties in international labour organising, a drastic tip in the balance of bargaining power between workers and employers and by extension, increasing employment vulnerability for workers at different points along the global commodity supply chain (Munck 2002; Fiorito and Gallagher 2006; Lévesque and Murray 2006; Webster 2015).

Mark Dickinson, then president of NUMAST, was a major advocate for, and leader of, the amalgamation. He later became the NI General Secretary and in a 2006 interview stated that in the context of growing employer power and declining state support "...[unions] had to be innovative and think outside the box in order to remain effective and strong for [their] members". This was, according to him, and many of the key leaders leading the transformation, the key impetus for seeking greater collaboration with similar unions across national borders, leading to the creation of Nautilus International. Thus it was conceived out of the need to survive and continue to function effectively in a changing industry and labour market.

The Nautilus International Project: Considering the Process, Motivation and Outcomes

As explained earlier, the two formerly independent maritime unions that initiated the merger—the UK's National Union of Marine, Aviation and Shipping Transport Officers (NUMAST) and the *Federatie van Werknemers in de Zeevaart* (FWZ) of the Netherlands—came together and joined in 2009 to create a single cross-border union. This was the culmination of a lengthy process of negotiation and consultation spanning a decade beginning in the late 1990s (Gekara 2010a). Prior to the conception of the amalgamation, the two unions had enjoyed a long, close working relationship. This was partly due to geographic proximity and the fact that their two countries have long intertwined maritime histories but also, and perhaps more importantly, as explained by the union leaders, because Dutch and British seafarers have traditionally worked side by side on-board Anglo-Dutch owned/operated vessels. What makes their move unique and novel is that the two unions, which had been independent and organised in different countries, agreed not just to collaborate more closely, as most international union alliances do, but to largely dismantle their national structures. This included abandoning their individual national identities and foregoing their independence to form a regional union with a new identity and structure set up across international borders as a single entity.

The separate histories of the two unions, prior to the amalgamation, present an informative case of national union restructuring, including mergers and splinters. The British arm of the union—Nautilus-UK—traces its roots to the Mercantile Marine Service Association (MMSA) in 1857. By 1920 the association had transformed itself through splinters, mergers and take-overs involving many other smaller marine unions. Further similar processes of restructuring over the following years resulted in the creation of NUMAST in 1985, when MMSA joined with the Merchant Navy and Airlines Officers Association (MNAOA) and the Radio and Electronics Officers' Union (REOU). Consequently, an inclusive union was created representing ship and airline officers and other shore-based maritime professionals. On the other side of the border FWZ had also gone through similar restructuring processes. Formed in 1901 by a group of officers at a bar in Amsterdam, the union grew and developed through mergers and take-overs culminating in the *Federatie van Werknemers in de Zeevaart* (FZW) in 1995. At that time Algemene Vakbond voor Zeevarenden (AVZ) the trade union for masters, officers and ratings on small merchant navy vessels and Vereniging van Kapiteins en Officieren ter Koopvaardij (VKO), mainly representing masters and officers on large merchant navy vessels, merged to form a wider union representing workers in the broader maritime profession. On both sides the restructuring seems to have involved a natural progression of mergers, beginning at the local and national level and eventually moving outward, across national borders. Later in 2011 and 2015 the new union further expanded with the joining of Unia, the Swiss maritime professionals' union and another Dutch seafarers' union—FNV Waterbouw, respectively. The commonly identified factors influencing union amalgamations including, declining memberships, reduced financial resources and political influence, strongly apply to the case of Nautilus International. The merger process was primarily driven by the need to regain political and financial ground in the industry's industrial relations, as the following interview extract shows:

> [unions] reach a critical mass and they know they can't go on like this, they've got declining membership, rising costs and no resources and they need to do something about it... They cannot go on increasing membership fees indefinitely just to stay afloat...this is what has happened with us. (NI Leader 1 2006)

Whereas mergers, takeovers and amalgamations are common within national borders, the NI case, illustrates an important point, which I term here as 'exhausted national possibilities' whereby a major impetus is created for the search for cross-border partners and a need is prompted for initiating closer working relations. Seemingly, by the close of the twentieth Century, the two unions involved had exhausted local possibilities for further mergers, so that,

> ...there were no more suitable, like-minded unions to merge with locally.... By this time all those who could be part of us were already with us, so we had to look outside. (NI Leader 1 2009)

This need illustrates the key point that national resources for labour organising are finite, particularly in the context of declining state protections and growing neoliberal policies in which business interests are preferenced over those of labour (Gekara

2010b). Consequently, room for further growth must be sought from without. For example, as a result of a continuing decline in the pool of seafarers locally, the possibilities of expanding membership in the vicinity were rapidly diminished. It appears that by this point, the Dutch and British maritime professional union amalgamation was almost a natural progression because they "already had a very long-standing relationship" and it was therefore "an inevitable choice" (NI Leader 1 2009).

It was in this context that active negotiations commenced in the late 1990s and, after almost a decade, the two unions moved on from the framework of an ad hoc cross-border collaboration, prevalent in the industry, to a more defined and structured association. In October 2006, they respectively dropped their individual identities and became the Nautilus Federation (NF). From then on they adopted the names Nautilus UK and Nautilus NL respectively. This move to a federation constituted a significant move. Not only did it signal the intention of creating a stronger bond, forged with the common goal of regaining both political and financial influence in the negotiation for seafarers' rights and labour standards in the region, but it also gained sufficient status to influence events on the international stage.

> The motivation for us was clear, we had lost a lot of ground and we could not afford to lose any more as our members depended on us... we had a responsibility as leaders to use every means to regain that ground and this was the most logical... (NI Leader 2 2010)

From the commencement of the negotiations the objective was to ultimately establish one single cross-border union. The NF was, therefore, meant as a temporary platform—a space for creating and testing the necessary structures for eventual full amalgamation. The federation period served three important functions. Firstly, it was during this time that the separate leaderships conducted final consultations and balloting to gain unequivocal grass-root approval for the eventual amalgamation. Secondly, it provided the space for rationalising and streamlining the two, hitherto, separate, and largely different organisational structures and creating one, which would enable the union to operate as one single entity transcending geo-political boundaries. Finally, it served as a platform for trialling the emerging structures for the new union. With regard to this last function, the NF stage was of great necessity, considering that there was till then no guiding model available for the kind of cross-border union merger envisaged by the leaders.

> The Nautilus Federation was just a stage and was never meant to remain as a lasting structure, it served its purpose, an important one but our aim was to quickly and strategically progress towards a complete merger and a single union body...it was important, just like a trial phase towards a marriage if you like. (NI Leader 3 2010)

Upon completion of the amalgamation process and the launch of the new union in May 2009, the Nautilus Federation was rendered dormant, with the provision that it would be reactivated as a temporary platform for initiating new national unions wishing to join Nautilus International in the future, as happened with the joining of Unia and FNV Waterbouw in 2011 and 2015 respectively. The organisational governance structure of 2010 resulted when the full merger was launched between the two principal partners.

Under the new union, an inclusive cross-border governance structure was adopted, which merged the formally separate organisational structures in a way that sought to maximise the advantages of both (see Fig. 13.6). The governance structure consists of a General Meeting (GM) of all members, which takes place every four years, at the top, followed by the Council of the Union (CoU), made up of thirty-two elected members, twenty-four of whom are British and eight Dutch. Reporting to the CoU are several council committees, including the Resolutions, Establishments and the Professional and Technical Committees. The next most significant level below the CoU comprises two national committees made up of the elected council members (24 UK and 8 NL) plus extra members from the national secretariats in the two countries. Regular national conferences are held on both sides where important matters affecting specific national aims are discussed, including the election of national committee members and representatives to the CoU. The GM is the highest organ in the decision-making hierarchy of the union where all members are represented and debate on important issues affecting all members and from where the effective running of the union takes place. Any resolutions carried at the GM are binding on the CoU according to the Nautilus Rule Book,

> The absolute control and administration of the affairs and property of the union and the furtherance of the objects of the union and the provision of all the benefits together with the necessary power to utilise union funds and monies shall be vested in the Council subject only to any direction of the Union given by its members at a general Meeting... (Rule 12.1)

The significance of the GM is that no important changes in the way the union is structured and operated may be effected without being discussed at the GM. For this reason, provision is made for the establishment of Special General Meetings (SGM) to handle important matters arising in-between the scheduled GMs. For example, a special GM was called on 30th June 2011, named the Rules General Meeting, to effect changes to the Rules in order to enable members of Unia (Switzerland union) to join NI. The national committees, on the other hand, "deal with policy issues relevant only to the specific country". The national committees also have the power to establish such further committees as necessary for the effective management and administration of the national branch (Rule 17.2).

The day-to-day management of the union is the responsibility of a General Secretary (GS) based in London. The GS is aided by National Assistant General Secretaries (AGS), based in the different countries represented coordinating several administrative departments. These departments oversee the implementation of various decisions and the running of the national branch. The national AGSs are also responsible for coordinating the activities of an Internal Senior Management Team that draws membership from the staff of the national administration. They also coordinate the activities of national administration teams from which an internal senior management team is constituted. This in turn, coordinates the activities of several joint committees, including a policy coordination committee, an industrial coordination seminar, a finance committee and a human resource committee. The idea behind this elaborate structure is that the management and governance of the union is as seamless as possible so as to

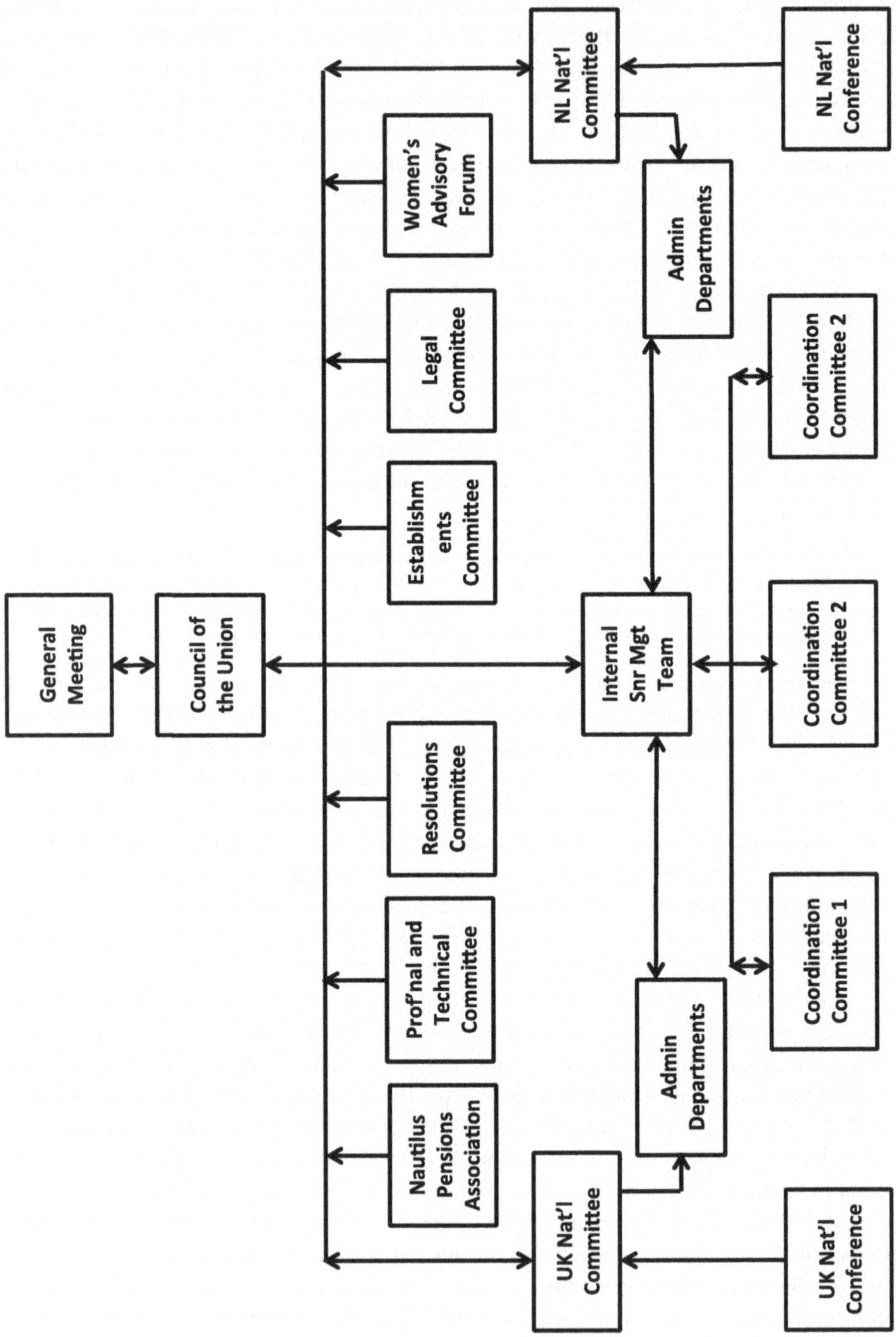

Fig. 13.6 Nautilus International organisational and governance structure. Source: Created by author from interview descriptions

encourage in all the members from different countries the development of a real sense of belonging and a feeling of common identity.

Concluding Assessment: Why Was the Merger Important and for Whom?

In order to assess the successes and appreciate the challenges of adopting the new structures one has to first look at the context in which the union exists and operates and also its specific objectives. First, as established earlier, Nautilus International was born of the necessity to survive in a declining labour market with the associated decline in its representational capacity as a workers' union. In this regard, as observed by many labour market commentators, unions can only serve their core purpose of reducing inequality, improving jobs, and widening income distribution, if they can maintain and/or increase density and grow their effectiveness through wide bargaining coverage and coordination (see e.g. Peters 2008; Swenson 2002; Western 1997). Accordingly, the key driving objective for the leaders of the NI project is easily understood and was expressed by one of the leaders as the need,

> ... [to] have a strong voice in Brussels [and] more power in negotiating with national governments and ship owners. (NI leader 1 2009)

Regarding this aspect, the immediate obvious outcome of the merger was an increase in membership numbers, as is evident from the rise in figures between 2008 (15,915) and 2009 (22,518) when the merger came into effect, as illustrated in Fig. 13.7.

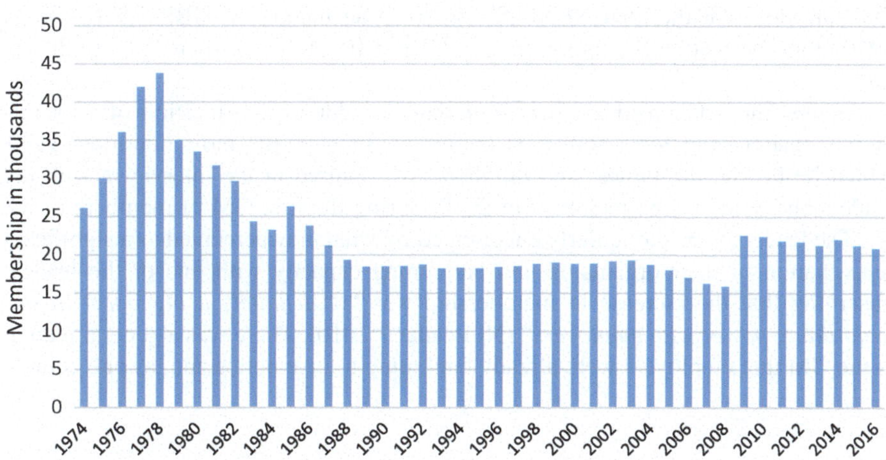

Fig. 13.7 Membership numbers pre and post-merger. Source: Created by author from Nautilus International annual reports, 1974–2016, The British Certification Officer, https://tinyurl.com/wgqeakw [24/11/1919]

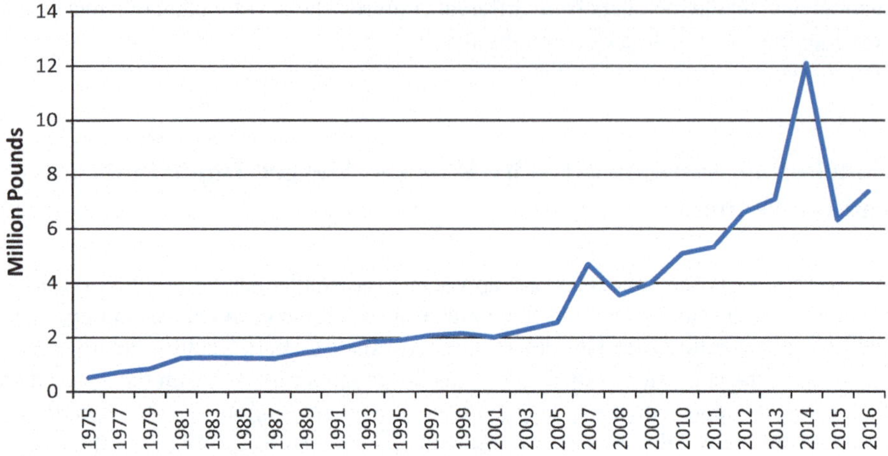

Fig. 13.8 NI income and expenditure. Source: Created by author from Nautilus International annual reports, 1975–2016, The British Certification Officer, https://tinyurl.com/wgqeakw [24/11/2019]

Another important and measurable indicator of success was the improvement in the collective financial resources of the union. Figure 13.8 shows that the financial income statement steadily increased from 2009 after a sudden dip between 2007 and 2009. The union's income is calculated according to members' subscriptions and contributions, memorandum agreements from employers and investment transfers (based on details in the annual returns) consequently it is easy to see how the pooling of financial sources from all members of the union could have such an immediate impact in comparison with the state of the NUMAST income before the merger. To illustrate, in 2008 the then NUMAST received an income of GBP 3,576,494. In 2010, after the merger the figure grew to GBP 5,101,440 and to GBP 7,118,205 in 2013.[1]

Against the set objectives, it is important to address the question of why this merger matters and for whom it is important. Perhaps the most important gains which lie behind the figures and numbers are captured in the interviews with the leaders and some of the members in 2010, during the first GM of members of the NI. The leaders were particularly encouraged by what they perceived as a significant rejuvenation of their organising and bargaining capacity with one of the leaders observing that the increase in membership was "*...definitely a big boost in our negotiating power with employers*" (NI Leader 2 2010). There was a general feeling at the GM that employers were already beginning to take notice and, as one council

[1]The Jump from 2013 to GBP 12,128,956 was due to a large lump-sum arrears transfer from the NI Netherlands office. The figure goes back to the normal trajectory in 2015.

member put it, "*...realise that we are one body of workers...they cannot win by bargaining with small, individual national unions*" (NI Council member 2010).

This observation, however, also represents Nautilus's main challenge and the one which undermines the extent of its power. While employers, i.e. shipping companies, are extensively global in their operation and have the ability to exploit the breadth of both political and economic resources available internationally with little restriction, unions have always been limited by their nationally embedded and path-dependent structures (see Gekara et al. 2013). Even with such cross-border mergers where they have tried, with notable effect, to emulate the seamless transnational workings of global business, the union still finds its influence limited to the individual countries it is organised across, i.e. Great Britain, the Netherlands and Switzerland. The second and more important challenge related to this limitation is the fact that, even collectively, the union represents and operates in a generally declining labour market where the number of seafarers will continue to decrease over time with natural attritions, since there is currently little replenishment occurring through new training.

Nevertheless, whilst recognising the challenges inherent in the situation, NI has adopted an unambiguous view of its role and a specific strategy for effective representation of its members. It sees its strategy as less expansionary and more targeted both in its spatial scope and its functional objectives. Its practical regional focus in Europe is not only to work towards maintaining and improving labour standards primarily for European seafarers but also for all seafarers, by lobbying national, regional and international policy as well as through strategic negotiations with employers. It has adopted the social partnership approach where it seeks to work with employers and governments towards a concerted goal of continuously improving workers' work and employment terms and conditions—to ensure high labour standards. According to one of the leaders in an informal conversation with the researcher in 2011,

> It is much easier to work with employers, work with government and Brussels and the rest of them. At the end of the day, we have to make them realise that we face the same challenges, at the end of the day, and they have realised...they need well qualified and motivated seafarers but to do this they must train and they must offer good conditions...as simple as that really. (NI Leader 1 2010]

As demonstrated in the foregoing analysis, Nautilus International, provides an illuminating case study of the significant challenges faced by labour in the current context of the ever increasing, exploitative power of capital. It reveals the potential strengths of global cross-border organising and sends one important message—that nothing less than globally coordinated, strategic alliances will help counter the power of capital and secure the future of workers' rights.

References

Alderton, T., M. Bloor, E. Kahveci, T. Lane, H. Sampson, M. Thomas, N. Winchester, B. Wu, and M. Zhao. 2004. *The Global Seafarer: Living and Working Conditions in a Globalised Industry*. London: ILO.

Beck, U. 2005. *Power in the Global Age: A New Global Political Economy*. Cambridge: Polity.

Brownrigg, M., G. Dawe, M. Mann, and P. Weston. 2001. Developments in UK Shipping: The Tonnage Tax. *Maritime Policy and Management* 28 (3): 213–223.

Carlisle, R. 1981. *Sovereignty for Sale: The Origins and Evolution of the Panamanian and Liberian Flags of Convenience*. Annapolis: Naval Institute Press.

Chomsky, N. 2017. *Global Discontents*. London: Penguin Books.

DeSombre, E.R. 2006. *Flagging Standards: Globalization and Environmental, Safety, and Labor Regulations at Sea*. London: MIT Press.

Dunning, J. 1993. *Multinational Enterprises in a Global Economy*. Workingham: Addison-Wesley.

Fiorito, J., and V.C. Gallagher. 2006. Renewal in the United Faculty of Florida: Class War in Paradise? *Labor Studies Journal* 31 (3): 39–64.

Gardner, B., M. Naim, B. Obando-Rojas, and S. Pettit. 2001. Maintaining the Maritime Skills Base: Does the Government Have a Realistic Strategy? *Maritime Policy and Management* 28 (4): 347–360.

Gekara, V.O. 2010a. Union Renewal Through Cross-Border Merger: Rationale, Processes and Challenges. *European Journal of Industrial Relations* 16 (4): 385–394.

———. 2010b. The Stamp of Neoliberalism on the UK Tonnage Tax and the Implications for British Seafaring. *Marine Policy* 34 (3): 487–494.

Gekara, V.O., I.L. Acejo, and H. Sampson. 2013. Re-Imagining Global Union Representation Under Globalisation: A Case of Seafaring Labour and the Nautilus International Cross-border Merger. *Global Labour Journal* 4 (3): 167–185.

Giddens, A. 2002. *Runaway World; How Globalisation is Reshaping Our Lives*. London: Profile Books.

Harvey, D. 2005. *A Brief History of Neoliberalism*. Oxford: OUP.

Held, D., A. McGrew, D. Goldblatt, and J. Perraton. 1999. *Global Transformations: Politics, Economics and Culture*. Cambridge: Polity Press.

Kahveci, E., and T. Nichols. 2006. *The Other Car Workers: Work, Organisation and Technology in the Maritime Car Carriers Industry*. Basingstoke: Macmillan.

Leggate, H., and McConville. 2005. Tonnage Tax: Is it Working? *Maritime Policy and Management* 32 (2): 177–186.

Lévesque, C., and G. Murray. 2006. How Do Unions Renew? Paths to Union Renewal. *Labour Studies Journal* 31 (3): 1–13.

Lillie, N. 2006. *A Global Union for Global Workers: Collective Bargaining and Regulatory Politics in Maritime Shipping*. London: Routledge.

McConville, J. 1999. The United Kingdom Shipping Industry and International Regulation. In *Transport Regulation Matters*, ed. J. McConville, 78–97. London: Pinter.

Metaxas, B.N. 1985. *Flags of Convenience: A Study of Internationalisation*. Aldershot: Gower.

Munck, R. 2002. *Globalisation and Labour: The New Great Transformation*. London: Zed Books Ltd.

Nautilus International Annual Reports (Various year 1974–2016), the British Certification Officer On-line., https://tinyurl.com/wgqeakw [24/11/2019]

Perraton, J. 2019. The Scope and Implications of Globalisation. In *The Handbook of Globalisation*, ed. J. Michie, 3rd ed., 50–96. Elgar Online.

Peters, J. 2008. Labour Market Deregulation and the Decline of Labour Power in North America and Western Europe. *Policy and Society* 27 (1): 83–98.

Sampson, H., and T. Schroeder. 2006. In the Wake of the Wave: Globalisation, Networks, and the Experiences of Transmigrant Seafarers in Northern Germany. *Global Networks* 6 (1): 61–80.

Scholte, J.A. 2000. *Globalisation: A Critical Introduction*. New York: Palgrave.

Stiglitz, J. 2002. *Globalisation and Its Discontents*. London: Penguin Books.
Strange, S. 1996. *The Retreat of the State: The Diffusion of Power in the World Economy*. Cambridge: Cambridge University Press.
Swenson, P. 2002. *Capitalists Against Markets. The Making of Labor Markets and Welfare States in the United States and Sweden*. New York: Oxford University Press.
Webster, E. 2015. *Labour After Globalisation: Old and New Sources of Power*. Institute of Social and Economic Research (ISER), Rhodes University. ISER Working Paper No. 2015/1
Western, B. 1997. *Between Class and Market: Postwar Unionization in the Capitalist Democracies*. Princeton, NJ: Princeton University Press.

Chapter 14
Trade Union Representation in the Philippines

Ralph Buiser

Introduction

This chapter discusses the various characteristics of maritime trade unions in the Philippines within the wider context of the history of the country's industrial relations and labour movement. The main historical focal points in the country's labour environment and how these shaped industrial relations today is introduced in the first section. In the second section the development of seafarers' representation in the country and the profile of their trade unions in the context of the country's labour history is discussed. The final section concludes with a discussion of the trends and challenges faced by unions representing Filipino seafarers today.

Philippine Industrial Relations: A Brief History

The history of the organisation of labour in the Philippines stretches back more than a century with the national union movement being formed as early as 1902. At this time the establishment of the *Union Obrera Democratica Filipina* (UODF) unified small-scale community-based workers' guilds *'gremios'* in Manila and its immediate environs (Carroll 1961). This was at the time when the country was transitioning from Spanish colonial rule to official American occupation and the labour movement in the decades that followed grew out of the nationalistic independence fervour of the times. Consequently labour unrest and organisation became a political concern prompting the colonial government to institutionalise the regulation of trade unions and their members. Despite this, unions and labour leaders grew in influence and

R. Buiser (✉)
University of Bristol, Bristol, UK
e-mail: ralph.buiser@bristol.ac.uk

V. O. Gekara, H. Sampson (eds.), *The World of the Seafarer*, WMU Studies in Maritime Affairs 9, https://doi.org/10.1007/978-3-030-49825-2_14

number and developed the collective aim of achieving national independence and self-governance. As a result there was a coalition of political party interests and those of union organisations. Subsequently, strong union leaders formed disparate union federations based on political ideologies and it is this fragmented nature of the labour movement which endures into the present day and could be said to account for much of the lack of progress made in the formation of a unified labour interest in the Philippines.

The early 1930s saw the beginnings of the Communist Party here and the socialist political movement that influenced the growth of communist-leaning trade unions in this country. The growing militant side of the labour movement prompted the new government to curtail its increasing membership by setting up the *Department of Labor* and the *Court of Industrial Relations* which in practice was used to identify union links to the militant movement and suppress strike action through a system of compulsory arbitration (Dejillas 1994). The hostility towards left-leaning trade unions continued up until the early 1950s, mitigated only by the *Industrial Peace Act* in 1953 that put an end to compulsory arbitration and paved the way to collective bargaining.

Collective bargaining agreements (CBAs) have since become the basis of labour relations and dispute management. By the early 1970s, unions had increased both in number and in influence. However, there was growing dissatisfaction with the enforcement of CBAs and ineffectual court decisions on labour conditions and wage determinations. This discontent was exacerbated by the failure of import substitution policies. Large-scale strikes resulted which disrupted major businesses and industrial progress. The state's response under the then President, Ferdinand Marcos, was to curtail union rights and freedoms, leading to the proclamation of Martial Law in 1972. The Marcos dictatorship would continue up until 1986 when the actions of various social movements culminated in the 1986 People Power Revolution that ushered in a democratic transition. The 1986 Constitution then established the basis for all political, economic, and social freedom in the country and its society (Table 14.1).

In 2015, there were 19,067 trade unions registered with the *Department of Labor and Employment* (PSA 2017). These had an estimated membership of 1.964 million workers. In these estimates, unionised workers in the Philippines in 2015 accounted for more than 5% of the total workforce. As a measure of real values, however Erickson et al. (2001) warn that union membership estimates by the Philippine government are based on self-reportage by unions and union federations—which, in order to project union power, are often largely overestimated. A more accurate depiction of the unionised workforce is the number of workers officially covered by CBAs, which the state has recorded since the early 1960s (Fig. 14.1).

Figure 14.1 shows that the highest number of CBA-covered workers was during the early 1990s (peaking at 1993 with 608,876 workers) which can be attributed to the positive structural and institutional changes made in line with democratisation project which started with the 1987 constitution (Abinales and Amoroso 2005).

Table 14.1 Distinct periods of industrial relations development in the Philippines

Period	General policy/ Period description	Period highlights	Latent political economic environment
Pre-1902	Feudal Economy	1870s–1890s—Workers' guilds or '*gremios*' emerge in Manila among 'printers, barbers, tobacco workers, and wood-workers' (Ramos 1978, p. 100)	Spanish colonial era establishes feudalistic ownership of land and labour enforced by Spanish governors, and the Filipino-Hispanic elite
1902–1908	Post-Hispanic beginnings	1902—establishment of the *Union Obrera Democratica Filipina* (UODF), unifying the *gremios* (see Carroll 1961) Union membership estimated to have reached the 20,000 mark and union leaders organise large-scale strikes (Ramos 1978)	Transition period from Spanish to American colonial rule Militancy of unions begins to emerge alongside the political independence movement of the times
1908–1935	Laissez Faire/ Union growth	1908—the American colonial government establishes the *Bureau of Labor* (Binghay 2007) entrenching elite interests over peasant groups 1930—Communist Party of the Philippines (PKP) is organised and is the nascent socialist movement in the early 1930s	Strong union leaders start to set up disparate union federations based on political ideology and merge with political parties Increasing civil strife and political unrest over American colonisers
1935–1952	Compulsory Arbitration/ Repressive state control	1936—Court of Industrial Relations is established, with jurisdiction over all labour disputes (Damaso 2001) Commonwealth Acts 103 and 213 imposes compulsory arbitration and compulsory registration of labor unions with the Department of Labor—which is used as a mechanism for supressing militant left-leaning labour movements (Dejillas 1994)	Commonwealth government is established giving Filipino elites greater political power Lack of meaningful reforms in the pre-war period (early 1940s); worsening political unrest among radical trade unions
1953–1972	Industrial Peace	1953—Magna Carta for Labor or the Industrial Peace Act is passed into law 1960s—Unprecedented increase in the number of strikes, losing man-days 'ranging from 523,000 in 1961 to 1.4 million to in 1972' (Ramos 1978), virtually disrupting economic activity on a national scale Number of registered unions rises from 836 in 1953 to 2522 in 1966 (Abinales and Amoroso 2005)	Collective bargaining is introduced together with the increasing influence of the International Labour Organization (ILO) (Damaso 2001) Post-war political climate now encourages union independence Ideological differences among union federations and their leaders prevails

(continued)

Table 14.1 (continued)

Period	General policy/ Period description	Period highlights	Latent political economic environment
1973–1986	Martial Law; Restricted labour movement	1972—Martial Law is declared by the Marcos administration 1974—*National Labor Relations Commission* and the *Overseas Employment Development Board* under a new *Labor Code* created to regulate both internal labour and emerging external migrant workers	Seeks to curtail freedoms of left-leaning organisations and restrict labour activities of trade unions and their federations (Abinales and Amoroso 2005) to prevent mass action and limit growth of communism
1986–1997	Tripartism and union growth	1986—Martial Law is lifted; new Philippine constitution is passed 1989—Act on voluntary arbitration 1994—Tripartite response to Structural Adjustment marks a consolidated effort of the state, representatives of the labour movement, and capital, to align its interests towards national economic growth	Late 1980s to early 1990s sees the early stages of democratic transition which guarantees state protection of freedoms of association, trade union rights, and voluntary arbitration (Damaso 2001) Tripartism, co-operation with government, unions, and businesses, is heavily promoted Unions put emphasis on legalism and minimum legal compliances of both workers and management but much less on collective bargaining negotiations
1997-present	Managing globalisation	1997 and 2008 Financial Crises	Since the late 1990s there has been a move towards neo-liberal policies promoted by the new democratic government policies (APL 2006) through alliance-building and social movement unionism (Ranald 1999; Aganon et al. 2008)

Currently however, the number of workers covered in CBAs is steadily declining and has done so since 2006. The dramatic drop in 2006 is seen as a culmination of two financial crises affecting the East Asian region. The country saw its export growth dropping to −16.2% and import growth rate to −13.3% in 2001 (Wang and Whalley 2010) which accompanied unprecedented job losses and the growth of the informal sector and the rise of labour flexibility in the formal sector (see for example, Bitonio 2012; Ofreneo 2013).

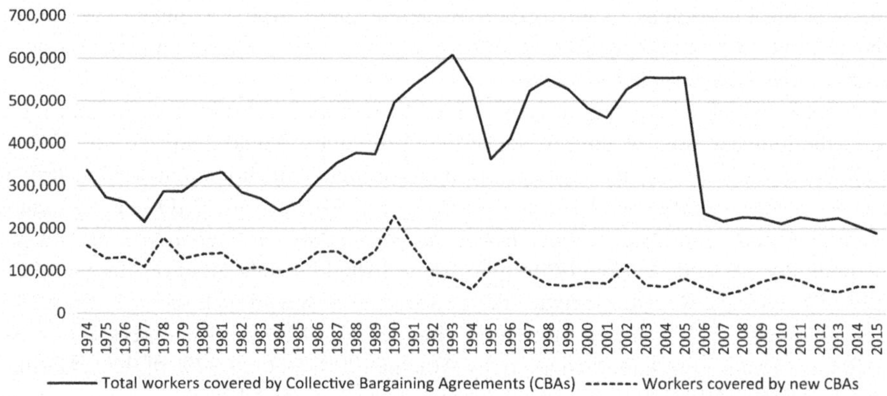

Fig. 14.1 Collective bargaining coverage in the Philippines. Adapted from: Philippine Statistics Authority (PSA) (2015, 2017)

Unionising Seafarers

The union movement among seafarers began to take shape during the *Industrial Peace* era. This was a time when unions and union federations from a wide range of industries in the Philippines began to grow in number and strength. During this period (early 1960s), two seafarer-led labour groups emerged focussing on the interests of workers employed on board foreign-flagged vessels. The Associated Marine Officers' Union of the Philippines (AMOUP) was established in 1960 by Captain Gregorio Oca, organising the marine officers within three major shipping companies and was centred in the port of Manila, one of the major ports in Asia-Pacific. On the ratings side, the Associated Seamen's Union of the Philippines (ASUP) was set up in the same year to organise unlicensed seafaring crew from the country. Issues surrounding unionism at the time revolved around low wages, compensation for occupational sickness, injury and death, and poor working conditions brought about by the emergence of open registries or flags of convenience (FOCs) where cheap unregulated labour in developing countries like the Philippines became an attractive source of manpower for the world's merchant fleet.

Growing concerns about the state of labour regulation and decent work on board ships gave rise to the increasing relevance of maritime trade unions on the home front. By 1970, the two Manila-based labour groups had merged to form the Associated Marine Officers and Seamen's Union of the Philippines (AMOSUP) under a conservative union federation namely the Philippine Transport Workers Organisation (PTWO).[1] Shortly afterwards, the union became the first maritime

[1]The union federation was founded by Roberto Oca Sr., kin of AMOUP founder Capt. Gregorio Oca. Today PTWO has evolved into the Philippine Trade and General Workers Organisation (PGTWO), one of the country's 135 union federations (in 2012) spanning unions from transport, services, manufacturing, textile, metal, paper, wood, food & beverage, and electronics industries.

union in the Philippines to be affiliated with the International Transport Workers' Federation (ITF)—the biggest most influential global union federation in the world's shipping and maritime labour sector.

A factor which proved significant in establishing a global minimum wage in the maritime industry was the emergence of the Philippines as a competitive supplier of seafarers to the world's ships outperforming traditional maritime countries in Europe and America. An additional factor was the ITF affiliation of AMOSUP and later other emergent maritime unions. Local statistical data on maritime trade union membership are irregular and oftentimes unpublished by state and non-state entities in the Philippines. Recent estimates derived from the Bureau of Labor and Employment Statistics (2013), suggest that more than a third of Filipino seafarers deployed in 2012 were unionised and in a study by Amante (2004), about 47% of the seafaring workforce in the Philippines were estimated to be unionised based on the study's survey using a randomised sample. This considerably exceeded union density as estimated in 2015 where out of the total workforce only about 5% were unionised (PSA 2017). The maritime sector is therefore a unique case when it comes to unionisation compared to the majority of industries in the country.

This high level of unionisation of workers may be partly attributed to the nature and structure of labour in a globalised industry. To a large extent it is shaped by flagging out and the ITF's 'Flags of Convenience' campaign. A diagram simplifying the unionisation of Filipino seafarers is depicted in Fig. 14.2. What may be identified here as one of the main determinants of whether seafarers will be unionised is the ship's status as an FOC vessel—which means they will be under strict regulation by the ITF through a global network of inspectors based in ports around the world. Under threat of collective action from seafarers' and dockers' unions in these ports, ships are pressured to meet minimum wage and labour conditions standards set by the ITF and the ILO (for a detailed discussion see Lillie 2006). These ports acting as 'choke points' along the industry's supply chain are crucial to the ITF's campaign to regulate the unregulated FOCs, according to the union's head of strategic research.[2]

It is within this globalised system that maritime unions in the Philippines operate. At present, there are six existing maritime trade unions in the Philippines representing seafarers who work on ocean-going ships (Table 14.2). These unions vary in size of membership, type of seafarers, union affiliations, services and benefits to its members, as well as size of their CBA portfolio (i.e. number of CBAs with ship owners).

AMOSUP The largest of these trade unions by far is the Associated Marine Officers' and Seamen's Union of the Philippines (AMOSUP). According to their own estimates, they had an active membership of more than 80,000 seafarers in 2010 (AMOSUP 2010). If this is an accurate depiction it suggests that AMOSUP members comprised about two-thirds of the total maritime trade union members in that year.

---

[2]Presentation by Dr Jeremy Anderson (28 March 2014), in the University of Westminster, London, UK, organised by the British Universities Industrial Relations Association (BUIRA).

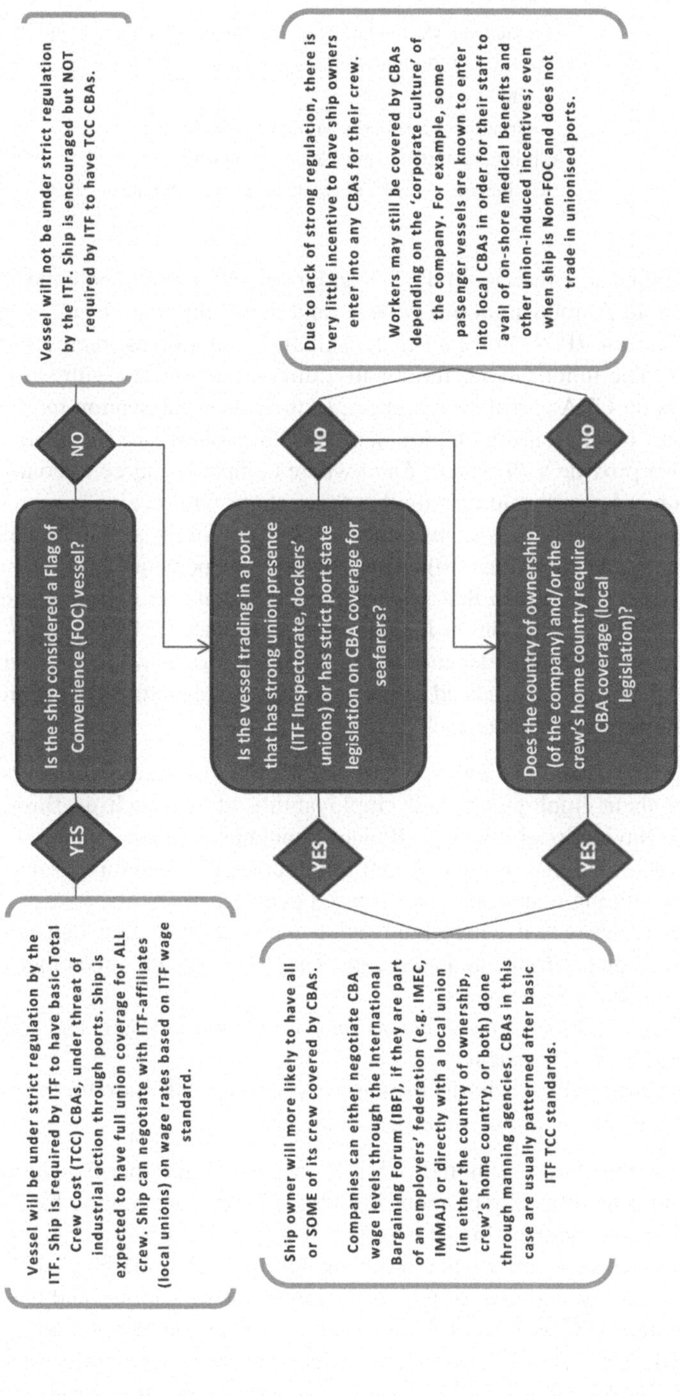

Fig. 14.2 Diagram of CBA coverage for Filipino seafarers

Table 14.2 List of maritime trade unions in the Philippines

Acronym	Trade Union Name
AMOSUP	Associated Marine Officers' and Seamen's Union of the Philippines
PSU	Associated Philippine Seafarers Union
UFS	United Filipino Seafarers
ISLA	International Seamen's Mutual Labor Association
POSU	Philippine Officers and Seamen's Union
MATEU	Mariners & Allied Transport Employees Union

It is also an affiliate and member of the ITF and maintains a seat in both the Overseas Workers' Welfare Administration (OWWA) and the Philippine Overseas Employment Administration (POEA) tripartite consultation committees, representing Filipino seafarers. The union, more importantly, directly negotiates with ship owners and companies on CBAs for their members. In their own publication in 2010, they report that apart from securing employment and 'fair wages' for members through CBAs they also provide a *Provident Fund* where companies agree to contribute an amount of money towards a lump sum that the seafarer will receive upon retiring at the age of 50 and also serves as an insurance mechanism for the seafarer member and their dependents (AMOSUP 2010). This serves as a pension fund that secures workers' retirement pay given that seafaring work is done on non-permanent contracts. Other services of the union include legal assistance, a *Welfare and Mutual Benefit Plan* for members and dependents, medical services as well as education and training. The union maintains a head office in Manila establishing adjacent properties for the benefit of their members such as:

(1) The *AMOSUP Training Center*, where members can attend short courses beneficial for their employment and employability at sea such as Basic Safety Training, Navigational Watch, Radar Simulator Course, General Tanker Familiarisation Course, Engine Room Simulator, Ship's Simulator and Bridge Teamwork, among many other skills based courses.
(2) The *Seamen's Hospital* where both union members and their dependants are given free medical service and medicine. They also operate three other regional hospitals for seafarer members.
(3) The *AMOSUP Sailors' Home* where they provide free board and lodging to official members in transient.
(4) The '*Slop Chest'* which is basically a grocery and supplies shop for the members and their dependents to purchase items on credit.

The Philippine Seafarers' Union (PSU) is the second largest maritime union in the Philippines with a membership of about 11,000 seafarers—accounting for 9% of the total maritime union membership. It was established in 1984 and is also an affiliate of the ITF. It is active in international labour discourse as a member of the Asian Seafarers' Summit (an initiative of the All Japan Seamen's Union), and the Norwegian/Asian Seafarers' Committee (NASCO) that is run in consultation with the ITF. Like AMOSUP, PSU (2013) reports that it has engaged successfully in securing CBAs for its members since 1984 as well as in delivering other services like the

Welfare Aid Program that provides medical and health aid/insurance benefits to members and free legal assistance.

Another maritime trade union operating nationally in the Philippines is the United Filipino Seafarers (UFS) that was established in 1994 and has since built a considerable membership of around 3000–4000 seafarers. It publishes a widely successful Filipino maritime newspaper *Tinig ng Marino* (Voice of the Mariner), circulated among the world's Filipino seafarers. The UFS engages in securing employment and CBAs for members and provides them with free employment-related legal assistance (UFS 2012). However, the union does not have well-established programmes like those of AMOSUP and PSU. Nonetheless, it does engage with lobbying, campaigning and social movement activities to push for seafarers' rights in national, and sometimes international, policymaking forums.

Similarly other seafarer trade unions, such as the International Seamen's Mutual Labor Association (ISLA), the Mariners and Allied Transport Employees Union (MATEU)—with a combined membership of around 15,000—engage in comparable social movement activities, although much of their work remains unreported and unpublished. Apart from these trade unions, there are also company-specific maritime trade unions that are estimated to have Filipino seafarer members numbering under 5000 workers.

Features of the Philippine Maritime Labour Movement

Cronyism

One of the main impediments to economic development has long been considered to be cronyism in Philippine state institutions, dating back to the Marcos administration (Kang 2003; Abinales and Amoroso 2005). Cronyism, a term referring to acts of favouritism and preferential bias based on kinship and close personal relationships, is endemic in Philippine politics and society and was borne out of its colonial heritage of drawing leaders and agents of the state from the powerful elite (Hutchcroft 1998). Such a feature of Philippine governance became firmly established during the Marcos administration (1965–1986) and was responsible for pushing the country into crippling debt (Wurfel 1988). Although the regime ended in 1986, propelling a nationwide democratisation project into the 1990s, crony capitalism has led to wide inequalities between the elite and poor. According to the World Bank (2015) income inequality between 2012 and 1988, with a GINI coefficient, was 40.8% in 1988 and 42.2% in 2012. Cronyism as a form of governance has permeated public and private institutions over the last half century, engendering widespread corruption in many ways and undermining the democratisation project in the Philippines, (see for example De Dios and Ferrer 2001).

Cronyism as a type of governance is apparent in the organisation of the maritime labour movement in the Philippines and is manifested among the more prominent maritime trade unions through the stranglehold of leadership by a select few. For instance, in its 60-year long history, the most prominent trade union in this sector, AMOSUP was instituted and led by a former seafarer Gregorio Oca up until his death in 2010. He was succeeded by his son, Conrado Oca, who whilst lacked seafaring experience, served in senior positions in the union and its affiliated organisations such as the Maritime Academy of Asia and the Pacific (MAAP) and the Seamen's Hospital in Manila (see AMOSUP 2016). Similar senior positions within the union and its affiliated organisations are held by Oca's immediate and extended family. Likewise, UFS and PSU, since their establishment in the late 1980s to the early 1990s, have been under the control of the same group of people for more than two decades.

Cronyism within the maritime labour movement is exacerbated by the virtual lack of democratic procedures within the unions. There is a complete absence of union elections despite some unions ostentatiously maintaining their commitment to democratic principles. For example in UFS' constitution and by-laws, the first aim of the union was to "To establish an effective, free and democratic trade union organization dedicated to the welfare of the workers" (UFS 2012). For these unions, however, the arbitrary appointment of a union president lies in a board of governors usually occupied by a close-knit group and supported by a similarly close-knit set of senior union management. In turn the appointment of cronies to senior union management, in the case of AMOSUP including its affiliated organisations, lies within the control and influence of the union president. Arguably cronyism in the maritime labour movement may be said to have been a key element in the continued strength and power of the industry as a whole without undue resistance. More generally, the lack of union democracy is argued by many unionists to make unions more efficient and create a less militant workforce, which is more agreeable to employers increasing job opportunities for Filipino seafarers. Nevertheless such an entrenched elite hampers the democratic processes within the unions since internal union democracy is 'likely to reduce chances for corruption' and build stronger, more participative membership' (Luce 2014). The result therefore in the case of the Philippine maritime labour sector is that of a passive union membership base led by crony leadership within the union organisation.

Servicing

Another common feature apparent across the Philippine maritime labour movement is its adoption of the servicing logic of action. Used in the context of trade unions strategy, Bacharach et al. (2001) define logics of action as frameworks of rationale informing union decisions with the aim of "legitimizing the union to its members, securing commitment of its members and attracting new members to the union" (p. 7). In this section I frame servicing as a form of union strategy whereby the union, working as a professionalised body is relied upon to translate members' interests into a set of services such as wage bargaining and the protection of members in employer disputes as well as providing other non-wage bargaining services to members in exchange for membership fees (Bacharach et al. 2001; de Turberville 2004). In the context of the Philippine maritime unions however, the adoption of the servicing logic goes only as far as the representation of members through centralised wage bargaining and the delivery of non-wage benefits to fee-paying members through a professionalised union organisation. What is unique in the Philippine case is that due to the way in which seafarers are employed with solely temporary contracts, unionising seafarers operates at a top-down level. That is to say the unions engage new employers into a collective bargaining agreement independent of the latter's employees. As such, seafarers when offered a contract by an employer with an existing collective bargaining agreement will automatically be required by employers to buy into a unionised contract. Seafarers therefore have very little agency over becoming fee-paying union members. Hence, the traditional rationale for servicing as an approach to attracting new individual workers may not fully apply in this case, what can apply however is that servicing can be seen as an approach to legitimise the union to its members.

In terms of centralised collective bargaining for members, ITF affiliated unions have the ability to negotiate at peak-level through the International Bargaining Forum (IBF) which brings to the bargaining table key global employers' organisations such as the International Maritime Employers' Committee (IMEC) and the International Mariners Management Association of Japan (IMMAJ) to negotiate an almost industry-wide pay scale in FOC ships (Lillie 2006). The result for union members of ITF affiliated maritime unions in the Philippines is a considerably higher base salary compared to those with non-CBA contracts and indeed compared to the minimum salaries prescribed by the POEA Standard Employment Contract. Arguably the positive pay differential is an incentive for workers to become union members.

More importantly in terms of legitimising the union to its members as a rationale for servicing, most prominent maritime unions in the Philippines are very advanced in terms of delivering non-wage services as we have seen earlier in this chapter. Services such as those offered by AMOSUP like free medical care through its seafarers' hospital, legal services, board and lodging, are mimicked by other unions, albeit on a smaller scale. Such non-wage benefits for union members are all geared towards justifying the union fees required from seafarers under CBA contracts.

Fragmentation

While there is a general trend among maritime trade unions in the Philippines to adopt a servicing logic to legitimise themselves to members, the ways in which they project themselves to advance seafarers' interests with the state and with capital is fragmented in approach. Generally, the union movement in this case adopts two competing approaches to advance workers' welfare in regulatory bodies, *co-operative* and *adversarial*. A co-operative union approach in this case refers to unions' involvement with multi-party discussions with state agencies and employer representatives to meet worker and employer interests. An adversarial union approach refers to unions' involvement in more militant ways to advance purely workers' interests.

The most prominent maritime trade unions in the Philippines are indeed divided between these two approaches. Whilst AMOSUP, PSU and to some extent ISLA adopt a more co-operative approach, UFS adopts a somewhat adversarial approach. Co-operative unions tend to be active in participating in committees on key sectoral issues with state agencies and employers' representatives to create dialogue and co-operation among the different stakeholders within the maritime labour industry. In 2011 for example, the Department of Labor and Employment (DOLE) established the Maritime Industry Tripartite Council (MITC) as a policy-consulting group consisting of maritime unions such as AMOSUP, ISLA, and PSU and employers' associations like the Filipino Association for Mariners' Employment (FAME) and the Filipino Shipowners' Association (FSA). MITC was instituted with the aim of developing new policies to advance maritime employment and enhance the welfare of Filipino seafarers and port workers (DOLE 2011). In particular it aims to co-opt key stakeholders from capital, labour and the state, in policymaking for the domestic and international maritime sector, as well as domestic port labour, such as the drafting and enactment of the *Rules and Regulations Governing the Employment and Working Conditions of Seafarers Onboard Ships Engaged in Domestic Shipping* in 2013 (DOLE 2013). In addition it responds to current issues requiring multi-sectoral attention. For example in January 2018 there was an MITC consultative meeting on the sinking of the MERCRAFT three passenger vessel in 2016 which was due to alleged shortcomings within government regulatory bodies (see Andes 2018). While independent assessments have yet to be made in relation to the impact of the MITC and other dialogue bodies within which maritime unions engage, in terms of enforcement, the policymaking function of such bodies is to a certain extent producing results.

For other maritime unions, advancing the welfare of maritime workers is done using a more adversarial approach. Some unions believe that a co-operative approach dilutes the ability of unions to fully represent workers' interests in the public sphere. The adversarial approach includes the mobilisation of union members to protest and express dissatisfaction towards government bodies as well as by means of legal recourse against individual government officials. In 2015 for example, UFS reports the holding of mass protests involving over 2000 seafarers including their families and other labour groups over a series of alleged malpractices within the Maritime Industry Authority (MARINA). Similarly in 2017, UFS filed individual graft charges to current and former MARINA officials in the Office of the Ombudsman pertaining to the "alleged arrogation of authority in the implementation of [the Executive Order 909, Series 2010] giving incentives in the use of brand new vessels" (Nonato 2017). Neither example however is unique and is in fact routine behaviour for UFS forming part of its overall strategy in representing workers and seafarers in general. In a self-published article by the UFS (2015), it proclaims that the "union never tire of calling on MARINA's doors to carry out what is right and just on behalf of Filipino seafarers".

Conclusion

Maritime trade unions in the Philippines are a reflection of traditional Philippine governance and are enduring institutions within an increasingly neo-liberal environment. There has been a decline in unionisation in the Philippines but the ways in which maritime unions have structured themselves have enabled them to break free from the narrative of union decline. One reason is that unions enjoy a large pool of labour in an industry where there is a high global demand for such labour. Consequently within this pool, unions are able to gain a strong base for membership in terms of volume. Another reason is that although this large pool of labour consists of temporary contract workers, unions here benefit from the ITF being a global union federation. FOC shipowners are forced to collectively bargain with a national union thus ensuring local ITF affiliates maintain their membership. A third reason is that unions are able to justify their role to members by adopting a servicing logic, thus benefiting members beyond wage bargaining.

Nevertheless there are several challenges to the continuing development of these maritime unions. First, unions are circumscribed by the entrenched system of cronyism which impinges on the ways in which their large membership is governed. A select few, with vested interests, prevent the implementation of democratic values within the union organisation. It could be argued that a passive membership is being engendered because members are not empowered to elect their leaders or to direct the activities of the union. An elite minority identifies and formulates union strategy and direction whilst neglecting to consider the interests and views of its members. Secondly, while the unions' adoption of the servicing logic helps them in legitimising their role among fee-paying members, they fail to represent workers' interests at the workplace level. Finally, while some unions have been able to advance workers' agendas, fragmentation among the major trade unions over the approach to adopt creates problems in delivering this agenda. For example, ITF affiliated unions tend to be more co-operative in their approach and work with the state and capital to strike a balance between the interests of workers and interests of employers in policymaking. In contrast, unions that are independent of ITF affiliation tend to reject a co-operative approach and adopt a more adversarial one by favouring mass mobilisation of members. In some cases they pursue legal cases against government agencies to increase pressure on policymakers to recognise workers' interests in many aspects of maritime regulation.

References

Abinales, P., and D. Amoroso. 2005. *State and Society in the Philippines*. Lanham: Rowman & Littlefield Publishers Inc.

Aganon, M., et al. 2008. *Revitalizing Philippine Unions: Potentials and Constraints to Social Movement Unionism*. Manila: Fridrich Ebert Stiftung and the University of the Philippines School of Labor and Industrial Relations.

Amante, M. 2004. Industrial Democracy in the Rough Seas: Case of Philippine Seafarers. In *Industrial Democracy Symposium*, ed. M. Amante. San Diego: Industrial Relations Research Association.

AMOSUP. 2010. *Looking Back, Sailing Forward 1960–2010*. Manila: Associated Marine Officers' and Seafarers Union of the Philippines.

———. 2016. *News & Updates. Passing of the Torch*. Manila, Philippines. Retrieved 24 November 2019 from http://amosup.org/news&updates/the-passing-of-the-torch/.

Andes, S. 2018, February 12. *DOLE tackles key maritime industry issues*. Retrieved 24 November 2019 from http://globalnation.inquirer.net/164098/dole-tackles-key-maritime-industry-issues.

APL. 2006. *Fighting Back with Social Movement Unionism*. Manila: Alliance of Progressive Labor.

Bacharach, S.B., P. Bamberger, and W.J. Sonnenstuhl. 2001. *Mutual Aid and Union Renewal: Cycles of Logics of Action*. Ithaca: Cornell University Press.

Binghay, V. 2007. *Trade Unions Today*. Antipolo City: VCB Research and Publications.

Bitonio, B.E.R. 2012. *Industrial Relations and Collective Bargaining in the Philippines (No. 994706933402676)*. Geneva: International Labour Organization.

Bureau of Labor and Employment Statistics. 2013. 2013 Yearbook of Labor Statistics. In *Department of Labour and Employment*, ed. Manila, Philippines.

Carroll, J.J. 1961. Philippine Labor Unions. *Philippine Studies* 9 (2): 220–254.

Damaso, J.M. 2001. Industrial Relations and Increasing Globalization: Case Study of the Philippines. In *Industrial Relations and Increasing Globalization in Selected Countries*, ed. N. Suzuki. Singapore: International Confederation of Free Trade Unions - Asian and Pacific Regional Organisation.

De Dios, E.S., and R.D. Ferrer. 2001. Corruption in the Philippines: Framework and Context. *Public Policy* 5 (1): 1–42.

de Turberville, S.R. 2004. Does the 'Organizing Model' Represent a Credible Union Renewal Strategy? *Work, Employment and Society* 18 (4): 775–794.

Dejillas, L. 1994. *Trade Union Behavior in the Philippines 1946–1990*. Manila: Ateneo de Manila University Press.

DOLE, Department of Labor and Employment. 2011, October 17. Press Release Archive. Tripartite partners push decent work for seafarers manning domestic shipping The Official Gazette. Manila, Philippines. Retrieved 24 November 2019 from https://www.officialgazette.gov.ph/2011/10/17/tripartite-partners-push-decent-work-for-seafarers-manning-domestic-shipping/.

DOLE, Department of Labor and Employment. 2013. *Department Order No. 129-13 Rules and Regulations Governing the Employment and Working Conditions of Seafarers Onboard Ships Engaged in Domestic Shipping*. Manila: Department of Labor and Employment. Retreived 29 November 2019 from https://www.dole.gov.ph/news/department-order-no-129-13-rules-and-regulations-governing-the-employment-and-working-conditions-of-seafarers-onboard-ships-engaged-in-domestic-shipping/.

Erickson, C., et al. 2001. *Recent Developments in Employment Relations in the Philippines*. Ithaca: Cornell University: School of Industrial and Labor Relations.

Hutchcroft, P.D. 1998. *Booty Capitalism: The Politics of Banking in the Philippines*. Ithaca: Cornell University Press.

Kang, D.C. 2003. Transaction Costs and Crony Capitalism in East Asia. *Comparative Politics*: 439–458.

Lillie, N. 2006. *A Global Union for Global Workers: Collective Bargaining and Regulatory Politics in Maritime Shipping*. London: Routledge.

Luce, S. 2014. *Labour Movements, Global Perspectives*. Cambridge: Polity Press.
Nonato, V. 2017, May 17. *Seamen's group files graft case versus Marina officials*. Retrieved 25 November 2019 from http://newsinfo.inquirer.net/900929/seamens-group-files-graft-case-versus-marina-officials.
Ofreneo, R.E. 2013. Precarious Philippines: Expanding Informal Sector, "Flexibilizing" Labor Market. *American Behavioral Scientist* 57 (4): 420–443.
PSA, Philippine Statistics Authority. 2015. *2015 Yearbook of Labor Statistics*. Manila: Philippine Statistics Authority.
———. 2017. *2017 Compilation of Industry Statistics on Labor and Employment*. Manila: Philippine Statistics Authority.
PSU, Philippine Seafarers Union. 2013. Services to the seafarers and to the nation. Retrieved 24 November 2019 from http://www.psu.org.ph.
Ramos, E. 1978. Trade Unions and Filipino Society. In *The Role of Trade Unions in Developing Societies*, ed. E. Kassalow and U. Damachi, 99–122. Geneva: International Institute for Labour Studies.
Ranald, P. 1999. Analysing, Organising, Resisting: Union Responses to the Asian Economic Crisis in East Asia, South Korea, and the Philippines. *Journal of Industrial Relations* 41 (2): 295–325.
UFS, United Filipino Seafarers. 2012. *Constitution and By-Laws*. Retrieved on 24 November 2019 from http://unitedfilipinoseafarers.com.ph/constitutionn-and-by-laws/.
———. 2015. *UFS conducts mass protest against MARINA*. Retrieved on 25 November 2019 from http://unitedfilipinoseafarers.ph/ufs-conducted-mass-protest-against-marina/.
Wang, J., and J. Whalley. 2010. The Trade Performance of Asian Economies During and Following the 2008 Financial Crisis. In *The Economies of China and India Cooperation and Conflict: Volume 1: China and India—The International Context and Economic Growth, Manufacturing Performance and Rural Development*, 143–173. Singapore: World Scientific.
World Bank. 2015. Data. Washington, D.C. Retrieved 24 November 2019 from https://data.worldbank.org/indicator/SI.POV.GINI?end=2015&locations=PH&start=2015&view=map.
Wurfel, D. 1988. *Filipino Politics: Development and Decay*. Ithaca: Cornell University Press.

Chapter 15
On-Line Support Groups for Families in China

Lijun Tang

Introduction

Seafarer-partners, which in this chapter refers to seafarers' wives or girlfriends, face a number of problems in everyday life. The first and major one is long-term and intermittent separation between seafaring couples. During the separation period, which can be up to 1 year, seafarer-partners lose their intimate companions temporarily and are likely to suffer loneliness (Tang 2007; Thomas 2003). Furthermore, despite advanced modern communication technologies, the communication between the ship and the shore is neither convenient nor cheap (Sampson et al. 2018; Thomas 2003; Thomas et al. 2003; Wu et al. 2007). Another problem seafarer-partners face is social isolation. They feel that non-seafaring people are not able to appreciate their experiences and concerns, and for this reason seafarer-partners are likely to set themselves apart from people not linked to seafaring (Tang and Chen 2017; Thomas 2003). In the era of the planned economy, state owned (shipping) companies in China took 'total' care of their employees in the sense that they were responsible for their employees' medical care, pension, and housing for a lifetime. These companies built seafarer villages—residential blocks—in the local port cities and allocated them to their employees. Those seafarers who did not live in the cities where their companies were located might be eligible for a one-off housing subsidy to buy a house locally. In practice obtaining a house or housing subsidy from companies was not easy and the waiting lists were usually long. With the reform of the economy, state companies gradually shed the function of housing their employees with the result that by the end of the twentieth century, seafarers working for state owned companies could no longer expect to be allocated a house and turned to the open estate market (Wu et al. 2007). In addition the transformation from a planned

L. Tang (✉)
University of Plymouth, Plymouth Business School, Plymouth, UK
e-mail: Lijun.tang@plymouth.ac.uk

V. O. Gekara, H. Sampson (eds.), *The World of the Seafarer*, WMU Studies in Maritime Affairs 9, https://doi.org/10.1007/978-3-030-49825-2_15

economy to a market one has encouraged the establishment of many non-state or non-local-government owned shipping companies whose employees also need to buy their own houses. As a result, most contemporary Chinese seafaring families live separately from each other rather than clustered as before in 'seafarer villages'. The issues identified above, mean that although seafarer-partners may wish to meet with, and share their concerns and experiences with, 'similar others' (Tang and Chen 2017; Thomas 2003) they are likely to be geographically dispersed and isolated.

In 2003, a seafarer set up a website called *Home of Chinese Seafarers* (HCS). The website provided a platform for Chinese seafarer-partners to share their experiences and concerns and to facilitate mutual support. This chapter aims to reveal some of the problems they experienced and discussed on the website, it examines the ways in which they helped each other to cope with these problems and discusses what encouraged them to do so online.

In order to grasp seafarer-partners' online experiences in more detail, I spent over 2 years observing their interaction on the website. During this period, I logged onto the website almost daily to view activity, taking notes of, and analysing, seafarer-partners' postings. To complement the observational data, I interviewed 30 seafarer-partner participants from different parts of China. Among the 30 respondents, 29 had received, or were receiving, higher education; 25 were below the age of 30; and 11 were married. According to my observations, the profile of the interviewees reflected the general population of seafarer-partner participants on the website—relatively young, well-educated and living in cities.

Sharing and Managing Problems on the Website

According to Baumeister and Leary (1995), intimate relationships entail frequent and affectively pleasant interactions between the involved parties within a stable and enduring context of concern and caring. Seafaring couples, however, are often deprived of frequent interaction by separation. Even long distance communication is not available most of the time (Ellis et al. 2012; Sampson et al. 2018). Without frequent and caring interaction, couples are likely to suffer from loneliness and distress (Tang 2012). Perhaps more importantly, tensions may arise because a couple cannot provide one another with the necessary support they require, either emotionally or physically, due to the separation.

In this context, the interview data indicated that seafarer-partners liked to share these problems on the website and helped each other to manage them. One informant revealed:

> I like to initiate, and respond to postings regarding emotions, for example, when seafarers' relations with their lovers meet problems, when some people are not confident about their relationships in the separation period, etc. These emotions and feelings are very similar to mine. I feel empathy with them. I will try my best to comfort them, to encourage them, and to support them.

In order to illustrate further, I use three discussion threads below to show how they 'comfort', 'encourage' and 'support' each other. The first one was written by Bluesky who was experiencing difficult times while her boyfriend was at sea:

> Example A: I have thought it over and over again. Maybe we should terminate the relationship, because I cannot sustain it any longer. I have not recovered from the illness... I just knew from a phone-call today that my father got injured in work and my brother has also been injured in the school. My mother has to take care of the shop, my father and brother alone, since I am not well and not together with them either. I feel so bad and useless....

The second seafarer-partner, Lotus, revealed her frustration caused by her parents' objection of her relationship with a seafarer. She wrote:

> Example B: Several days ago when my parents knew that I was still in a relationship with my boyfriend, they admonished me. They are not happy with his job and family and are forcing me to terminate the relationship. What should I do? Please give me some suggestions!

The third posting was made by Lily, who was not entirely sure about whether her boyfriend loved her or not:

> Example C: Having seen that most sisters' lovers here are working in the deep sea fleet, I used to feel fortunate that I could keep in touch with him through messages and phone-calls... After he left, I make use of every little spare time to send messages to him. Gradually, sending messages becomes the main theme of my life and it is my source of happiness.... But he always replies me at the ratio of 1:3. This hurts me. I warned him several times. But after only few days, he would be back to his former attitude. This time I feel that I have had enough.... I sent him a message: Since it continues like this, we'd better break up....

These three postings clearly indicate a sense of frustration. It is suggested that bad feelings signal a gap between the perceived reality and tacitly held expectations (Hochschild 1983; Tang 2009; Turner and Stets 2006). Bluesky's (example A) bad feelings can be regarded as resulting from those unexpected and unfortunate events that she described. In example B, it could be argued that Lotus possibly expected that her parents would support her but this was not the case. While in example C, apparently, Lily hoped very much for reciprocation from her boyfriend only to be disappointed by his failure.

By revealing their problems in a public forum, the three seafarer-partners invited others, either explicitly or implicitly, to help them manage these emotional tensions and to provide support. Fifteen seafarer-partners replied to Bluesky's posting, eleven to Lotus, and another fifteen to Lily. In those replies, the seafarer-partners did what Hochschild (1983) terms as 'emotion work' to help the initiators. An analysis of the replies suggested several strategies involved in the emotion work on the HCS website, although the boundaries between these strategies are not clear-cut. To avoid repetition, I only use some representative replies to illustrate these tactics.

The first one is *acknowledgement that it is not easy to be a seafarer-partner*. To posting A, one replied:

A1[1]: Seafarer-partners do sacrifice a lot, especially in difficult times. I hope that together with your friends you can overcome the current problems. Problems are always fleeting.

One participant answered to posting B:

B1: There are lots of problems in our way. I think the best way forward for both of us and our parents is to move and change our parents, and to make them understand and support our choice. Maybe by that time, I think we will be the happiest persons in the world.

Both respondents first acknowledged the difficulties of being a seafarer-partner. By doing so, on the one hand, they offered sympathy and understanding; on the other, they suggested implicitly that hard times were common for seafarer-partners and thus *normalised* the problems. Acknowledgement, however, did not seem enough, since it did not give any practical suggestions to help solve the problems. Therefore, A1 went on to *encourage* Bluesky to overcome the problem; and B1 offered *advice*.

The second strategy of providing help is *encouragement to the frustrated to be strong*, as shown in A1. Another two also offered encouragement to Bluesky:

A2: Do not feel too sad. Things will be going better. Believe yourself, believe your love!

A3: The suffering will be over soon. The sun will come out after the rain.

One seafarer-partner replied to Lotus urging continuance:

B2: If you love each other, do not give up! I give you my best wishes and may you be happy forever!

By replying to different postings, all three seafarer-partners encouraged the initiators to overcome their difficult times: hold on to your love, do not give up; although there are problems, they are fleeting; happiness lies just ahead! Thus, the encouragement also served, on the one hand, to *play down* difficulties, since the latter were regarded as fleeting; on the other, to offer hope—suffering will end soon. These encouraging words arguably provided some strength and confidence to the initiators to tide them over the hard times.

The third type of response is a *reframing of the situation* for the initiators. For example:

A4: This is just your temporary feeling. In fact, you are blaming him, since so many things have happened but he is not with you! I can understand your feeling, for this happened to me before. In fact, you do not really want to terminate the relationship. Think twice and have confidence in yourself and him. Do not let yourself feel regret in the future.

This replier started her response by *playing down* the situation—it was temporary and thus was not as serious as the initiator had thought. Following that, she *reframed* the situation for the initiator. In this seafarer-partner's view, Bluesky was blaming, rather than intending to break up with, her boyfriend and therefore the action of terminating the relationship should not be taken; otherwise, it would be costly. The

[1]A1 indicates the first quoted reply to posting example A. The same pattern is used afterward, such as B1, A3, and C4, for easy reference.

fact that 'this has happened to me' justified her competence in doing this on the one hand, and *normalised* the situation for Bluesky on the other—you are not the only one and many of us have experienced this problem. In the end, this replying seafarer-partner served the purpose of *encouraging* Bluesky to 'have confidence' and offered *advice*—'think twice' and 'do not let yourself feel regret'. The reframing strategy was widely used in replies to posting C:

C1: Do not mind this too much. In the past, we could only expect letters, which take several months. How fortunate now we are that we have mobiles! On board the ship, he cannot carry the mobile everywhere. He cannot receive your messages on time. Even if he can, he may not be able to reply to you immediately since he has got job to do. Moreover, not the whole coastal sea is covered by a network service. Some areas are not covered at all.. . .

C2: Many times, our environments and moods are not synchronised.. . . When you are full of passion, maybe he is busy with working; when you are sleeping, maybe he becomes passionate.. . . We are all different. Especially with those in distance relationships, synchronisation is very difficult.

C3: In the past, I also used to hasten my husband to reply to my messages. Only after I visited his ship did I realise how hard and tiresome his job is. There are always reasons for not responding to messages. Do not take it seriously.

C4: All men are careless. My partner only replies to me once after receiving one hundred of messages from me.. . .

These replies reframed and reinterpreted the situation from different perspectives. C1 first *downplayed* the problem: compared with the past, you are in a better position and should feel satisfied. Then the replier continued to give two possible reasons to justify the failure of Lily's boyfriend: either he was working or there was no network coverage. C2 offered another reason—tempo-spatial dislocation and asynchronization. Based on her own experience, the third replier believed that seafarers had to work hard and therefore did not have much energy left for messaging. The first three replies also gave Lily a sense of what could be happening at sea. The last one generalised men's 'nature' and suggested that it was 'natural' for men not to reciprocate women's intimacy.

Reframing, as indicated by the examples, was at the same time *normalising*. It served to convince initiators that the situations were widely experienced and normal and therefore there was no need to feel unhappy or distressed. Playing down and normalising the situation, arguably, would change the initiators' perception of reality and thus reduce the difference between the expectation and the perception.

Reframing also helped frustrated seafarer-partners to make sense of what was happening to them. The initiators' bad experiences disrupted their lives and made them feel insecure about themselves and their relationships. In a sense, they felt a loss of control. Others' reinterpretations threw a positive light on the situations and thus helped the initiators to understand things in a less threatening way. Orgad's (2004a, b) study of breast cancer patients' web-pages and online help groups suggests that their sharing of illness experiences and the knowledge gained from this served to empower patients in the sense that they were able to make sense of, and manage, the threat and disruption that cancer posed to their routine everyday lives.

Similarly, reframing on the HCS seemed to make it easier for distressed seafarer-partners to reflect more upon, and to better manage, their disrupted lives and to regain a sense of security and control. Maybe for this reason, Lily came back to the thread and thanked others for their support.

The final support strategy which was identified was *offering advice*, which as indicated earlier, was sometimes intertwined with other forms of tactics. Here, I show more examples:

> **B3**: Try your best to get your parents' consent. When you become a seafarer's wife, you will be home alone for a long period of time, during which you will need your parents' support.

> **B4**: If you are deep in love with each other, and if you are really prepared for the future difficulties of being a SP, take action to change your parents' attitude.

> **C5**: Do not hold it too tight. Learn to release it a bit sometimes. Like chocolate, it melts if you hold it too tight.

B3 not only gave a suggestion, but also pointed out the implication of not acquiring consent from parents. B4 advised Lotus to transform her parents' attitude. Although the two suggestions were a bit different, the aim was the same—try to change the parents. Based upon her understanding of love, C5 offered her advice to Lily: give your boyfriend some freedom. These suggestions, arguably, helped the initiators to take informed actions.

The four strategies, as shown above, served to downplay and normalise problems, throw positive light on negative experiences, and offer hope and advice to seafarer-partners in distress. As such, they contributed to alleviating tensions for seafarer-partners and nurturing their well-being. Mermaid, a seafarer's girlfriend aged 24, for example, said in the interview:

> I feel that... since he is not home, there is a kind of longing. I want very much to talk to other seafarer-partners about my situation, the problems I experienced in work and everyday life, and my pressure. Then they would reply to me... some of them give me advice, which I feel gives me guidance in life. Their replies also help to remove some of my pressure [stress].

Nurturing Seafaring Relationships

The 'emotion work' performed on the HCS website between seafarer-partners is not new. Previous research revealed that friendship between women could allow them to share marital problems, reveal emotional vulnerabilities, and provide mutual support (Jerrome 1984; Oliker 1989). Oliker (1989), for example, in a study of friendship among a group of married American women, noted that through friendship, these women disclosed marital problems and helped each other to diffuse these problems and to sustain the marriage through emotion work. As such, it is argued that women's friendship provides a safety valve, serving to discharge their discontent with, and strengthen their commitments to, marriages (Jerrome 1984; Oliker 1989).

The 'emotion work' on the website, however, was not performed face-to-face. Furthermore, it might be between anonymous strangers rather than friends.

Nevertheless, it similarly had a positive impact on couple-relationships. Firstly, it diffused seafarer-partners' dissatisfaction with the relationship. Snow, a seafarer's girlfriend in her mid-twenties, stated in the interview:

> It makes my mind more at peace. Having read others' experiences, I feel that life should be like this. In the past, before I came to this website, I did not know how hard and tiresome his work is. I felt that he should make a phone call to me immediately once his ship was moored to a wharf. Otherwise, I would be very angry. Now I know that their job is hard and busy.

Thus, Snow's anger and disappointment at her boyfriend's failure to answer her phone-calls was abated. This seems to have been achieved because, after advice from others, Snow started to see the situation differently—the failure was not because her boyfriend did not care about her but because he was too busy and had little time outside of work. Online observation revealed that several seafarer-partner participants revealed, on the website, that reading others' postings helped them to change the negative feelings created by their partners' failures or faults in 'doing intimacy'.

Secondly, the nurturance serves to foster seafarer-partners' commitment to the relationship as illustrated in the following interview extract:

> Interviewer: In which respect(s) do you think this website gives you help?
> Breeze: I feel mainly in the respect of the relationship with my boyfriend.
> Interviewer: How does it help in this respect?
> Breeze: When I cannot see any hope, many people give me support and encourage me to stand firm. (Interview with Breeze, a 27 year old seafarer-partner)

As a result, the mutual support on the website helped seafarer-partners to release and alleviate emotional tensions, to reduce dissatisfaction and discontent with partners and to sustain and foster commitment to the relationships.

This does not mean, however, that seafarer-partners always nurture couple-relationships on the HCS. When they sense from a posting that the relationship has already broken down or mutual love does not exist anymore, for example, if one party has formed another relationship, seafarer-partners encouraged the posting initiator to move on and wished her good luck in the future.

A Specialised Community

We have seen that seafarer-partners were willing to share their emotional problems and provide support to each other on the HCS, even though they might be strangers. What made and encouraged them to do so?

For seafarer-partners, the HCS can be seen as a 'specialised community' (Wellman 2001). It is 'specialised', because community members tend to relate to each other through narrowly defined but shared interests or identities. This 'specialised' nature makes it easy for members to empathise and identify with each other (Bernardi 2016; Parr and Davidson 2008). Empathy encourages not only disclosure but also mutual support (Bernardi 2016; Wallace 1999).

This specialised community provided a vital space for seafarer-partners to talk about their problems. Such a space was not available offline for most seafarer-partners as they lived far apart and they felt that their non-seafaring friends could not appreciate their situation. One seafarer-partner explained:

> They [non-seafaring friends] have little idea about seafarers; they cannot empathise with seafarer-partners' feelings! Even though we talk, the conversations can never go as deep as I wish. Moreover, there are many things that they do not understand.

Similarly, another seafarer-partner, Yangtze-Girl, indicated that in real life she had difficulty in finding an opportunity to share her negative feelings with others and therefore she had to bear them alone:

> In real life, I bear it alone! It is quite natural that my family members are not happy with my choosing of a seafarer. If taking this and that kind of unhappiness into consideration, probably, he and I would not come together today [if I complain to my parents]! Therefore, I can only shoulder pressures in work and unhappiness in real life alone!

By contrast, Yangtze-Girl seemed to feel 'at home' on the website, as she stated:

> Since I entered the HCS, I discovered sisters who, like me, are waiting. Probably, sea and seafarers draw us very near; there is nothing to hide! I discovered that they also experienced what I did and we encourage each other. We are like sisters, family members!

It was common that seafarer-partners called each other 'sisters'. They likened the HCS to their parents' homes where they could always find support. Another seafarer-partner wrote on the website:

> The HCS is our warm home. Here we should comfort each other, encourage each other, and support each other.

Therefore, there was a strong sense of solidarity and closeness among seafarer-partners in this community due to their shared experience and identity, even though they were physically far away from each other. This sense of closeness further encouraged them to reveal problems and provide mutual support.

Conclusion

This chapter has revealed some problems that seafarer-partners are likely to face due to consecutive long-term separations. It demonstrates how seafarers' partners find it difficult to talk about these problems with their non-seafaring friends and family members even though they are physically close to them. In this context, the virtual and 'distant' HCS provided them with a valuable space to talk about problems and to both offer and receive support. Despite the physical distances between forum members they felt closely connected to each other on the HCS because they were all seafarer-partners and had similar concerns and experiences. The chapter reveals the ways in which such on-line forums may offer, essential, largely unseen, informal, support to seafarers by serving to protect their very vulnerable relationships in their absence.

References

Baumeister, R.F., and M.R. Leary. 1995. The Need to Belong: Desire for Interpersonal Attachment as a Fundamental Human Motivation. *Psychological Bulletin* 117: 497–529.

Bernardi, R. 2016. *How Do Online Communities of Patients Aggregate on Twitter? An Affordance Perspective. The International Conference on Information Systems*. Dublin: ICIS.

Ellis, N., H. Sampson, I. Acejo, L. Tang, N. Turgo, and Z. Zhao. 2012. *Seafarer Accommodation on Contemporary Cargo Ships*. Cardiff: SIRC Publication, December, ISBN: 1-900174-43-X.

Hochschild, A.R. 1983. *The Managed Heart: Commercialization of Human Feeling*. London: University of California Press.

Jerrome, D. 1984. Good Company: The Sociological Implications of Friendship. *Sociological Review* 32 (3): 696–718.

Oliker, S.J. 1989. *Best Friends and Marriage: Exchange Among Women*. Berkeley: University of California Press.

Orgad, S. 2004a. Just Do It! The Online Communication of Breast Cancer as a Practice of Empowerment. In *Internet Researcher Annual: Selected Papers from the Association of Internet Researchers Conferences 2000–2002, Volume 1*, ed. M. Consalvo, N. Baym, J. Hunsinger, K.B. Jensen, J. Logie, M. Murero, and L.R. Shade. New York: Peter Lang Publishing.

———. 2004b. Help Yourself: The World Wide Web as a Self-Help Agora. In *Web. Studies*, ed. D. Gauntlett and R. Horsley, 2nd ed. London: Arnold.

Parr, H., and J. Davidson. 2008. "Virtual Trust": On-Line Emotional Intimacies in Mental Health Support. In *Trust*, ed. J. Brownlie, A. Greene, and A. Howson. London: Routledge.

Sampson, H., N. Ellis, I. Acejo, N. Turgo, and L. Tang. 2018. *The Working and Living Conditions of Seafarer on Cargo Ships in the Period 2011–2017*. Cardiff: SIRC Publication, October, ISBN: 1-900174-50-2.

Tang, L. 2007. The "Presence" of the Absent Seafarers: Predicaments of Seafarer-Partners. In *SIRC Symposium 2007*. Cardiff: Cardiff University, July.

———. 2009. Shaping Feelings in Cyberspace: The Case of Chinese Seafarer-Partners. *Emotion, Space and Society* 2 (2): 104–110.

———. 2012. Waiting Together: Seafarer-Partners in Cyberspace. *Time and Society* 21 (2): 223–240.

Tang, L., and G. Chen. 2017. Costs and Benefits of Mobility: The Case of Chinese Seafarers. In *Maritime Mobilities*, ed. J. Monios and G. Wilmseier. London: CRC Press.

Thomas, M. 2003. *Lost at Sea and Lost at Home: The Predicament of Seafaring Families*. Cardiff: SIRC.

Thomas, M., H. Sampson, and M. Zhao. 2003. Finding a Balance: Companies, Seafarers and Family Life. *Maritime Policy and Management* 30 (1): 59–76.

Turner, J.H., and J.E. Stets. 2006. Sociological Theories of Human Emotions. *Annual Review of Sociology* 32: 25–52.

Wallace, P.M. 1999. *The Psychology of the Internet*. Cambridge: Cambridge University Press.

Wellman, B. 2001. Physical Place and Cyberplace: the Rise of Personalized Networking. *International Journal of Urban and Regional Research* 25 (2): 227–252.

Wu, B., G. Shen, and L. Li. 2007. *The Transformation of the Chinese Labour Market for Seafarers*. Cardiff: SIRC.

The manufacturer's authorised representative in the EU is Springer
Nature Customer Service Centre GmbH, Europaplatz 3, 69115 Heidelberg,
Germany. If you have any concerns regarding our products, please
contact ProductSafety@springernature.com

Printed and bound by CPI Group (UK) Ltd, Croydon, CR0 4YY
06/10/2026
02228482-0001